THE WORLDWIDE GUIDE TO

MOVIE LOCATIONS

PRESENTS

LONDON

TONY REEVES

TITAN BOOKS

The Worldwide Guide to Movie Locations Presents London
1 84023 499 7
Published by
Titan Books
A division of
Titan Publishing Group Ltd
144 Southwark Street
London
SE1 0UP

First edition September 2003
10 9 8 7 6 5 4 3 2 1

ACKNOWLEDGEMENTS
Thanks to: Ian Aegis; London Borough of Barnet; Geoffrey Bayldon; Simon Bosanquet; London Borough of Camden; Ian Carmichael; James Cary-Parkes; George Cole; Simon Crook; Malcolm Davis; Terry Deal; Dallas Denton-Cox; Harvey Edgington and the London Film Commission; The Edmonton Hundreds; Peter Elford; Assheton Gorton; Ben Greenacre; Greenwich Film Unit; Peter Hannan BSC; Jon Hardy; Nigel Hatton; Herts Filmlink; Matthew Hodson; Peter Jaques; Pat Karam; Sir Alec McCowen; Louise McManus Fernandes; Christian McWilliams; Steen Mangen; Angus More Gordon; Tony Nuttall; Carolyn Partrick; Glen Platts; Paul Raphael; Adam Richards; Shoreditch Town Hall Trust; Norman Warwick; West London Film Office; Russ Williamson; Working Title Films.

PUBLISHER'S NOTE
Every effort has been made to ensure that the information given in this book was correct at the time of going to press. However, details such as travel information and phone numbers can change. The publishers cannot accept responsibility for any consequences arising from the use of this book. We would, however, be delighted to receive any corrections for incorporation into the next edition.

PRIVACY
Please note that many of the locations detailed in this book are private property, and are not open to the general public. Please respect the privacy of the owners, and be aware that access of any kind is often prohibited.

Visit our website: **www.titanbooks.com**
Visit the Worldwide Guide to Movie Locations website: **www.movie-locations.com**
(and **www.movie-locations.com/update** for updates, corrections and amendments)

Did you enjoy this book? We love to hear from our readers. Please email us at **readerfeedback@titanemail.com** or write to Reader Feedback at the above address. To subscribe to our regular newsletter for up-to-the-minute news, great offers and competitions, email **titan-news@titanemail.com**.

Titan books are available from all good bookshops or direct from our mail order service. For a free catalogue or to order, phone **01536 764646** with your credit card details, email **asmltd@btinternet.com** or write to **Titan Books Mail Order, ASM Ltd, Unit 6, Pipewell Industrial Estate, Desborough, Northants NN14 2SW.** Please quote reference ML/LO.

A CIP catalogue record for this title is available from the British Library.

Printed and bound in Great Britain by MPG Books Ltd, Bodmin, Cornwall.

CONTENTS

LONDON BELONGS TO YOU...

If you haven't read *The Worldwide Guide to Movie Locations*, then perhaps *The Worldwide Guide to Movie Locations Presents: London* needs a word of explanation. *The Worldwide Guide to Movie Locations* was originally published in 2001, and the title pretty much says it all. I wanted to produce a travel guidebook to the world's filming sites for fans and historians, plus holidaymakers with a taste for the offbeat – one that would cover all genres, periods and countries. My goal was a comprehensive guide encompassing wild Western landscapes and elegant stately homes, urban mean streets and exotic beaches, grand European castles and the seediest of backstreet bars: the full gamut of the cinematic experience from John Wayne through Merchant-Ivory to Luc Besson. Although the book contains far more than I could ever have envisaged when I started the project (around 1,600 film titles, arranged alphabetically from *A Bout de Souffle* to *Zulu*), practical limitations on the size of a travel guide meant that I ended up leaving out more than I included. It seems that, while *The Worldwide Guide to Movie Locations* remains the central resource for film locations, the way to do full justice to our cinematic heritage is with site-specific guides, and *London* is the first of these.

At first glance, researching *London* seemed to be not quite so glamorous as researching many of the far-flung locations in the *Worldwide Guide*, but it turned out to be no less fascinating. Feature films set in London go way back, though in the early days of cinema the city was more often than not fabricated in the studio. Hitchcock recreated Wapping for his 1934 version of *The Man Who Knew Too Much* and Borough for *Sabotage* in 1936. Though 1938's *St Martin's Lane* mixed real locations with studio sets to create a fascinating picture of the West End's theatreland, in the early forties, confections such as *Spring in Park Lane* and *Maytime in Mayfair* were still studio-bound, and Hollywood continued to conjure up its own version of the capital with the likes of 1945's *Hangover Square* – peopled with Gower Gulch Cockneys and ex-pat aristocrats, a London perpetually fog-shrouded, yet with a clear view of Big Ben and St Paul's from every window.

The real London can occasionally be glimpsed before WWII, but it was afterwards, when cameras really began to leave the confines of the studio, that the capital came into its own cinematically. The Ealing studios, based in West London, gave their name to a whole genre of comedies celebrating the triumph of the individual over bureaucracy, often with a streak of surprisingly dark humour. In 1950, Jules Dassin achieved the seemingly impossible by successfully transplanting that most American of genres, film noir, to London, with the hard-as-diamonds *Night and the City*. In 1947, Robert Hamer put the working class centre-screen with the East End-set *It Always Rains On Sunday*, while, as part of the late fifties Free Cinema movement, cineastes such as Lindsay Anderson and Karel Reisz produced ever-so-slightly patronising documentaries about chirpy working class Londoners (*Every Day Except Christmas* and *We Are the Lambeth Boys* respectively), before the New Wave finally broke over England in the early sixties.

Although Tony Richardson's 1959 film of *Look Back in Anger* still has the stagey feel of theatre actors slumming, the director was soon out on the streets with a new generation of actors, producing movies like 1961's *A Taste of Honey* (set in the North, but partly shot in London). The capital provided a wealth of backdrops: Notting Hill, an area of ruthless landlords and immigrant tenants, became a crucible for social tensions in films including *West 11* and *The L-Shaped Room*, while Carnaby Street and the King's Road were portrayed as 'swinging' long after the real swingers had moved on.

The sharp, bleached-out monochrome and day-glo colours of the sixties gave way to the grainy, hand-held murkiness of the seventies, with crooked cops and anti-hero robbers inhabiting the same glum streets in the likes of *Villain*, *Brannigan* and *Sweeney!* One-word titles. Hard. Terse. By this time, two long-running British institutions were well into their stride: the Carry On and James Bond film series. For a while, the downbeat, bespectacled Harry Palmer threatened to scupper Bond's frivolous glossiness, but 007 was capable of being reinvented, while Palmer could only ever be Caine, even with Ken Russell applying baroque flourishes to *Billion Dollar Brain*.

Britain has never quite recaptured the giddy enthusiasm of the sixties, when film-makers managed the neat trick of being boldly innovative and wildly crowd-pleasing at the same time. Apart from slickly crafted romcoms, contemporary London cinema is apparently engaged in a competition with itself to produce the grimmest, most drug-ridden estate drama, the coolest gangster movie (with least comprehensible street slang) and the most humour-free comedy. Wish-fulfilment is the current common link. Jess *will* get to play professional soccer, a bookish nerd *can* get to marry a Hollywood superstar and Home Counties actor chaps *do* get to play with the rough boys.

Yet among these broad trends, it's the one-off oddities that gleam as the unique gems of London cinema.

The bizarre collision of Donald Cammell's perversity and Nicolas Roeg's virtuosity produced *Performance*, the most eye-popping bag of cinematic tricks since *Citizen Kane*, and left Warner Bros execs frozen in horror like the *Springtime for Hitler* audience. *Withnail & I* launched squalor chic and pulled off the trick of convincing audiences they were witnessing authentic Camden life, even though the Westway is clearly visible in the background. The remorselessly macho Douglas Hickox suddenly came up with the campest film of all time – cheap laughs! stomach-churning gore! genuine pathos! poodle pie! – in *Theatre of Blood*. Michael Powell's universally reviled *Peeping Tom* drove every film critic in the land to rewrite history and pretend they'd liked it all along (though Dilys Powell, bless her, admitted that the first act she wanted to do in Heaven was to search out the director and apologise for her review). *The Krays*, which promised to be the most dully predictable plod through familiar thuggery, turned out to be by turns infuriatingly 'poetic' and breathtakingly insightful. And outsider David Lynch brought the suffocating industrial physicality of *Eraserhead* to our cosy Victorian era in *The Elephant Man*.

This guide aims to take you to the eclectic heart of London cinema: to swanky hotels and lowlife pubs, forgotten corners of the old city and here-today, gone-tomorrow style bars. Without leaving London, you can sink a pint of Guinness in the Irish pub of *The Long Good Friday*, explore the Moscow church visited by Izabella Scorupco in *GoldenEye*, enjoy a night in the Fhloston Paradise opera house where the blue alien diva performs in Luc Besson's *The Fifth Element*, hang out in the Berlin airport from *Indiana Jones and the Last Crusade* or see the Cuban cigar factory from *Die Another Day*.

Prepare to follow in the footsteps of names as familiar – or perhaps not so familiar – as Harold Shand, Lara Croft, Robert Rusk, Hortense Cumberbatch, Edward Lionheart, Mrs Wilberforce, Melville Farr, Morgan Delt, Diana Scott, Harry Fabian, Alex Greville, Louis Mazzini, Hugo Barrett, Dr Nookie and Charlie Croker...

HOW TO USE THIS GUIDE

Unlike the *Worldwide Guide*, which is arranged by film title, *London* is arranged by area, putting the emphasis firmly on travel. There are seventeen sections laid out as walking tours, but this is simply for convenience. I don't recommend following these routes scrupulously, but rather using each tour as a suggested itinerary. Dip in and pick out what you want to see. Take your time, live the experience, sample the bars and restaurants.

For convenience, filming locations and other sites of interest are picked out in **bold type**. Where appropriate, I've listed useful phone numbers, websites and tube and railway stations. You'll find separate sections on Bars & Restaurants, Hotels, Shopping, Entertainment and Historic Sites, which are cross-referenced with the walks.

I can't stress how important it is to remember that, while there are plenty of commercial establishments who'll be pleased with your custom, many of the locations listed are private homes. The occupants are unlikely to have any connection with, or in some cases any knowledge of, the films. By all means look, but please don't ever disturb or annoy residents, and please do respect people's privacy. Discretion is the word.

VISITING LONDON

If you're visiting the city, here are a few tips to help. Check out the London Tourist Board for further details (*website: www.londontouristboard.com*). If you want to investigate London streets in advance, look at *www.streetmap.co.uk*.

ARRIVING BY AIR
City Airport
℗ *020.7646.000*
website: www.londoncityairport.com
A comparatively new airport in the Docklands area. Serving only Europe, it's used mainly for business flights. A shuttle service connects with the Docklands Light Railway (DLR).

Gatwick
℗ *020.7646.000*
website: www.baa.co.uk

The capital's second major airport, 30 miles south of the city. A regular train service, the Gatwick Express (© *0990.301530; website: www.gatwickexpress.co.uk*), connects to Victoria Station, every fifteen minutes during peak service, every thirty minutes off-peak. The journey time is half an hour. Gatwick is rarely used for filming, though the Beatles do caper about on its helipad in *A Hard Day's Night*.

Heathrow
© *0870.0000123*
website: www.baa.co.uk
The busiest airport in the world, this is where you're most likely to touch down. London Underground's Piccadilly line runs into central London from here, and if you're on a limited budget, this is the cheapest way. The tube service is frequent, but the trains can be uncomfortably packed and the journey takes up to an hour. The excellent Heathrow Express (© *0845.600.1515; website: www.heathrowexpress.co.uk*) is much more expensive, but will whisk you, every fifteen minutes, in relative comfort, direct to Paddington Station in a quarter of an hour. The setting for the glossy 1963 film *The V.I.P.s*, the airport was also used for the climax of *A Fish Called Wanda*, but most memorably for the arrival of Harold Shand in *The Long Good Friday*.

Luton
© *01582.405100*
wesite: www.london-luton.com
A bargain basement airport, 30 miles north of London, used by charter flights. A regular rail service, taking about forty minutes, runs to Kings Cross Station, North London, every fifteen minutes.

Stansted
© *01279.680500*
website: www.baa.co.uk
Small but perfectly-formed, this new Norman Foster-designed airport has a regular rail service to the recently-refurbished Liverpool Street Station, close to the City. Journey time is around forty-five minutes. It became New York's JFK Airport for *Bridget Jones's Diary*.

NATIONAL RAIL & COACHES
© *rail: 08457.484950*
website: rail: www.nationalrail.co.uk; coaches: www.transportforlondon.gov.uk/vcs
Despite its reputation, I've generally found the national rail system to be punctual and efficient, but this may be because I tend not to travel during the rush hour when the system is really stressed. The monopoly of British Rail is a thing of the past and you now have choice on the railways (though the assumption seems to be that your choice of train depends less on its destination than on whether it has green carriages with a buffet car or blue carriages with trolley service). What this means in practice is that phoning for information or finding the cheapest deal can be a nightmare, as you need to know which company runs the trains to your destination. twenty-four-hour information, and numbers for the various rail companies, can be found by calling national rail enquiries or visiting their website (details above). If you're travelling at weekends, particularly on Sunday, always check beforehand, as there are frequent disruptions due to track maintenance – Sod's Law dictates that this will inevitably affect the journey you had planned.

Central London is served by eleven major railway stations. Coming from Scotland, the North or the Midlands, you'll arrive north of the city at King's Cross, St Pancras or Euston. Liverpool Street and Fenchurch Street serve the East and East Anglia. Marylebone and Paddington serve the West of England. Victoria and Waterloo serve the South and Southwest. Charing Cross and London Bridge serve the South and Southeast. Coaches arrive at Victoria Coach Station, close to Victoria Railway Station.

TRAVELLING AROUND LONDON
By car is one of the least convenient and least pleasant ways of exploring the city; traffic is generally slow and parking can be a nightmare. Keep the car for exploring the surrounding countryside. Taxis are expensive and can be excruciatingly slow in the centre of town, but if you must, only hire licensed Black Cabs – unregulated minicabs can be even more expensive, and sometimes even dangerous. Buses can be useful, but traffic delays render them unpredictable. There are numerous railway stations across London, and these can sometimes be quicker and more direct than the Underground service, especially if you are travelling to a des-

tination outside the city centre. However, if you are fit and confident, and weather permits, cycling remains one of the quickest ways to get around. The downside is the apparent ease with which thieves can deal with the most sophisticated bike lock.

The London Underground is expensive and constantly maligned – certainly it can't hold a candle to, say, the Paris Metro or the New York Subway – but it remains one of the most convenient ways to navigate the city centre. Trains are more frequent during rush hours, but also more crowded and uncomfortable, and the individual lines vary enormously in speed and frequency: the Piccadilly line is fast and reliable, the Northern line notoriously fickle. The colour-coded tube map is geographically misleading, but a classic of design simplicity (though as the number of lines increases, you need the visual acuity of a master colourist to distinguish the various shades). Ticket pricing is by zone rather than distance, which results in all kinds of anomalies, so check out the zones carefully before buying your ticket. If you travel after 9.30 on weekdays (or any time at weekends), it pays to buy a Travelcard, which allows unlimited travel within the zones you pay for. A Travelcard covering zones 1 and 2 currently costs £4.10 and takes in much of Central London, though for a mere 30p extra you can get a card covering zones 1 to 4, which will take you to all but the most outlying stations. The Travelcard is valid on mainline trains, the DLR and buses, too. There's also a seven-day Travelcard (for any longer periods, you will need a London Transport photocard as ID).

Unlike the New York system, London Underground makes it easy to get onto stations, but don't be tempted to try travelling without a ticket as, once on, you need a ticket to exit, and fare dodging is taken seriously. And remember that, since the horrific fire at King's Cross Station, there is no smoking anywhere on the Underground system, not even at overground stations.

The Underground closes shockingly early. Even if trains are still running after you leave the bar or restaurant, you'll need to check that late trains go all the way to your destination and that connecting lines will still be running. There are plenty of night buses (their route numbers are prefixed with 'N'), but they're wildly unpredictable.

HOTELS

London accommodation is notoriously expensive, and service can often fall short of standards found in other countries. Bayswater, between Marble Arch and Paddington, seems to consist almost entirely of cream-painted hotels. The area around Victoria is similarly blessed with countless lodgings, varying wildly in quality from cheap boarding houses to the glitziest palaces. Plenty of budget accommodation can be found around Earl's Court (conveniently close to the West End, courtesy of the Piccadilly line), but remember, you get what you pay for.

BARS

The great London bar experience remains the good, old fashioned pub: polished wood, gleaming brass, etched glass and surly bar staff. However, the traditional London pub is something of an endangered species. Unique names and styles are increasingly subsumed by large chains, lumbered with names involving any combination of slugs, lettuces and firkins. The good news is, the notoriously stringent licensing laws, left over from WWI, are finally being relaxed, and it's not usual to tip bar staff – unless you happen to have landed in a style-conscious bar pretending it's on the Continent.

TRAVEL ADVICE

The usual advice about taking care in unfamiliar areas applies, but probably more so, as many movie locations are off the tourist track. If you're not a native of the city, some districts may make you feel a little uncomfortable, but this has more to do with unfamiliarity than any physical threat. The biggest crime risk you will probably face are pickpockets, especially on the tube or in crowded shopping streets. There are few areas that are actually dangerous, though of course any poorly-lit side-street at night in any city in the world can pose a risk. Check out unfamiliar areas during daylight.

Don't stand out. Checking routes carefully before you set out can avoid the uncontrollably flapping street map which signals 'vulnerable tourist' to every scam artist in the district. Dress down. Buy something from a local supermarket and get a branded carrier bag. Keep your camera in it. Nobody steals groceries.

Hotels

If you're on a tight budget, then staying in a film location in London is probably not an option. New York can offer a quirky little hideaway. LA can offer the traditional sleazy motel. But in London, you'll have to fork out for one of the great names at the top end of the range. Maybe Britain just doesn't have the same hotel culture as the USA. We're talking The Ritz, Savoy, Dorchester…

CENTRAL LONDON
LEICESTER SQUARE TO COVENT GARDEN
Savoy Hotel, 1 Savoy Hill, Strand
✆ 020.7836.4343
website: www.savoy-group.com
tube/rail: Charing Cross (Backerloo and Northern lines)
Once a traditional turn-of-the-century hotel, the Savoy – an adjunct to the Savoy Theatre, built to stage the operettas of Gilbert and Sullivan – was perked up in 1929 with an unmistakable stainless steel, art-deco frontage on the Strand. The gleaming entrance court is straight out of an RKO musical, even down to the fact that traffic drives on the right (which is allowed nowhere else in Britain). Movie actress Anna (Meryl Streep) stays at the Savoy in the modern-day scenes of *The French Lieutenant's Woman*, and Catherine Zeta-Jones tails Sean Connery to the 'Cryptonic' building from here at the opening of *Entrapment*. Most famously, though, the ferociously patriotic Harold Shand (Bob Hoskins) gives the coolly dispassionate mafia bosses a mouthful when they unceremoniously dump him here, before being abducted by the IRA (with a young Pierce Brosnan wielding the gun) at the end of *The Long Good Friday*.

OXFORD STREET TO SOHO
Langham Hilton, 1c Portland Place
✆ 020.7636.1000
website: www.langham.hilton.com
tube: Regents Park (Bakerloo line), Great Portland Street (Metropolitan, Circle and Hammersmith & City lines)
This hotel gleams beautifully as the exterior of the 'Grand Hotel Europe', Bond's 'St Petersburg' base in *GoldenEye*.

Mayfair Westbury Hotel, Conduit Street
✆ 020.7629.7755
tube: Bond Street (Jubilee and Central line)
Convenient for upmarket shopping – Bond Street, Versace, Tiffany's, Armani and Sotheby's are all close

by. Jerry Lee Lewis (Dennis Quaid), though, is less interested in shopping than in his teen bride Myra (Winona Ryder) when he stays here in the colourful 1989 biopic *Great Balls of Fire!*

WESTMINSTER TO BELGRAVIA
51 Buckingham Gate
✆ 020.7769.7766
website: www.51-buckinghamgate.com
tube: St James's Park (District and Circle lines)
tube/rail: Victoria (Victoria, District and Circle lines)
Previously the St James Court Hotel, a converted Edwardian block, the complex consists of 82 luxury suites and apartments, and there's butler service. So it's not a budget hostel… The courtyard of this prestigious lodging became the exterior of Anthony Hopkins' London home in *Howards End*.

Jolly St Ermin's, 2 Caxton Street
✆ 020.7222.7888
website: www.jollyhotels.co.uk
tube/rail: Victoria (Victoria, District and Circle lines)
Built in 1887 on the site of a former monastery, St Ermin's became a hotel in 1900 and features a striking art nouveau interior, which is the 'American restaurant' where editor Horace Whigham (George Plimpton) comes on to Louise Bryant (Diane Keaton) in Warren Beatty's *Reds*. It is also the hotel where Bob Hoskins turns up in his flash new gear, appropriate to his new role as minder to high-class callgirl Cathy Tyson, in *Mona Lisa*. The ballroom of St Ermin's was transformed into the dining room of the Savoy, circa 1890, for Oliver Parker's misguided film adaptation of Oscar Wilde's play *The Importance of Being Earnest*. Take note: the immediate area can be a bit dead at weekends. On the bright side, the building has to be one of the safest in London – as the *Sid and Nancy* crew discovered while shooting a scene on the roof of the hotel (standing in for Bayswater's Inverness Court) when Sid Vicious and Nancy Spungen enjoy a spot of gunplay. The commotion drew the attention of the neighbours directly opposite: New Scotland Yard, headquarters of the Metropolitan Police.

TRAFALGAR SQUARE TO MAYFAIR
Dorchester Hotel, 53 Park Lane
✆ 020.7629.8888
website: www.dorchesterhotel.com
tube: Marble Arch (Central line), Hyde Park Corner (Piccadilly line)
Built on the site of the palatial old Dorchester House, the hotel opened in 1931 as the last word in stylish modernity, with an elegant deco-ish frontage peer-

ing through foliage at Deanery Street. Less stuffy old-school than other great names, and boasting extravagant suites created by stage designer Oliver Messel, the hotel has always been a favourite with showbiz celebs – Alfred Hitchcock stayed here, as did Marlene Dietrich, Judy Garland, Laurence Olivier and Vivien Leigh. Elizabeth Taylor and Richard Burton gave legendary parties here, and Peter Sellers made it his London base. Villain Ben Larkin (John Vernon) stays at the Dorchester in *Brannigan*. On-the-way-up Bongo Herbert (Cliff Richard) nestles down in a Dorchester suite with on-the-wane star Dixie Collins (Yolande Donlan) in the 1959 music biz satire *Expresso Bongo*. Vanessa Redgrave and Robert Stephens hold their wedding reception on its roof terrace in Karel Reisz's seminal *Morgan – A Suitable Case For Treatment*, until gorilla-suited Marxist David Warner gatecrashes the proceedings, before tootling off down Park Lane on his scooter.

London Hilton, 22 Park Lane
✆ 020.7493.8000
website: www.hilton.com
tube: Hyde Park Corner (Piccadilly line)
In American movies, suspected murderers on the run end up in sleazy motels, where there's always a sinister, weasely desk clerk and one letter missing from the neon sign. In Hitchcock's *Frenzy*, Jon Finch is helped out by his RAF chum Clive Swift, who is staying at the Hilton on Park Lane… Opposite the Hilton is the tiny patch of grass where Finch meets Anna Massey after slipping out of the Coburg Hotel. Cathy Tyson and Bob Hoskins fall out by the Achilles statue, behind the tacky Queen Elizabeth Gates, in *Mona Lisa*. The Hilton is close to the West End and Mayfair, and to a clutch of other big name hotels. The balcony views over Hyde Park are gorgeous, but Park Lane itself is scruffy, dismal and traffic-clogged.

Le Méridien Grosvenor House Hotel, Park Lane
✆ 020.7499.6363
tube: Marble Arch (Central line)
Yet more gangsters in Mayfair. Reluctant robber Ray Winstone stays here under the carefully chosen alias 'Rowntree' – "like Smarties [made by Rowntrees], like *Shaft* [starring Richard Roundtree]" – once he's been cajoled back to London for the bank job by Ben Kingsley in *Sexy Beast*.

Metropolitan Hotel, 19 Old Park Lane
✆ 020.7447.1000
website: www.metropolitan.co.uk
tube: Hyde Park Corner (Piccadilly line)
Drably unimaginative or audaciously minimalist? This concrete and glass block houses the dizzyingly expensive **Nobu** restaurant (see **Bars & Restaurants**, p14), which can be seen in *Notting Hill*.

The Ritz, 150 Piccadilly
✆ 020.7493.8181
website: www.theritzhotel.co.uk
tube: Green Park (Jubilee, Piccadilly and Victoria lines)
'The law, like The Ritz, is open to anyone', goes the old saying, and it's true. If you're rich enough, you can stay and enjoy the Louis XVI opulence, or just stop in for afternoon tea. Be warned though, tea at The Ritz is a popular experience so you'll probably need to book ahead. The Ritz is another hangout for working girl Cathy Tyson in *Mona Lisa*. It is also where Julia Roberts invites Hugh Grant for the disastrous press interview in *Notting Hill*. Modesty Blaise (Monica Vitti) visits her Arab chums here in Joseph Losey's heavy-handed film of the famous cartoon strip.

Sheraton Park Lane Hotel, Piccadilly
✆ 020.7499.6321
tube: Green Park (Jubilee, Piccadilly and Victoria lines)
The British puritanical streak, which likes to equate the sybaritic luxury of Mayfair with criminality, is neatly summed up in the opening scene of *Gangster No. 1*, when Malcolm McDowell *almost* drinks a flute of pee-contaminated champagne in the Sheraton's toilets (though the boxing match he's attending was filmed on a studio set). High class hooker Cathy Tyson works the hotel in *Mona Lisa*, while its art deco splendour stood in for the Café Royal in Neil Jordan's *The End of the Affair*.

NORTHWEST LONDON
Avoca House Hotel, 46 Belsize Park
✆ 020.7722.7777
website: www.avocahousehotel.co.uk
tube: Swiss Cottage (Jubilee line)
Convenient for both leafy Hampstead and the 'goth' bustle of Camden Town, this comfortable little hotel was where much of Vadim Jean and Gary Sinyor's 1992 offbeat, low-budget Jewish comedy *Leon the Pig Farmer* was filmed.

Swiss Cottage Hotel, 4 Adamson Road
✆ 020.7722.2281
website: www.swisscottagehotel.co.uk
tube: Swiss Cottage (Jubilee line)
Recently restored, this 59-room hotel is a conversion of four Victorian properties built in 1860. The interior was used for the drunken night-time shenanigans in 'Brazil' in *Mike Bassett: England Manager*.

THE CITY OF LONDON
Thistle Tower, St Katherine's Way
℗ 0870.333.9106
website: www.thistlehotels.com
tube: Tower Hill (District and Circle lines)
DLR: Tower Gateway
Located on the Thames riverfront alongside Tower Bridge, there's no getting away from the fact that, on the outside, the Thistle is just plain nasty – classic lines of the seventies teamed with the uplifting joy that is beige. Judy Geeson bids farewell to John Wayne here at the end of *Brannigan*. The hotel can also be seen in another cop drama, *Sweeney!*

WEST LONDON
FITZROVIA TO HATTON GARDEN
Radisson Marlborough Hotel, 9-14 Bloomsbury Street
℗ 020.7636.5601
tube: Tottenham Court Road (Northern and Central lines)
Outside the Marlborough, Shirley Valentine (Pauline Collins) bumps into her old school friend (Joanna Lumley) in the film of Willy Russell's play. Good for the British Museum and the literary haunts of Bloomsbury and Fitzrovia.

WEST LONDON
PADDINGTON TO NOTTING HILL
The Halcyon Hotel, 81 Holland Park
℗ 020.7727.7288
website: www.thehalcyon.com
tube: Holland Park (Central line)
The exclusive hideaway of visiting rockstars and Hollywoodsters evading the paparazzi. It was the London base of Simon Templar (Val Kilmer) in the disappointing film of *The Saint*.

Hempel Hotel, 31-35 Craven Hill Gardens
℗ 020.7298.9000
website: www.the-hempel.co.uk
tube/rail: Paddington (District, Circle, Bakerloo and Hammersmith & City lines)
tube: Bayswater (District and Circle lines), Queensway, Lancaster Gate (Central line)
One of the new breed of minimalist designer hotels, actress-turned-architect-and-interior-designer Anouska Hempel's soothing white-on-white style classic is the ideal place to unwind and calm down. The Hempel's Zen Garden, across the road from the hotel, is the suitably chic venue for the wedding reception of Hollywood glam queen Anna Scott (Julia Roberts) and her unlikely new husband William Thacker (Hugh Grant) at the end of *Notting Hill*.

Hilton Hyde Park, 129 Bayswater Road
℗ 020.7221.2217
website: www.hilton.com
tube: Queensway (Central line)
It sometimes seems that hotel names change weekly as chains snap up famous landmarks and are, in turn, absorbed. The anonymously-named Hilton Hyde Park was for many years the Coburg Hotel, which is where Richard Blaney (Jon Finch) blows the money given to him by his ex-wife by staying with barmaid Anna Massey, in Hitchcock's *Frenzy*. The couple check in as 'Mr and Mrs Oscar Wilde', a witty improvement by actor Jon Finch on the 'Mr and Mrs Smith' of the script. The 'Cupid Room' (I bet that was real) costs him £10. It may cost you a little more now. After his ex is found murdered, Blaney escapes down the back stairs. Located alongside Queensway tube station, the 129-room hotel is not to be confused with London's famous first Hilton, the London Hilton.

Inverness Court Hotel, 1 Inverness Terrace
℗ 020.7229 1444
tube: Queensway (Central line), Bayswater (District and Circle lines)
The definitely not cleaned-up Sid Vicious and Johnny Rotten cause chaos when they visit cleaned-up American rock star Rock Head (a character not a million miles from Iggy Pop, or perhaps Johnny Thunder of the New York Dolls) here in Alex Cox's *Sid and Nancy*. "This is a respectable hotel." announces pompous manager Eddie Tudor-Pole, "Lillie Langtry stayed here." And it's true. The hotel was built as a private home for the actress by Edward VII, during his affair with her. For such a respectable hotel, the Inverness Court has been the scene of some raucous cinematic goings-on. In Ken Russell's 1977 biopic *Valentino* it is the 'American' bar, where the silent heart-throb (played by dancer Rudolph Nureyev) drinks macho Rory O'Neil (Peter Vaughan) under the table after demonstrating his masculinity in the boxing ring. The same year the Inverness Court became 'The Dunchester Club', hangout of slippery PR man Barry Foster, quizzed by disgraced cop Regan (John Thaw) in *Sweeney!*

Royal Eagle Hotel, 26-30 Craven Road
℗ 020.7706.0700
website: www.royaleagle.com
tube: Lancaster Gate (Central line)
tube/rail: Paddington (Bakerloo, District, Circle and Hammersmith & City lines)
Believe it or not, this is the exterior of the hotel where Renton and co meet dealer Keith Allen to do the skag deal in *Trainspotting*. Empty and dilapidated at the time of filming, the five grand Victorian houses which

make up the hotel have since been totally renovated and spruced up into quite a classy establishment. You can't stay in the room featured in the movie, though, since the hotel interior was filmed in Glasgow.

Royal Lancaster Hotel, Lancaster Terrace

℡ *020.7262.6737*

website: www.royallancaster.co.uk

tube: Lancaster Gate (Central line)

A luxury hotel. The site of the 'coming out' bash for Charlie Croker (Michael Caine) on his release from Wormwood Scrubs at the beginning of *The Italian Job.*

EAST LONDON
The Great Eastern Hotel, Liverpool Street

℡ *020.7618.5000*

website: www.great-eastern-hotel.co.uk

tube/rail: Liverpool Street (Metropolitan, Hammer-smith & City, Circle and Central lines)

Housed in the eastern section of the spectacularly revamped Liverpool Street Station, this hotel was used for scenes in Lindsay Anderson's anarchic *O Lucky Man!* Its exterior was also glammed up to become the 'Grand Plaza London', where Bill Murray ends up perched on a ledge in Jon Amiel's 1997 comedy thriller *The Man Who Knew Too Little.* And, yes, that really is Murray clinging on for dear life. Built in 1884, the Great Eastern once boasted its own tracks and sidings, but had fallen into neglect until a multi-million pound makeover from the Conran group enabled it to reopen in February 2000 as a top-of-the-range establishment – so now it really is as glitzy as it looks in Amiel's movie.

SOUTHWEST LONDON
Lanesborough Hotel, 1 Lanesborough Place

℡ *020.7259.5599*

website: www.lanesborough.com

tube: Hyde Park Corner (Piccadilly line)

If you can afford to stay in this frightfully exclusive luxury hotel, you certainly don't need to know the nearest tube station. The huge complex, built in the 1830s by William Wilkins, the architect of the National Gallery, once housed St George's Hospital (originally established in 1733 in a country home construsted by Viscount Lanesborough). In 1980, the hospital had 'outgrown' the premises and moved south of the river to Tooting. (Only a hardened cynic, surely, would suggest that such a prime piece of real estate was wasted housing the sick.) The hotel's Royal Suite was used for the fraught meeting between Tom Cruise and Sydney Pollack in Stanley Kubrick's *Eyes Wide Shut.*

FAR NORTHWEST LONDON
Landmark Hotel, 222 Marylebone Road

℡ *020.7631.8000*

tube/rail: Marylebone (Bakerloo line)

Close to the sadly quiet Marylebone mainline station, including this hotel might be considered a bit of a cheat – Gwyneth Paltrow is mugged on the pavement in front of the Landmark after losing her job in *Sliding Doors* (this is odd, since the underground station she's just emerged from is Waterloo).

Bars & Restaurants

CENTRAL LONDON

LEICESTER SQUARE TO COVENT GARDEN

The Black Friar, 174 Queen Victoria Street

© 020.7236.5474

tube/rail: Blackfriars (Circle and District lines)

Built in 1875 on the site of the Dominican priory that gave the area its name, what makes the pub such a treasure is that, in 1902, it was given a makeover that is, frankly, high camp. The gilt and marble interior is overlaid with bronze art nouveau friezes depicting piously industrious monks, and admonishing the drinkers with severe warnings: 'Finery is foolery', 'Haste is waste' and 'Industry is all'. Lord Risley, the aristo with a taste for the military, gets into trouble with a guardsman here in the Merchant-Ivory film of EM Forster's posthumously-published *Maurice*. Take note that The Black Friar is closed on Saturdays and Sundays, as are most of the pubs in the City of London area, which becomes a ghost town at weekends.

Café Rouge, Wellington Street

© 020.7836.0998

tube: Covent Garden (Piccadilly line)

A good place for that getting-to-know-you date. This branch of the ubiquitous restaurant chain was once the Dome, the restaurant where Andie MacDowell catalogues her sexual track record for the benefit of Hugh Grant in *Four Weddings and a Funeral*.

The Globe, 37 Bow Street

© 020.7836.0219

tube: Covent Garden (Piccadilly line)

The Globe has been given quite a makeover since it featured as the pub where Richard Blaney (Jon Finch) works as a barman, before being sacked by landlord Felix Forsythe (Bernard Cribbins – far nastier than he was as Stationmaster Perks in *The Railway Children*), in Alfred Hitchcock's *Frenzy*. The pub once displayed photographs of Hitch directing the movie, now replaced by blandly generic pics of old London. Why?

The Lamb and Flag, 33 Rose Street

© 020.7497.9504

tube: Covent Garden (Piccadilly line)

Located in a tiny alleyway off Garrick Street, this is the oldest pub in Covent Garden (dating from 1623), with a somewhat colourful past reflected in its old name, The Bucket of Blood. Charles Dickens sank a pint or two here. It's the site of the money pick-up

in George Cukor's *Travels With My Aunt*.

Nell of Old Drury, 29 Catherine Street

© 020.7836.5328

tube: Covent Garden (Piccadilly line)

Directly opposite the Theatre Royal Drury Lane, it's the pub where Jon Finch overhears city gents drooling over the wave of necktie killings – "Well, we haven't had a good juicy series of sex murders since Christie. And they're so good for the tourist trade" – in Hitchcock's *Frenzy*. Drop in during the day to people-watch from the large window.

Rules Restaurant, 35 Maiden Lane

© *table reservations: 020.7836.5314,*

private room reservations: 020.7379.0258

tube: Covent Garden (Piccadilly line)

It's London's oldest restaurant, and you only have to glimpse Rules to get the idea: old world class. This is no place for committed vegetarians though, specialising as it does in all kinds of game. It was a favourite of writer Graham Greene, who set key scenes of his novel *The End of the Affair* here. The exterior can supposedly be seen in Neil Jordan's film of the book, but to be perfectly honest, I can't see it.

The Salisbury, 90 St Martin's Lane

© 020.7836.5863

tube: Leicester Square (Piccadilly and Northern lines)

Located on the southeast corner of St Martin's Court, you can hardly miss the splendid Victorian glitter of the Salisbury. An eye-popping dazzle of brass and glass, it's now packed and touristy, but it used to be one of London's old theatrical gay bars, and as such naturally figured as the West End bar in *Victim*. In-joke or coincidence – gay director George Cukor set Maggie Smith's digs above the Salisbury in his film of *Travels With My Aunt*?

Sarastro, 126 Drury Lane

© 020.7836.0101

website: www.sarastro-restaurant.com

tube: Covent Garden (Piccadilly line)

Atmosphere is everything in this delirious theatre set of red and gilt kitsch orientalism. Banquettes become opera boxes and there's a soundtrack of arias. The food is suitably rich, middle eastern cuisine. An appropriately dramatic backdrop for that confrontation you've been planning – it's here that Jenny Seagrove disrupts the evening of Charles Dance and Anthony Edwards in the 1998 romantic comedy *Don't Go Breaking My Heart*.

Simpson's-in-the-Strand, 100 Strand
© 020.7836.9112
website: www.simpsonsinthestrand.co.uk
tube: Covent Garden (Piccadilly line)
tube/rail: Charing Cross (Bakerloo and Northern lines)
From its beginnings in 1828 as the Grand Cigar Divan – where upper crust gents smoked, drank coffee and, oddly, played chess via runners with opponents in other coffee houses – Simpson's has gone on to become a world-famous British institution. Dickens ate here (Just when did he find time to write?), as did *bon viveur* Alfred Hitchcock. Its West Room is where Anthony Hopkins advises Emma Thompson to try "roast beef and Yorkshire pudding, and cider to drink... So thoroughly old English", in *Howards End*. The tradition of carving joints at the table continues. The interior of Simpson's was recreated in the studio for Alfred Hitchcock's 1936 film *Sabotage*.

OXFORD STREET TO SOHO
Café de Paris, 3 Coventry Street
© 020.7395.5806
website: www.cafedeparis.com
tube: Piccadilly Circus (Piccadilly and Bakerloo lines)
Opened in 1924, this exclusive nightclub secured real cachet when the then-Prince of Wales became a regular. Lord and Lady Mountbatten dined on oysters here, Cole Porter entertained and Merle Oberon – Cathy in the classic 1939 film of *Wuthering Heights* – started her careeer here. During the Blitz, when most of the West End closed down, the club remained open on the assumption that it was bomb-proof. Tragically, this turned out not to be the case, and a direct hit killed 80 people. Rebuilt, it continued to provide entertainment for the glitterati until it hit a slump in the eighties, when it found fame as a movie backdrop in films such as *King Ralph*. In Julien Temple's *Absolute Beginners*, the smooth Henley (James Fox) hosts a *très chic* fashion show here. Mandy Rice Davies (Bridget Fonda) and Christine Keeler (Joanne Whalley) sample the high life at the nightclub in *Scandal*. And Reggie and Ronnie bask in their celebrity status here in Peter Medak's *The Krays*. The nightclub was relaunched in 1996. There's a slim chance you could get in by joining the queue, but if you really want to party in style, best to book in advance or, better still, wangle yourself a place on the VIP list.

Its, 56-60 Wigmore Street
© 020.7224.3484
tube: Bond Street (Central and Jubilee lines)
If you're hungry (and the weather's fine), you can enjoy a plate of pasta *al fresco* here at a pavement table. Hopefully, you'll enjoy your meal more than Jeff (Derek Thompson), Harold Shand's (Bob Hoskins) right-hand man, who gets spat on during his clandestine meeting with the shady Councillor Harris (Bryan Marshall) in *The Long Good Friday*.

Lupo, 50 Dean Street
© 020.7434.3399
tube: Leicester Square (Piccadilly and Northern lines)
This classy, dark, velvet-curtained Italian restaurant and bar was once the famed celeb eaterie Mario and Franco's Terrazza, where Chicago cop John Wayne enjoys a meal with Judy Geeson in *Brannigan*.

Momo, 25 Heddon Street
© 020.7434.4040
tube: Piccadilly Circus (Piccadilly and Bakerloo lines)
Hidden away in a tiny side-alley off Regent Street, you're not likely to stumble across Mahgreb restaurant Momo by accident. The creation of Mourad Mazouz, the owner of the 404 restaurant in Paris, this North African fantasia, embracing Tunisian, Algerian and Moroccan cuisine, is a riot of exoticism and a fave celeb hangout. This is where Bridget is given loads of advice by her friends before the date with caddish Daniel Cleaver (Hugh Grant) in *Bridget Jones's Diary*.

The Pitcher and Piano, 69 Dean Street
© 020.7434.3585
tube: Piccadilly Circus (Piccadilly and Bakerloo lines)
Packed Soho drinkery, one of the many real locations used in Michael Winterbottom's slice of London life, *Wonderland*.

Planet Hollywood, 13 Coventry Street
© 020.7287.1000
tube: Piccadilly Circus (Piccadilly and Bakerloo lines)
Not quite the exclusive place it was when it opened in 1993 (68 branches and counting). Go to get jostled by the crowds, gulp down a burger and gawp at that fabulous movie paraphernalia.

Ronnie Scott's Club, 47 Frith Street
© 020.7439.0747
website: www.ronniescotts.co.uk
tube: Leicester Square (Piccadilly and Northern lines)
Ronnie Scott's has been catering to the jazz *cognoscente* on this site since 1965. Craig Ferguson turns on the charm here in *Born Romantic*.

The Spice of Life, 6 Moor Street, Cambridge Circus

© 020.7437.7013

tube: Leicester Square (Piccadilly and Northern lines)

This pub stands alongside the Palace Theatre, so caters to the Les Mis audience, though downstairs is quieter. Sid Vicious stumbles out of the pub with his pal Wally, maybe not having got tickets for the show, in Alex Cox's Sid and Nancy.

The Three Greyhounds, 25 Greek Street

© 020.7287.0754

tube: Leicester Square (Piccadilly and Northern lines)

A 1920s faux-Tudor pub in the heart of touristy Soho, where Jess relaxes after buying football boots in Carnaby Street in Bend It Like Beckham.

WESTMINSTER TO BELGRAVIA
Villa Elephant on the River, 135 Grosvenor Road

© 020.7834.1621

tube: Pimlico (Victoria line)

This Italian restaurant supplied the interior of the casino owned by Harold Shand (Bob Hoskins), where a bomb is discovered, and the lads collect their guns, in The Long Good Friday.

TRAFALGAR SQUARE TO MAYFAIR
Nobu, Metropolitan Hotel, 19 Old Park Lane

© 020.7447.4747

tube: Hyde Park Corner (Piccadilly line)

If you're dining here, then you probably won't need the tube station, since your driver will be dropping you off. Nobu is not a budget night out. Pale, minimal and Japanese, it's perfect for that really special occasion, when you find yourself needing to impress the Hollywood megastar who wandered into your corner shop. Yes, it's in Nobu that Julia Roberts gives as good as she gets to a bunch of mouthy lads while on a date with Hugh Grant in Notting Hill. The fashionably low-key entrance is on the corner of Hertford Street.

Shepherd's Tavern, 50 Hertford Street

© 020.7499.3017

tube: Green Park (Piccadilly, Victoria and Jubilee lines), Hyde Park Corner (Piccadilly line)

A pub tucked away behind Park Lane in the classy heart of Mayfair, it's where Eve Gill (Jane Wyman) downs a brandy with DI Wilfred 'Ordinary' Smith (Michael Wilding) in Hitchcock's 1950 film Stage Fright.

NORTHWEST LONDON
The Assembly House, 292-294 Kentish Town Road

© 020.7485.2031

tube/rail: Kentish Town (Northern line)

A burst of Victorian exuberance overlooking Kentish Town tube station, the Assembly House takes its name from the days when stagecoach travellers would gather together for the scary trip to Hampstead and the north. The proximity of Camden keeps the place buzzing, but the recent sprucing up hasn't destroyed the pubby old charm it showed as the 'East End' local in 1971's Villain, with Richard Burton miscast as a Krayish gangster. A great publicity shot of the time shows Liz Taylor, visiting Burton on location, pulling pints behind the bar.

The Boston Arms, 178 Junction Road

© 020.7272.8153

tube: Tufnell Park (Northern line)

Another staging post, more elaborate than the Assembly House, though a bit shabbier and with more of a local feel, being further from Camden but not quite into the orbit of Hampstead. It houses The Dome, the club which became 'Hamburg's Top Ten Club', where the Beatles headline their first legit gig after graduating from strip joints, in Iain Softley's 1993 movie Backbeat.

The Holly Bush, 22 Holly Mount

© 020.7435.2892

tube: Hampstead (Northern line)

This thankfully unchanged warren of wood panels and bench seats was built in the 17th century as the stable of painter George Romney's house, which still stands next door. When Romney retired to the Lake District, the building became local assembly rooms, and the stable was upgraded to become a kitchen and, eventually, the pub it is today. Past customers include famous travellers Boswell and Dr Johnson, playwright Oliver Goldsmith and essayist Charles Lamb. Music hall entertainer Marie Lloyd drank here, as did 'Two Ton' Tessie O'Shea, the ukulele-strummer Dirk Bogarde uses to establish his alibi in The Blue Lamp. The Hollybush was transformed into 'The Marquis of Granby', where TV soap star June Buckridge (Beryl Reid) knocks back the gin and tonics after hearing that her district nurse soap opera character has been killed off, at the opening of The Killing of Sister George.

NORTHEAST LONDON
The Angelic, 57 Liverpool Road

© 020.7278.8433

tube: Angel (Northern line)

A trendy pub/wine bar in the centre of Islington, serving alcoholic drinks and fresh fruit juice. It was the Moriarty Bar when they filmed scenes for Brit-gangster movie *Love, Honour and Obey* here.

Café Lazeez, 88 St John Street

℃ *020.7253.2224*
tube/rail: Farringdon (Metropolitan, Circle and Hammersmith & City lines)
Forget red flock walls and chicken tikka, Lazeez is a new generation Indian restaurant – large and modern. How many curry houses could be transformed into a glitzy wine bar, as Lazeez was, when it became 'Slammers', the expansive, glass-fronted bar where Jasper Rawlins (Steven Mackintosh) looks for barman Guy (Matthew Blackmore), only to find him dead in the gents, in *The Criminal*.

The Cock Tavern, East Poultry Avenue

℃ *020.7248.2918*
tube/rail: Farringdon (Metropolitan, Circle and Hammersmith & City lines)
A simple door leads down to this extensive basement bar beneath Smithfield Market. The Cock is one of those market pubs with an extended licence which allows the porters to drink at all hours – a nice, blood-spattered white coat should get you served at 6.30am. There's a restaurant and a café, with menus featuring an all-day breakfast and the tempting promise of the biggest steaks in London. It closes at 4pm, though. This is the bar where the older gangster, Gangster 55 (Malcolm McDowell), discovers that Karen (Saffron Burrows) has survived the murder attempt in *Gangster No. 1*, which kind of carries through the theme of blood and butchery…

The Gate, 18-20 St John Street

tube/rail: Farringdon (Metropolitan, Circle and Hammersmith & City lines)
Another lively bar, the decor of which is a cool update on the classic polished wood and mirrors look. It's here that Jasper (Steven Mackintosh) sounds off about the iniquities of dance music to the mysterious Sarah Maitland (Natasha Little) at the opening of Julian Simpson's nifty paranoia thriller *The Criminal*.

Mint 182, 182-186 St John Street

℃ *020.7253.8368*
website: www.mintbar.co.uk
tube: Barbican (Metropolitan, Circle and Hammersmith & City lines)
What London thoroughfare could be cooler than St John Street, linking Angel to Clerkenwell? Scruffy office buildings metamorphose into designer bars faster than you can say *passé*. One such is the chillout bar and restaurant Mint 182, which until recently was Bar Rock, the minimalist bar where Jude Law and Jonny Lee Miller sample the pink champagne after a fraught meeting with Sean Pertwee's 'Saaf' London gang in the desperate-to-be-cool gangster flick *Love, Honour and Obey*. By the time you read this, St John could be the next Carnaby Street, and Mint 182 may already have peaked.

The Three Kings, 7 Clerkenwell Close

℃ *020.7253.0483*
tube/rail: Farringdon (Metropolitan, Circle and Hammersmith & City lines)
Just off Clerkenwell Green, opposite St James's Church, the folky and funky Kings has a bit of a student union feel: part art gallery (the quirky exhibits are for sale) and part music bar (with an eclectic policy), there are regular Beat Club nights (admission charge). Poetry alert: readings can sometimes be brilliant, but can also have you staring into your drink praying for deliverance. The pub stands in for the real Magdala Tavern, the Hampstead pub where Ruth Ellis shot dead her upper-class boyfriend David Blakeley, in *Dance With a Stranger*. An endangered species in an age of designer makeovers, the exterior of the pub has been jazzed up a little, but the comfortingly traditional wooden interior remains.

Vic Naylor and Vic's Bar, 38-40 and 42 St John Street

℃ *020.7608.2181*
tube/rail: Farringdon (Metropolitan, Circle and Hammersmith & City lines)
Vic Naylor's is a large and busy bar/restaurant serving up modern Brit cuisine (with a menu changing daily) to a young and pretty lively crowd. It quietened down a bit to become 'JD's', the bar run by Eddie's dad (Sting) in *Lock, Stock and Two Smoking Barrels*. Closed Sundays.

The small, minimal Vic's Bar next door is one of three bars at the Smithfield end of St John Street which have featured in movies. In prison drama *Mean Machine*, washed-up soccer ace Danny (Vinnie Jones) screeches to a halt outside the bar, before having a little run-in with the law inside which lands him in the clink. This prison drama, tailored to exploit Jones' hardman image, is a remake of Robert Aldrich's 1974 film, which starred Burt Reynolds as the banged-up footie pro.

THE CITY OF LONDON
The Jamaica Wine House, St Michael's Alley

℃ *020.7626.9496*
tube/DLR: Bank (Central, Northern, Circle, District and Waterloo & City lines)

tube: Monument (Circle and District lines)
Relax in this odd-looking terracotta pub, which started life in 1652 as a coffee house – London's first, in fact. In the 17th century, much of the business of the day was conducted in coffee houses (which is how insurance giant Lloyd's began) and the businesslike attitude is reflected in the severe bare boards-and-benches interior. It reopened in 2002 after renovation, and is now part of the Tup chain. Robbie Ross (Michael Sheen) consoles John Gray (Ioan Gruffudd), Oscar Wilde's discarded lover, here in *Wilde*.

The Lamb, Leadenhall Market
℘ *020.7626.2454*
tube/DLR: Bank (Central, Northern, Circle, District and Waterloo & City lines)
tube: Monument (Circle and District lines)
This is a lunchtime pub, catering to city office workers (it's at the foot of the Lloyds Building). It's here that, while tracking down villain Drexel (Del Henney), Brannigan (Wayne) and Sir Charles Swann (Richard Attenborough) kick off one of those brawls only ever seen in the movies, where everyone in the bar punches out everyone else.

Pizza Express, Leadenhall Market
tube/DLR: Bank (Central, Northern, Circle, District and Waterloo & City lines)
tube: Monument (Circle and District lines)
Diagonally opposite the Lamb, this branch of the high street chain used to be Thai restaurant Saigon Times, where hostage negotiator Russell Crowe is assigned to the Latin American case in *Proof of Life*.

WEST LONDON:
FITZROVIA TO HATTON GARDEN
AKA, 18a West Central Street
℘ *020.7836.0110*
website: www.akalondon.com
tube: Tottenham Court Road (Central and Northern lines)
This bar and restaurant is the cool little sister of the End nightclub (next door), and boasts a liver-curdling array of spirits and cocktails. It's here that Mark Rylance works as head barman in Patrice Chéreau's groundbreaking 2000 film of Hanif Kureishi's *Intimacy* . AKA is open until 3am and, as a special treat, there's Monday Night at the Movies, where you can enjoy indie and classic films while munching on popcorn or a hotdog, washed down with a beer – heaven.

Bertorelli's, 19-23 Charlotte Street
℘ *020.7636.4174*
tube: Goodge Street (Northern line)

A long-established Italian restaurant. During the 1930s, waiters had to run across the road to the Fitzroy Tavern to fetch drinks for diners, before the restaurant had a licence for alcohol. Refurbished and updated, it's the restaurant where Gwyneth Paltrow either drinks or works to support John Lynch in the alternating realities of Peter Howitt's *Sliding Doors*.

Hakkasan, 8 Hanway Place
℘ *020.7927.7000*
tube: Tottenham Court Road (Central and Northern lines)
Forget the rather dingy side-street, it's high, high style in this Chinese restaurant from the creators of the Wagamama chain – the interior did scoop a restaurant design award. The restaurant boasts a dazzling array of cocktails, all with an eastern twist. Try Green Destiny – named after the fabulous sword in *Crouching Tiger, Hidden Dragon*: Zubrowka bison grass vodka, cucumber, kiwi fruit and apple juice. If the occasionally unpredictable door policy means you don't get in, you can ogle the decor in *About a Boy* as Hugh Grant tries to unravel his web of deceit to Rachel Weisz.

The Newman Arms, Newman's Court, 23 Rathbone Place
℘ *020.7636.1127*
tube: Tottenham Court Road (Central and Northern lines)
A stone's throw from Oxford Street, this busy little West End pub was a favoured watering hole of writer George Orwell. Prostitute Brenda Bruce takes Carl Boehm up to her room above the Newman Arms, where the unbalanced photographer films her murder, in Michael Powell's *Peeping Tom*. In real life, rather than obliging hookers, upstairs you'll now find a restaurant specialising in substantial pub fare.

Ye Olde Mitre Tavern, between 8 and 9 Hatton Garden
℘ *020.7405.4751*
tube: Chancery Lane (Central line)
tube/rail: Farringdon (Circle, Metropolitan and Hammersmith & City lines)
Tucked away in a narrow alley, and marked by an old crooked street lamp and a small sign in the shape of a bishop's mitre, this tiny pub with wood-panelled bars can still get pretty busy at lunchtimes. The original tavern was built in 1547 for servants of the Palace of the Bishops of Ely, Cambridgeshire (and is technically still part of Cambridgeshire). The bishops' palace and the original tavern were subsequently demolished in the 18th century, but the pub was quickly re-built. Shades of *Passport to Pimlico* –

since the bar is technically not part of London, legend has it that police must ask permission to enter, which is quite possibly why it's the local of Doug the Head, and where director Ritchie puts in a microcameo as Man Reading Newspaper, in *Snatch*.

PADDINGTON TO NOTTING HILL
Babushka, 41 Tavistock Crescent
© 020.7727.9250
tube: Westbourne Park (Hammersmith & City line)
Facing the end of St Luke's Road, Babushka has had a radical makeover since its fame in the movies. It's now hard to believe that this heaving, raucous bar was Camden's woozy old Irish boozer the Mother Black Cap, where Withnail (Richard E Grant) orders "Two large gins. Two pints of cider. Ice in the cider", in 1987's *Withnail & I*. For a while the bar was lumbered with the laddish name of Fudrucker's, but it's now one of the trendy Russian Babushka chain, with a fabulous range of vodkas (savoury garlic and chilli, anyone?). Babushka, in its current incarnation, is glimpsed briefly near the opening of sex-swap comedy *Virtual Sexuality*.

The Bramley Arms, Freston Road
tube: Latimer Road (Hammersmith & City line)
This pub has a long history as a film location. Outside the Bramley, the police chase ends with a pile-up in Ealing's *The Lavender Hill Mob*. Twenty-eight years later, Spider (Gary Shail) is attacked by Rockers on the same spot, after his scooter breaks down in *Quadrophenia*. In a gesture inspired by Ealing's *Passport to Pimlico*, when threatened with eviction in the late seventies, local residents appealed to the UN, and the *Quadrophenia* film crew needed to get 'passports' for the 'Kingdom of Frestonia' in order to film here. And from Mod to Punk – the Bramley is both 'The Old Mahon', where Sid Vicious (Gary Oldman) boozes, and the office of Malcolm MacLaren (David Hayman), filmed in rooms above the bar, in *Sid and Nancy*. Jeremy Irons drinks here in the film of Harold Pinter's reverse-timescale drama *Betrayal*. The pub can also be seen in John Boorman's offbeat drama of West London life *Leo the Last*.

Cash Bar, 105-107 Talbot Road
© 020.7221.8059
tube: Westbourne Park (Hammersmith & City line)
An upmarket music bar, which used to be Coins Café, a much-missed coffee house with a terrific reputation for good, basic grub. It was transformed into 'It's Only Natural', the organic bakery run by sexually curious James Purefoy, cheating on Jennifer

Ehle with her gay pal, in Rose Troche's *Bedrooms & Hallways*.

Coffee Shop, 303 Westbourne Park Road
© 020.8964.5484
tube: Notting Hill Gate (Central, Circle and District lines)
What it says. This tiny refreshment spot (overshadowed by Coffee Republic next door) is a good place to grab a refreshing shot of caffeine, and is, in fact, where Hugh Grant grabs the coffee and orange juice he proceeds to slop all over Julia Roberts in *Notting Hill*. In good weather, you can sit outside at a rather wobbly tall table.

The Earl Derby, 50 Bosworth Road
© 020.8969.2879
tube: Westbourne Park (Hammersmith & City line)
This Notting Hill local is the pub Mark Rylance follows Kerry Fox to, where she's performing in *The Glass Menagerie*, in Patrice Chéreau's surprisingly explicit 2000 film of Hanif Kureishi's *Intimacy*.

The Earl of Lonsdale, 277-281 Westbourne Grove
© 020.7727.6335
tube: Notting Hill Gate (Central, Circle and District lines)
Located at the southern, antiquey end of the Portobello Road market, the Lonsdale used to be Henekey's, a pub with a reputation as a rock'n'roll hangout in the sixties and seventies. Villain James Villiers sees Tom Courtenay with agent Edward Hardwicke here, and draws the wrong conclusions, plunging Courtenay into a murky world of intrigue, in Dick Clements' swinging sixties spy spoof *Otley*.

The Frog and Firkin, 96 Ladbroke Grove
© 020.7229.5663
tube: Ladbroke Grove (Hammersmith & City line)
This pub used to be the Elgin, a notoriously characterful Notting Hill bar. Not just full of character, but full of characters – serial killer John Christie was one of its customers. The footie crowd watch Mike Bassett (Ricky Tomlinson) recite Rudyard Kipling's poem *If...* on the big-screen TV here in *Mike Bassett: England Manager*.

Ground Floor Bar, 186 Portobello Road
© 020.7243.0072
tube: Notting Hill Gate (Central, Circle and District lines)
You can't fault the name – Ground Floor Bar is exactly what it says, as is First Floor Restaurant above.

Smack in the middle of the fruit and veg stretch of Portobello Road market, the bar is your standard revamped boozer, complete with leather sofas. Stephen Baldwin and Sadie Frost relax here after shooting the crime reconstruction show, in George Sluizer's *Crimetime*.

Manor, 6-8 All Saints Road

℃ *020.7243.0969*

tube: Westbourne Park (Hammersmith & City line)

This used to be the West Indian Mas Café, now re-invented in cool classic shades and serving up modern Euro cuisine. It became the restaurant whose grand opening Gwyneth Paltrow organises in *Sliding Doors*.

FAR NORTH LONDON
The Queen's Hotel, 26 Broadway Parade

℃ *020.8340.2031*

rail: Hornsey

A Grade II listed building, built for businessman John Cathles Hill, the Queen's is another of those huge and fussy Victorian pubs dominating the local high street. It became the bar where ??? (Ray Winstone, giving a performance that deserves a much better movie) indulges his passion for karaoke in smug gangster flick *Love, Honour and Obey*. And, OK, 'Avenues & Alleyways' does make a great theme tune.

The Salisbury, 1 Grand Parade, Green Lanes

℃ *020.8800.3600*

rail: Harringay, Harringay Green Lanes

Built for the same entrepreneur as the Queen's Hotel in Harringay, the Salisbury lies just to the east, at the corner of St Ann's Road. For a culture synonymous with repression and self-discipline, the Victorians certainly let rip with their public houses. This elaborate, three-storey temple to the trinity of beer, wine and spirits became the 'Covent Garden' drinking house where a vociferous drunk (Robert Stephens) convinces the now-famous Charlie Chaplin (Robert Downey Jr) that his hometown no longer has a welcome for him in Richard Attenborough's biopic *Chaplin*. Possibly its most notable screen appearance is as the 'Northern Ireland' pub 'Fagan's' at the begining of *The Long Good Friday*, where Harold Shand's right-hand man Colin (Paul Freeman) gets involved in some very shady financial dealing and hits on the doomed Irish lad. The Salisbury appears most recently under its own name as the big, bustling pub where Miranda Richardson looks for Gabriel Byrne in David Cronenberg's *Spider*.

EAST LONDON
Bacchus, 177 Hoxton Street

℃ *020.7739.7176*

tube/rail: Old Street (Northern line)

A quiet – apart from the huge video screen – little local in the middle of Hoxton street-market, which has changed little since it stood in for the real pub where George Cornell was gunned down, in Peter Medak's *The Krays*. The Blind Beggar, where a cocky Ronnie popped Cornell in a pub full of witnesses, much changed and spruced up, can still be seen in Whitechapel.

City Spice, 138 Brick Lane

℃ *020.7247.1012*

website: www.city-spice.co.uk

tube: Shoreditch (East London line)

Bangladeshi restaurant City Spice was previously the famed Clifton Restaurant, one of the longest established curry houses in Bangla Town, where Irish terrorist Miranda Richardson spies on Jaye Davidson and Stephen Rea in *The Crying Game*.

Fifteen, 15 Westland Place

℃ *020.7251.1515*

tube/rail: Old Street (Northern line)

TV chef Jamie Oliver's bold venture to turn fifteen deprived youngsters into top chefs gave rise to this restaurant, and the wave of publicity generated by the TV series which charted the rocky progress of the project ensured that the restaurant was, in the short term at least, solidly booked out. The building can be seen on screen, before it was a restaurant, as the spacious New York-style loft apartment of Kevin McKidd in Rose Troche's *Bedrooms & Hallways*.

Mother, 333 Old Street

℃ *020.7684.0723*

website: www.333mother.com

tube/rail: Old Street (Northern line)

For many years this was the London Apprentice, a large and really quite frisky gay bar, which appears as the far more discreet 'Metro Bar' where Col (Jim Broadbent) tends bar and Dil (Jaye Davidson) performs in *The Crying Game*. It has now been relaunched as this refreshingly informal (for increasingly style-conscious Hoxton), and straight, club, visited by Minnie Driver and Mary McCormack in *High Heels and Low Lifes*.

The Royal Oak, 73 Columbia Road

℃ *020.7739.8204*

tube/rail: Old Street (Northern line)

A gay bar in the evenings, on Sunday mornings the Oak caters to the crowds flocking to the famous

Columbia Road flower market. The faded, period charm of the neighbouring streets has resulted in numerous large and small screen appearances. It became 'Samoan Jo's', the South Seas theme pub where Bacon is served, not a refreshing drink, but a bleedin' rainforest in *Lock, Stock and Two Smoking Barrels*. It was also the local 'East End' boozer in David A Stewart's *Honest*, while the exterior was the pub smashed up in *The Krays*. The Royal Oak was also the time-warping local in UK TV sitcom *Goodnight Sweetheart*.

The Ten Bells, 84 Commercial Street

✆ 020.7377.2145

tube/rail: Liverpool Street (Hammersmith & City, Circle, Metropolitan and Central line)

Thankfully, after being called the Jack the Ripper for many years, the pub has now reverted to its original name. Located on the corner alongside Christ Church Spitalfields, the pub is where the prostitutes congregate in the Hughes brothers' Ripper movie *From Hell*, though for the film it was reconstructed in Prague. The pub also has memorabilia from the case.

The Waterman's Arms, 1 Glenaffric Avenue

✆ 020.7538.0712

DLR: Island Gardens Station

A legendary waterfront pub with live entertainment, once owned by writer and broadcaster Dan Farson, one of the fifties Bohemians of the Colony Room. It is 'The Governor General', where Harlod Shand (Bob Hoskins) finds Billy (Nick Stringer) – "Walk to the car Billy, or I'll blow your spine off!" – while Victoria (Helen Mirren) is placating the Americans, in *The Long Good Friday*.

SOUTHEAST LONDON
The Five Bells Public House, New Cross Road

tube/rail: New Cross Gate (East London line)

This striking Italianate palazzo – it's a Grade II listed building – is the boozer in Gary Oldman's intense but glum film about domestic violence, *Nil by Mouth*.

The Gloucester, 1 King William Walk

✆ 020.8858.2666

rail/DLR: Greenwich

A large and popular gay bar, which appeared as itself in feelgood romance *Beautiful Thing*.

The Wishing Well, 79 Choumert Road

✆ 020.7639.5052

rail: Peckham Rye

If the exterior of the fictitious 'Coach and Horses' in Fred Schepisi's *Last Orders* seems oddly different from the interior (just look at the windows), it's

because they were filmed at two different pubs. While the interiors were filmed in a disused pub (the Larkhall Tavern, in Clapham), the exterior – which is Bermondsey in the book – is the Wishing Well. And it looks even less like its counterpart without the set dressing. Oh, and if you're a real fan of the movie, you can stay here, as the Wishing Well is also a hotel.

SOUTH-CENTRAL LONDON
The Brewery Tap, 68 Wandsworth High Street

✆ 020.8870.2894

rail: Wandsworth Town

Ale has been brewed on this site since 1581. For a long time, it's been Young's Brewery, with the Tap as its outlet. Unlikely as it seems, the Tap was home to Robert Mitchum in Robert Clouse's 1977 international thriller (largely filmed in Hong Kong) *The Amsterdam Kill*.

Caesars Nightclub, 156-160 Streatham Hill

✆ 020.8671.3000

rail: Streatham Hill

The site of the rigged and unlicensed bareknuckle 'boxing match' in *Snatch*, when the cheerfully incomprehensible Mickey O'Neil (Brad Pitt) refuses to go down in the fourth. The boxing ring was erected over the club's dancefloor, and seventies and eighties music is the more usual entertainment. Cheap and cheerful or huge and cheesy? It probably amounts to the same thing.

Cantina del Ponte, Butler's Wharf Building, 36c Shad Thames

✆ 020.7403.5403

tube: Tower Hill (District and Circle lines)

tube/rail: London Bridge (Northern and Jubilee lines)

Terence Conran's riverside Italian restaurant is part of the redevelopment of the old warehouse area southeast of Tower Bridge. It was the site of caddish Daniel Cleaver's date with Bridget in *Bridget Jones's Diary*.

Dogstar Bar, 389 Coldharbour Lane

✆ 020.7733.7515

website: www.dogstarbar.co.uk

tube/rail: Brixton (Victoria line)

The Dogstar Bar is probably more famous in its previous incarnation as Jamaican hangout the Atlantic, which was burned down twice in two separate riots during the eighties. It can be seen as the 'Dog Bar' – "formerly the Atlantic, famous Jamaican hangout 'til it got burned down twice in two separate riots" – where the mix of scammers, druggies and flakes congregate in *South West 9*. So you'd never figure that one out then... It is now a hectic music bar with a different club night every night, a late licence and free entry on week days.

The George Inn, 77 Borough High Street

✆ *020.7407.2056*
tube/rail: London Bridge (Northern and Jubilee lines)
Not many pubs are owned by the National Trust, but the George, hidden away in a courtyard off the High Street is London's last remaining galleried inn. It can be a bit touristy at times, but the long series of dark oakwood bars, dating from 1676, are a joy. What stands is a third of the original building, which once enclosed three sides of the courtyard. Two wings were demolished, which apparently provided an opportunity to design a courtyard for devotees of council block chic. The George became the coaching tavern Tom's coach departs from in the 1951 film of *Tom Brown's Schooldays*.

The Globe, 8 Bedale Street

✆ *020.7407.0043*
tube/rail: London Bridge (Northern and Jubilee lines)
Located beneath the railway lines alongside Borough Market. Renée Zellweger lives her singleton life and writes her eponymous diary above the Globe in *Bridget Jones's Diary*. The pub appeared far less cosy as the sleazy 'Critchley Hotel' in the Michael Caine-Bob Hoskins caper movie *Blue Ice*.

The Jolly Gardeners, 49 Black Prince Road

tube/rail: Vauxhall (Victoria line)
This became 'The Drowning Trout', the big old pub where Bullet Tooth Tony (Vinnie Jones) is confronted by Sol (Lennie James) and co before the bloody shoot up in *Snatch*. Despite its proximity to Westminster, do remember that this is a local boozer, not a Mayfair winebar.

SOUTHWEST LONDON
La Bersagliera, 372 King's Road

✆ *020.7352.5993*
tube: South Kensington, Gloucester Road (Circle, District and Piccadilly lines)
This small Italian restaurant in a cavern-like space was, in fact, the 'Cavern' coffee house where those groovy teens gather after summoning the Count in *Dracula A.D. 1972*. At the fag-end of the Hammer series, the Count is dragged into the 20th century, but the biggest horrors on display are those seventies fashion nightmares.

El Blason, 8-9 Blacklands Terrace

✆ *020.7823.7383*
tube: Sloane Square (District and Circle lines)
Amazingly, this Spanish restaurant, just off the King's Road, remains pretty much as it was when Michelangelo Antonioni shot photographer David Hemmings showing his portfolio of images of working class men to his agent Peter Bowles for *Blowup* in 1966.

The King's Head, Kenway Road

tube: Earl's Court (Piccadilly and District lines)
In the days when the area was still known as Kangaroo Valley, Bazza (Barry Crocker, whose other contribution to Antipodean culture is singing the *Neighbours*' theme song) was approached by ad exec Groove Courtenay (Jonathan Hardy) to advertise 'High Camp Cigarettes' here in Aussie gross-out *The Adventures of Barry Mackenzie*. Since the scene was filmed, the pub has had a serious wine bar makeover.

Roof Garden and Rainbow Room, 99 Kensington High Street (entrance on Derry Street)

✆ *020.7937.7994*
website: www.roofgardens.com
tube: High Street Kensington (Circle and District lines)
One of Kensington's best kept secrets is the Roof Garden atop the old Biba/Derry and Toms department store (now housing Marks and Spencers and British Home Stores). On the sixth floor, a hundred feet above the bustle of the high street, are one-and-a-half acres of garden, woodland and, believe it or not, flamingos. It's open to the public from 11am to 5pm (the entrance is actually around the corner, on Derry Street).The *très* exclusive nightclub, the Rainbow Room (open Thursdays and Saturdays, members only), became the pink deco 'Chapel of Our Lady of the Checkout Counter' for the nightmare climax of Terry Gilliam's dazzling *Brazil*. It was also once the legendary Regine's nightclub, which became the elaborately mirrored restaurant where Victoria (Helen Mirren) struggles to convince potential American partners that a few bomb explosions are all in a day's work, in *The Long Good Friday*.

FAR WEST LONDON
The Blue Anchor, 13 Lower Mall

✆ *020.8748.5774*
tube: Hammersmith (Hammersmith & City, Piccadilly and District lines)
Hearty pub on the Thames, and just the place to sink a pint after pulling on the oars – the rowing club is

next door. Site of the "sponsored epileptic fit" in *Sliding Doors*.

FAR NORTHWEST LONDON
Crocker's Folly, 24 Aberdeen Place
℗ *020.7286.6608*
tube: Warwick Avenue (Bakerloo line)
One of three gorgeously photogenic Maida Vale establishments, this grand Victorian hotel with elaborate marble decoration was built in 1898 by businessman Frank Crocker. The legend goes that Frank built the hotel on the assumption that the new West Country line would terminate at Maida Vale, but when he discovered the terminus was to be Marylebone, he killed himself by leaping out of an upstairs window. However, like the Ploughman's Lunch (an ad-man's invention to sell pub food), this seems to be an urban myth. The nickname Crocker's Folly only became the official monicker in 1987, before which it was called the Crown Hotel. And although Frank Crocker did indeed shuffle off at the early age of 41, he died of natural causes. The pub became the 'New York' writers club where Pete Van Wherry (Gene Hackman) drinks with Jack Reed (Warren Beatty) in Beatty's *Reds*. Hackman, who was suffering from a bad cold, reportedly tired of director Beatty's continued retakes. However, the perfectionism paid off with a Best Director Oscar. It's also the gentlemen's bar where Gwendolen (Frances O'Connor) raises eyebrows by following 'Jack' (Colin Firth) in *The Importance of Being Earnest*.

The Crown, 152 Cricklewood Broadway
℗ *020.8452.4175*
rail: Cricklewood
This popular and photogenic pub has been a backdrop to plenty of TV shows, and is the 'Camden' pub where Catherine McCormack drowns her sorrows after her short-lived marriage to Douglas Henshall, before quickly hooking up with feckless painter Dougray Scott, in *This Year's Love*. Since a recent major revamp though, it's no longer the rather down-at-heel boozer seen in the film.

The National Club, 234 Kilburn High Road
℗ *020.7328.3141*
tube: Kilburn (Jubilee line)
Another London club masquerading as Hamburg in Iain Softley's *Backbeat*, the biopic of Stuart Sutcliffe. It features as the 'Star Club', where the Beatles perform 'Twist and Shout'.

Otto Dining Lounge, 215 Sutherland Avenue
℗ *020.7266.3131*

tube: Maida Vale (Bakerloo line)
The determinedly isolationist Will (Hugh Grant) chooses this spacious and coolly minimal restaurant for his series of disastrous dates in *About a Boy*. Cheekily, it's also the glass-fronted restaurant where Marcus (Nicholas Hoult) tries to set Will up on a date with his mum (Toni Collette) in the same movie. The glass walls look out onto Maida Vale.

The Prince Alfred, 5a Formosa Street
℗ *020.7286.3287*
tube: Warwick Avenue (Bakerloo line)
A real joy, with glistening mahogany and sinuously curving etched glass windows, the Alfred is an irresistible draw to film-makers. It was slightly scruffier when they shot the scene in *King Ralph* where Ralph (John Goodman), having inherited the English throne, discusses the car industry with the King of Zambesi (Rudolph Walker) over a game of darts. However, all those location fees seem to have been put to good use – the pub positively gleams in Neil Jordan's *The End of the Affair*, when Maurice Bendrix (Ralph Fiennes) receives evidence of supposed 'intimacy' from private detective Parkis (Ian Hart). The pub can also be seen in Michael Radford's unbearably pretentious 1998 film *B Monkey*, with Rupert Everett, Asia Argento (daughter of Italian horrormeister Dario) and Jonathan Rhys Meyers. Don't be put off by the ordinary public bar. There are, in fact, more private bars, which you reach by crawling through what are basically glorified catflaps (these openings were intended for use by cleaners). Go on, you know you want to try it. The rear has also been opened up as the Formosa Dining Room restaurant.

The Warrington Hotel, 93 Warrington Crescent
℗ *020.7286.2929*
tube: Warwick Avenue (Bakerloo line)
Overflowing with crimson and gilt, the hotel's glorious art nouveau bar could be the anteroom of a Parisian bordello, and rumours persist that you could once be entertained in the Warrington's private rooms. Music hall star Marie Lloyd certainly enjoyed quaffing Champers in the theatrical ambience. Detective Laurence Olivier comforts a distraught Carol Lynley here in Otto Preminger's delightfully wacky psycho-thriller *Bunny Lake Is Missing*.

Shopping

CENTRAL LONDON
LEICESTER SQUARE TO COVENT GARDEN
Cinema Store, 4B&C Orion House, Upper St Martin's Lane
✆ *4B: 020.7379.7838, 4C: 020.7379.7895*
website: www.the-cinema-store.com
Mail order service (worldwide)
tube: Leicester Square (Piccadilly and Northern lines)
4B stocks movie-related magazines, toys, T-shirts, DVDs and collectibles of all sorts, while 4C stocks books, laser discs and rare videos. Look out for occasional celebrity signings.

Dress Circle, 57-59 Monmouth Street, Upper St Martin's Lane
✆ *020.7240.2227*
website: www.dresscircle.co.uk
tube: Covent Garden (Piccadilly line)
Dress Circle is the specialist shop for soundtracks. Closed for refurbishment at the time of writing, you can still visit online.

Forbidden Planet, 179 Shaftesbury Avenue
✆ *020.7420.3666*
website: www.forbiddenplanet.com
Mail order service
tube: Piccadilly Circus (Piccadilly and Bakerloo lines)
The store for everything sci-fi, horror, fantasy and comics. There are also branches in Croydon and Dartford, if you're in the area.

Fraser's Autographs, 399 Strand
✆ *020.7836.9325*
website: www.frasersautographs.com
rail/tube: Charing Cross (Northern and Bakerloo lines)
Part of the Stanley Gibbons group (which started out stamp collecting), Fraser's deals in authenticated autographs, and claims to have over 60,000 – one of the largest selections – from Oliver Cromwell to Liz Hurley. It also deals in celebrity memorabilia (they've offered Al Capone's silk scarf and Monroe's bathing suit). You can buy online, and there are also online auctions.

Pleasures of Past Times, 11 Cecil Court
✆ *020.7836.1142*
tube: Leicester Square (Northern and Piccadilly lines)
Another unpredictable mix of nostalgia, including books, memorabilia and postcards.

Stage Door Prints, 9 Cecil Court
✆ *020.7240.1683*
tube: Leicester Square (Northern and Piccadilly lines)
Located in the narrow alleyway of antiquarian bookshops specialising in travel, theatre and the like, where Anthony Hopkins browses in *84 Charing Cross Road*, Stage Door Prints specialises in period prints and memorabilia, as well as stocking a selection of classic movie star autographs.

OXFORD STREET TO SOHO
Flashbacks, 6 Silver Place
✆ *020.7437.8562*
website: www.dacre.org/flash
Mail order service
tube: Piccadilly Circus (Piccadilly and Bakerloo lines)
This shop specialises in memorabilia, including vintage and modern posters and front-of-house stills, as well as those precious pressbooks.

Foyles Bookshop, 113-119 Charing Cross Road
✆ *020.7437.5660*
website: www.foyles.co.uk
tube: Tottenham Court Road (Northern and Central lines)
Though no longer London's biggest bookstore, Foyles is still something of an institution and remains almost wilfully eccentric. Cluttered and sometimes confusing, it's still possible to come across that oddity you wouldn't find elsewhere.

Grant & Cutler, 55-57 Great Marlborough Street
✆ *020.7734.2012*
website: www.grantandcutler.com
tube: Russell Square (Piccadilly line)
Foreign language book specialists, stocking books on world cinema and screenplays.

Vintage Magazine Company, 55 Charing Cross Road
✆ *020.7494.4064*
website: www.vinmag.com
tube: Leicester Square (Northern and Piccadilly lines)
A vast array of magazines of all periods, some in mint condition (and priced accordingly). The store's remit covers all forms of printed material, including newspapers, adverts, ephemera and stills.

It has expanded to five stores plus online marketing, and now stocks mousepads, T-shirts and kids' clothing.

Vintage Magazine Company, 39-43 Brewer Street
℗ 020.7439.8525
website: www.vinmag.com
tube: Piccadilly Circus (Piccadilly and Bakerloo lines)

Zwemmer Media & Contemporary Art Shop, 80 Charing Cross Road
℗ 020.7240.4157
website: www.zwemmer.com
Mail order service
tube: Leicester Square (Piccadilly and Northern lines)
Part of the stretch of dusty old bookshops on Charing Cross Road between Leicester Square and Cambridge Circus, Zwemmer is one of the great art bookshops, with an excellent cinema section. The area seems to be under threat from commercialisation – the famous number 84 is now a bar – so visit while you can.

TRAFALGAR SQUARE TO MAYFAIR
Institute of Contemporary Arts Bookshop, Nash House, the Mall
℗ 020.7766.1452
website: www.ica.org.uk
tube/rail: Charing Cross (Northern and Bakerloo lines)
If you're catching a film or exhibition here, don't forget the art and cinema bookshop.

NORTH-CENTRAL LONDON
Offstage Theatre and Film Bookshop, 37 Chalk Farm Road
℗ 020.7485.4996
tube: Chalk Farm (Northern line)
While predominantly a theatre bookshop, it also has an excellent film section, with a fine range of technical and professional books if you're wanting to get into the profession.

NORTHWEST LONDON
Owl Bookshop, 209 Kentish Town Road
℗ 020.7485.7793
tube/rail: Kentish Town (Northern line)
A leading indie shop specialising in modern fiction, biography and children's books, this is where Sinead Cusack works in Les Blair's Bad Behaviour.

Everyman Cinema, 5 Holly Bush Vale
℗ 0870.0664777

website: www.everymancinema.com
tube: Hampstead (Northern line)
Film scholars and movie enthusiasts alike will find a range of materials at this famed repertory cinema.

NORTHEAST LONDON
Decorum Books, 24 Cloudesley Square
℗ 020.7278.1838
website: www.decorumbooks.co.uk
Mail order only
tube: Angel (Northern line)
Specialises in film, theatre and music books and scores.

Terence Kaye, 52 Neeld Crescent
℗ 020.8202.8188
tube: Hendon Central (Northern line)
Specialising in theatre, film and the performing arts, this shop is a treasure trove of rare and collectible books.

WEST LONDON
FITZROVIA TO HATTON GARDEN
Cinema Bookshop, 13-14 Great Russell Street
℗ 020.7636.0206
tube: Tottenham Court Road (Northern and Central lines)
One of a dying breed of independent bookshops – small, cramped and packed with all manner of rare, out-of-print and obscure books on film. It's easy to spend hours here.

SOUTHEAST LONDON
Spread Eagle Book Shop, 8 Nevada Street
℗ 020.8305.1666
website: www.spreadeagle.org
rail/DLR: Greenwich
A second-hand bookshop with a good selection of film books, along with movie ephemera such as posters and stills.

SOUTH-CENTRAL LONDON
Cinegrafix Gallery, 4 Copper Row, Shad Thames
℗ 020.7234.0566
tube/DLR: Tower Hill (District and Circle lines)
Movie poster specialists.

The Screenwriter's Store, Friars House, 157-168 Blackfriars Road
℗ 020.7261.1908
website: www.screenwriterstore.co.uk
tube/rail: Blackfriars (District and Circle lines)
Suppliers of screenplays and screenwriting software.

Entertainment: Cinemas

Before the video revolution of the eighties, and in the days when television closed down before midnight, many of the capital's arthouse cinemas kept afloat with wildly imaginative double bills every night of the week. Catching a classic art movie meant scouring listings magazines for a rare screening, rather than slipping a cassette into the VCR. The Curzon (now the Curzon Mayfair, since a new sister screen opened in the West End) still survives, but the Paris Pullman, off Old Brompton Road, which offered a double bill every night of the week – pairing *Badlands* with *Edipo Re* or *Psycho* with *if...* – is now a block of flats, and the Academy Cinemas on Oxford Street, with their distinctive woodcut posters, are just a memory. With the relentless encroachment of multiplexes, indie cinemas are now becoming a rarity. The following is a listing of some of the remaining London independent cinemas, along with movie houses of particular interest.

CENTRAL LONDON
LEICESTER SQUARE TO SOHO
Curzon Soho, 99 Shaftesbury Avenue
℃ 0871.871.0022
website: www.curzoncinemas.com
tube: Leicester Square (Northern and Piccadilly lines)
The newer West End sister to the old, established Curzon in Mayfair.

Prince Charles Cinema, 7 Leicester Place
℃ 020.7494.3654
website: www.princecharlescinema.com
tube: Leicester Square (Northern and Piccadilly lines)
In the 19th century, the Barker-Burford Panorama stood on this site. Since 1991, the Prince Charles has been a repertory house with a different rota of films every day, making it a useful place to catch up with those recent movies you missed on first release.

Odeon West End, 40 Leicester Square
℃ 0870.505.0007
website: www.odeon.co.uk
tube: Leicester Square (Northern and Piccadilly lines)
The second Odeon cinema in the square.

Odeon Leicester Square, 22-24 Leicester Square
℃ 0870.505.0007
website: www.odeon.co.uk
tube: Leicester Square (Northern and Piccadilly lines)
This single-screen cinema's striking black granite tower defines the streamline moderne Odeon style, but its thirties interior was appallingly revamped in 1967. Premières are often held here. It's outside the Odeon that innocent murder suspect Jon Finch waits for Anna Massey, after spending an unpleasant night in a dosshouse, in Alfred Hitchcock's *Frenzy*.

UCI Empire Leicester Square, 5-6 Leicester Square
℃ 0870.010.2030
website: www.uci-cinemas.co.uk
tube: Leicester Square (Northern and Piccadilly lines)
Originally one of the theatres which filled the square in the 19th century, the Empire was later remodelled into a cinema. Located on the north side, this is the site of the glitzy movie première that ends *Notting Hill*. Outside, where you'll usually find street performers and living statues, Hrithik Roshan conjures up a bevy of dancing girls for the 'Vande Mataram' number in *Kabhi Khushi Kabhi Gham*.

Warner Village West End, 3 Cranbourn Street
℃ 0870.240.6020
website: www.warnervillage.co.uk
tube: Leicester Square (Northern and Piccadilly lines)
A huge complex of nine screens just off the east corner of the square.

OXFORD STREET TO SOHO
The Other Cinema, 11 Rupert Street
℃ *info: 020.7437.0757, box office: 020.7734.1506*
website: www.picturehouse-cinemas.co.uk
tube: Piccadilly Circus (Piccadilly and Bakerloo lines), Leicester Square (Northern and Piccadilly lines)
A new addition to the West End, specialising in cult, offbeat and independent powerful cinema, The Other Cinema claims to be "*the* place to see films that make you think."

TRAFALGAR SQUARE TO MAYFAIR
Curzon Mayfair, 38 Curzon Street
℃ 020.7495.0500
website: www.curzoncinemas.com
tube: Green Park (Piccadilly, Victoria and Jubilee lines), Hyde Park Corner (Piccadilly line)

One of the surviving classic arthouse cinemas, it is a Grade II listed building, but has recently undergone extensive refurbishment which included splitting the original auditorium into two screens, of 320 and eighty-three seats.

Institute of Contemporary Arts Cinema, Nash House, the Mall

℗ 020.7930.3647
website: www.ica.org.uk
tube/rail: Charing Cross (Bakerloo and Northern lines)
The cinema screens art house films from the ICA's repertory in this avant garde arts centre on the Mall. It's also the site of the book launch in *Bridget Jones's Diary*.

NORTHWEST LONDON
Everyman Cinema, 5 Holly Bush Vale

℗ 0870.066.4777
website: www.everymancinema.com
tube: Hampstead (Northern line)
The UK's oldest repertory cinema. Built in 1913 as a community centre, the Everyman became a theatre in 1920 with a reputation for staging avant garde works (Noël Coward's *The Vortex* premièred here – drugs! homosexuality!). Having been converted into a cinema in 1933, this is one of the great London arthouses to have survived the home video revolution, and recently staved off redevelopment with a little help from a high profile campaign spearheaded by Britpack stalwarts including Ewan McGregor and Jude Law. Oh, and it has good old-fashioned love seats…

Phoenix Cinema, 52 High Road

℗ 020.8444.6789
tube: East Finchley (Northern line)
Opened in 1912 as the East Finchley Picturedrome, it was called the Rex in the thirties. The building still retains many of its original Edwardian and deco features and shows indie and arthouse presentations.

NORTHEAST LONDON
Barbican Screen, Barbican Centre, Silk Street

℗ box office: 020.7638.8891,
hotline: 020.7382.7000
website: www.barbican.org.uk/film
tube: Barbican (Circle, Hammersmith & City and Metropolitan lines)
There are two cinema screens in Europe's biggest arts and conference complex, which also houses theatres, concert halls and restaurants. The screens show mainstream movies, arthouse and special seasons – which recently included the Australian Film Festival, an art deco film season and a Spike Lee retrospective, with a personal appearance by the director.

Rio Cinema, 107 Kingsland High Street

℗ 020.7241.9410
website: www.riocinema.ndirect.co.uk
rail: Dalston Kingsland
A mainstream and arthouse cinema with occasional seasons. The Turkish Film Festival has been held at the Rio in December for the last ten years, and has recently been joined by the Kurdish Film Festival, held in November.

WEST LONDON
PADDINGTON TO NOTTING HILL
Electric Cinema, 191 Portobello Road

℗ 020.7908.9696
website: www.electriccinema.co.uk
tube: Notting Hill Gate (Central, District and Circle lines)
One of the UK's oldest purpose-built cinemas, the Electric was built in 1910 when Portobello Road was a snazzy shopping street. It has remained largely unchanged, and still has a screen suited to the old Academy 4x3 proportion. By the sixties it had degenerated into something of a fleapit (where serial killer Reginald Christie worked), and in the seventies it became a friendly, scruffy arthouse cinema. It has changed hands several times since the mid-eighties but has now been comprehensively restored as a cinema club and brasserie complex, and now boasts leather seats, footstools and, unfortunately, the inevitable tables for food and drink. Sadie Frost and Stephen Baldwin have a raunchy sex session in the doorway alongside the Electric in *Crimetime*. Geeky Chas (Luke de Lacy) gets a few home truths here from Justine (Laura Fraser) in *Virtual Sexuality*. The Electric stands in for Brighton's Duke of York cinema, where John Hannah and Famke Janssen have a clandestine meeting with Peter Stormare during a showing of Orson Welles' *The Lady From Shanghai*, in Rob Walker's convoluted mystery *Circus*. It can also be seen in Hanif Kureishi's *London Kills Me*. You can even glimpse the Electric's (then) crumbly exterior on Portobello Road, which Hugh Grant passes during the bravura 'four seasons' sequence in *Notting Hill*.

Gate Cinema, 87 Notting Hill Gate

℗ 020.7727.4043
website: www.gatecinema.co.uk
tube: Notting Hill Gate (Central, District and Circle lines)

Originally the Electric Palace, built in 1911, this indie cinema now has a modern frontage, which was rebuilt after bomb damage, but still retains the original Edwardian plasterwork.

Notting Hill Coronet, 103 Notting Hill Gate
℃ 020.7727.6705
tube: Notting Hill Gate (Central, District and Circle lines)
Built as a theatre in 1898 (where legends such as Henry Irving and Sarah Bernhardt performed), it was converted into a cinema in the 1920s and survives as a mainstream movie house. Hugh Grant watches *Helix*, the sci-fi movie short on both horses and hounds starring Anna Scott (Julia Roberts), here in *Notting Hill*.

FAR NORTH LONDON
Muswell Hill Odeon, Fortis Green Road
℃ 0870.505.0007
website: www.odeon.co.uk
tube: Highgate (Northern line)
As far as programming goes, this is just another link in the Odeon chain, but the 3-screen cinema itself is a deco classic.

EAST LONDON
Genesis Cinema, 93-95 Mile End Road
℃ 020.7780.2000
website: www.genesiscinema.co.uk
tube: Mile End (Central, Hammersmith & City and District lines)
The Genesis Cinema stands on a site which has been used for entertainment since 1848, when a pub-cum-music hall, The Eagle, stood here. It subsequently became Lusby's Music Hall and, after a fire, it reopened in 1885 as the Paragon Theatre of Varieties, where Charlie Chaplin performed with Fred Karno's troupe before heading off to Hollywood. With music hall in decline, by the time it was re-named the Mile End Empire in 1912 it was already unofficially functioning as a cinema. In 1928 it became a UPT cinema, which was subsequently purchased by ABC in 1934. The current cinema was built in 1939. In 1963, it hosted the Royal Première of *Sparrows Can't Sing*, filmed locally and based on Joan Littlewood's stage production. It's now a 5-screen independent cinema, and hosts the Raindance Film Festival.

Stratford Picture House, Gerry Raffles Square, Salway Road
℃ 020.8555.3366
website: www.picturehouse-cinemas.co.uk
tube/rail/DLR: Stratford (Central and Jubilee lines)

A 4-screen cinema, alongside the famous Theatre Royal (not to be confused with the same name, same owner cinema located in Stratford-Upon-Avon), which shows the latest big releases along with indie fare. It is part of the same organisation as the West End's The Other Cinema.

SOUTH-CENTRAL LONDON
BFI London IMAX Cinema,
1 Charlie Chaplin Walk, South Bank
℃ 020.7902.1234
website: www.bfi.org.uk/showing/imax
tube/rail: Waterloo (Northern, Bakerloo and Jubilee lines)
You can't miss the giant illuminated cinema in what used to be the old concrete 'bullring' in front of Waterloo Station. Big, big, big is the order of the day. Overwhelming cinematic experience or monumental headache? Your call. Part of the BFI, the 477-seat cinema, with the UK's largest screen (20 by 26 metres) opened in 1999, with the emphasis on spectacular travelogues, occasional 3D features and showings of classic movies (which don't occupy the full giant screen). Hugh Grant waits for his date outside the IMAX in *About a Boy*.

National Film Theatre, South Bank
℃ 020.7928.3232
website: www.bfi.org.uk/showing/nft
tube/rail: Waterloo (Northern, Bakerloo and Jubilee lines)
The showcase of the British Film Institute, with a varied repertory: rarities, special seasons and lectures. Recent interviewees have included Robert Altman, Richard Widmark and Ethan Hawke.

Ritzy Cinema, Brixton Oval, Coldharbour Lane
℃ 020.7733.2229
website: www.ritzycinema.co.uk
tube/rail: Brixton (Victoria line)
The Ritzy opened in 1911 as the Electric Pavilion, but after a couple of name changes it closed in the mid-seventies, but was restored in 1978 to become – with 5 screens – the UK's largest arthouse complex.

SOUTHWEST LONDON
Ciné Lumière, Institut Français,
17 Queensberry Place
℃ 020.7073.1350
website: www.institut-francais.org.uk
tube: South Kensington (District, Circle and Piccadilly lines)
Un peu de France in South Ken. The emphasis is obviously on French cinema, though you'll also

find international classics. Being French, the venue is a triumph of style in the beautiful brick and glazed South Ken institute, with its art deco lobby. There's also food and drink – excellent, though not cheap.

Watermans, 40 High Street
℡ *020.8232.1010*
website: www.watermans.org.uk
tube: Gunnersbury (District line)
An arts centre overlooking Kew Gardens, with a theatre, gallery, workshops and an intimate 125-seat cinema.

FAR WEST LONDON
Himalaya Palace, 14 South Road
℡ *020.8813.8844*
website: www.himalayapalacecinema.co.uk
rail: Southall
Built in 1928, and looking like a more modest cousin of Grauman's Chinese Theater in Hollywood, this Grade II listed cinema has since been renovated as a showcase for both Bollywood and Hollywood blockbusters.

Riverside Studios Cinema, Crisp Road
℡ *020.8237.1111*
website: www.riversidestudios.co.uk
tube: Hammersmith (Piccadilly, District and Hammersmith & City lines)
Built as a water pump factory, the building was converted into a film studio in 1934 by Triumph Films (*The Seventh Veil*, with James Mason and Ann Todd, was shot here), and into a TV studio in 1954 by the BBC. *Hancock's Half Hour*, *Z-Cars*, *Doctor Who* and *Blue Peter* are among the classic television shows which were broadcast from here, until the 'Beeb' moved out in 1975 and the Riverside became an arts and media centre. The cinema hosts special events, which have included the Italian Film Festival and a season of contemporary Greek cinema.

FAR NORTHWEST LONDON
Tricycle, 269 Kilburn High Road
℡ *020.7328.1000*
website: www.tricycle.co.uk
tube: Kilburn (Jubilee line)
rail: Brondesbury
Behind the quirky period façade lies a smart arts complex, with a theatre, gallery and spanking new, award-winning cinema. It shows Thursday matinees and world cinema at weekends. In April-May, the Tricycle hosts the Ballygowan London Irish Film Festival. Take a look alongside Kilburn tube

station to see the site of the 'Bijou' frontage in *The Smallest Show On Earth*.

Festivals

Apart from the obvious London Film Festival, a host of specialist seasons can be found. Some, like the Lesbian and Gay Festival, are long established; some flourish for a year and disappear. Check the internet or a regular London listings publication such as *Time Out* for what's coming up.

Australian Film Festival
℡ *Barbican box office: 020.7638.8891*
website: www.barbican.org.uk/australianfilm
Held at the Barbican, March 2003 saw the ninth Australian festival, with premières of the latest releases from the busy film industry, along with documentaries and shorts.

BFM International Film Festival
website: www.bfmfilmfestival.com,
Black Filmmaker Magazine: www.blackfilmmakermag.com
This festival, organised by Black Filmmaker Magazine, has been running for four years and celebrates black world cinema with UK premières and seasons of older films. Every year there is the presentation of a Lifetime Achievement Award, which in 2002 went to Pam Grier. Venues include West End Odeons, Ciné Lumière, the Rio in Dalston and Kilburn's Tricycle.

London Film Festival
website: www.rlff.com
2002 saw the forty-sixth annual London Film Festival, Europe's largest public film event. For the last three years, it's borne the name Regus, but the festival is now looking around for a new sponsor. It's usually held in November, with screenings at the NFT on the South Bank and at various West End cinemas.

London Lesbian & Gay Film Festival
website: www.llgff.com
Another long-runner – April 2003 saw the seventeenth festival. As the name indicates, the LLGFF is a celebration of queer film-making from around the world, with plenty of indie contributions and UK premières. Venues include the National Film Theatre on the South Bank and the Odeon West End.

Mosaiques

website: www.ambafrance.org.uk/institut
A film festival of cultural diversity, hosted by the Institut Français, enters its fourth year, with contributions from Maghreb, Africa and Asia. Screenings at Ciné Lumière in South Kensington.

Onedotzero

website: www.onedotzero.com
New forms of moving image are explored in the world's largest independent digital film festival. Check the website for venues.

Raindance Film Festival

website: www.raindance.co.uk
The East End's answer to Redford's Utah binge, now in its eleventh year, Raindance promotes independent, international film-making, specialising in work by first-time directors. It's your chance to spot the next wonderkid and boast that you saw their first-ever screening... Venues include the Genesis Cinema, Stratford Picture House, Rhythm Factory (also the home of film club Peep Show) and Brady Arts Centre (192-196 Hanbury Street). Spin-off festivals include Raindance East, showcasing Asian film, and Raindance Kids, for children.

Sci-Fi-London

website: www.sci-fi-london.com
The London science fiction and fantasy film festival is now in its second year and is a little sensitive about image, billing itself as 'strictly non-geeky'. Ken Russell's little-seen *The Fall of the Louse of Usher* (no, that's not a typo) premièred at the festival in 2002. Venues include Curzon Soho and The Other Cinema.

Venues change, but currently screenings are held at the Hatcham Social Club, 369 Queens Road in New Cross (itself a location for Gary Oldman's *Nil by Mouth*).

kinoKULTURE, The Horse Hospital, Colonnade

website: www.thehorsehospital.com
tube: Russell Square (Piccadilly line)
'Rarities, cult classics, uncensored cuts, B-movie gems and experimental animations' is the remit for kinoKULTURE at this avant garde arts venue, though what's on offer is likely to be much more off-the-wall. Recent events included a nude film showing. So, no *Sound of Music* karaoke, then?

Peep Show, Rhythm Factory, 16-18 Whitechapel Road

tube: Whitechapel (Hammersmith & City, District and East London lines), Aldgate East (Hammersmith & City and District lines)
Music and film just didn't work together in the same space, so this is a venue with two areas: live music and cutting edge shorts in separate spaces.

Straight8

website: www.straight8.net
Remember Super8, the 8mm film cartridge you couldn't rewind or edit or do fancy tricks with? Straight8 celebrates these limitations: 'One Super8mm cartridge, no editing'. Go to watch, or submit your own entry.

Clubs

Beyond the mainstream. If you fancy being a little more adventurous, take a chance on one of the many specialist clubs. It's always a bit of a gamble, but for every evening of bum-numbing self-indulgence, there's the chance of a genuinely thrilling experience that will expand your idea of just what cinema can be.

Exploding Cinema

website: www.explodingcinema.org
'No stars, no funding, no taste' and 'deeds not words' are the mottos of this fiercely independent collective, dedicated to non-mainstream cinema.

Historic Sites

The opening hours listed are guides only, and may change according to the time of year – always check ahead to confirm. Admission charges are not given, as these are subject to constant change.

CENTRAL LONDON
WESTMINSTER TO BELGRAVIA
Westminster Abbey
© 020.7654.4900
website: www.westminster-abbey.org
opening times: Monday-Tuesday and Thursday-Friday, 9.30-16.45, Wednesday, 18.00-19.00, Saturday, 9.30-14.45, admission charge (unless attending worship)
tube: St James's Park (District and Circle lines)
The site of every coronation since the 11th century, the abbey is also the last resting place of many of the country's monarchs (including Richard II, Henry V and Elizabeth I), as well as writers Chaucer, Dickens and Kipling, composers Handel and Purcell, and actors Garrick, Irving and Lord Olivier. *The Quatermass Xperiment* climaxes with the blobby alien being cornered and incinerated in the Abbey, but though the exterior is the real thing, with all those flaming tentacles flailing about in the nave, the interior had to be faked in the studio.

Westminster Cathedral, Victoria Street
website: www.westminstercathedral.org.uk
tube/rail: Victoria (District, Circle and Victoria lines)
Despite the plaza, this exotically Byzantine Catholic cathedral feels hemmed in by shops and office blocks. The darkly glittering interior remains unfinished, though it does contain Stations of the Cross sculpted by Eric Gill (also responsible for Broadcasting House's Prospero and Ariel). The Cathedral's campanile, from which cuddly retired assassin Rowley (Edmund Gwenn) plummets to his death in *Foreign Correspondent*, was one of the few real London locations (captured by a second unit) in the film. This very un-English cathedral was the site of Alfred Hitchcock's London memorial service in 1980. In 1978 the brick and Portland stone red-and-white striped exterior provided the exterior of the decadent disco run by Borgia Ginz (Jack Birkett, credited as Orlando) in Derek Jarman's *Jubilee*. You can take the lift up to the top of the belltower for £2 if you want an endless vista of ugly rooftops.

TRAFALGAR SQUARE TO MAYFAIR
Buckingham Palace
© 020.7766.7300
website: www.royal.gov.org
opening times: State Rooms: 1 August-28 September, 9.30-16.30; Queen's Gallery: 10.00-17.30
tube: Green Park (Piccadilly, Victoria and Jubilee lines)
The monarch's London residence is, visually, something of a disappointment, though there is a 'Lifestyles of the Rich and Famous' fascination in touring the handful of staterooms. On screen, the exterior of 'Buck House' – the interior is, for obvious reasons, rarely used for filming – is usually glimpsed behind the credits or as it whizzes past the window of a taxi, to signify 'tourist newly arrived in London'. Rita Tushingham, in just such a situation in *The Knack*, ponders whether the building might be the YWCA she's looking for. Oliver Reed and Michael Crawford find that it doesn't offer enough of a challenge for their planned caper in *The Jokers*: "Flag's not flying. That's making it too easy!" Austin Powers collects his knighthood here in *Austin Powers in Goldmember*, as does villain Gustav Graves (Toby Stephens), after making a spectacular parachute entrance, in *Die Another Day*. The palace's longest screen time must be in *Ooh, You Are Awful*, a vehicle for British TV character-comedian Dick Emery, in which, as con-man Charlie Tully, he marries off Princess Anne to a gullible Italian businessman's son in the Queen's Picture Gallery (*© 020.7930.4832*). The recently expanded gallery displays works by Rembrandt, Vermeer, Michelangelo, Rubens and Gainsborough.

NORTHWEST LONDON
Kenwood House, Hampstead Lane
© 020.8348.1286
opening times: April-October, 10.00-18.00, November-March, 10.00-16.00
tube: Hampstead, Highgate (Northern line)
rail: Hampstead Heath
A sumptuous mansion, remodelled in the 18th century by Robert Adam and once home to Lord Mansfield, which was bought in 1925 by Guiness Brewery magnate Lord Iveagh. It now houses the Iveagh Bequest of old masters, including works by Rembrandt, Vermeer, Turner, Reynolds and Gainsborough. The exterior is the location for the 'Henry James' movie Julia Roberts is making when Hugh Grant eavesdrops on her in *Notting Hill*. The pond became the grounds of the public school, where Oliver Reed is beaten up, in Michael Winner's *I'll Never Forget What's' is Name*.

NORTHEAST LONDON
Church of St Bartholomew the Great, Smithfield

website: www.greatstbarts.com
tube/rail: Farringdon (Circle Line)

Founded, like the adjoining hospital (affectionately known as St Bart's), by Rahere – one-time jester to King Henry I – in 1123, after he saw a vision of St Bartholomew while stricken with a bout of malaria on a trip to Rome, what you see today is only a fraction of the original church. After Henry VIII's dissolution of the monasteries, the church was variously used as stables and a printing works (where Benjamin Franklin worked). It's thick-set, stone interior is 'Nottingham Cathedral' in *Robin Hood: Prince of Thieves* (don't expect to see the cathedral's grand frontage though – it was a set built on the Shepperton backlot). The exterior of St Bartholomew's can be seen at the end of *Four Weddings and a Funeral* as 'St Julian's', where Charles (Hugh Grant) wriggles out of marriage to 'Duckface' (Anna Chancellor). It's to St Bartholomew's that William Shakespeare (Joseph Fiennes) goes to pray for forgiveness after the murder of Christopher Marlowe (Rupert Everett) in *Shakespeare in Love*. *The End of the Affair* sees Julianne Moore remonstrating with God here, as private investigator Ian Hart and his son spy on her.

THE CITY OF LONDON
College of Arms, Queen Victoria Street

© 020.7248.2762
website: www.college-of-arms.gov.uk
opening times: Monday-Friday, 10.00-16.00
tube: Blackfriars, Mansion House (District and Circle Lines)
rail: Blackfriars

There has been a college of arms on this site since 1555, but the original structure burnt down in the Great Fire of London in 1666 and this handsome brick building dates from the 1670s. A uniquely British institution, the college is home to the heralds who grant and keep records of the coats of arms of the nobility, and the wannabe-nobility. Where better for James Bond (George Lazenby) to get a crash course in heraldry, in order to pass himself off as Sir Hilary Bray (George Baker, who's voice Lazenby does an impressive job of imitating) in *On Her Majesty's Secret Service*? Bray reveals the Bond family motto, *orbis non sufficit* ('the world is not enough'), which proved such a handy title for the 19th Bond movie. To get your own coat of arms, you must prove a pedigree showing direct male-line descent from an ancestor already entitled to arms. Or can simply try applying for arms to be granted.

St Paul's Cathedral, Ludgate Hill

© 020.7236.4128
website: www.stpauls.co.uk
opening times: Monday-Saturday, 8.30-17.00
tube: St Paul's (Central line)

Wren's masterpiece, replacing the cathedral destroyed in the Great Fire of 1666, occupies a special place in the cinema of London. If we are to believe Hollywood, its dome has the amazing property of being visible from every window in the capital. The Cathedral contains the impressive tombs of the Duke of Wellington and Lord Nelson, as well as that of the architect himself, bearing the famous inscription (in Latin): "If you seek his monument, look around". The Cathedral is where Pip arrives in London in David Lean's 1946 film of *Great Expectations*. The director returned in 1962 to film the acquaintances of TE Lawrence offering a chorus of opinions after his memorial service in *Lawrence of Arabia*. The royal family assembles on the steps at the end of *The Madness of King George*. The cathedral is at its most imposing at night, floodlit, as it is when Richard Widmark flees his creditors across the wide sweep of steps at the opening of *Night and the City*. The illuminated frontage also glows in the background as Bob Hoskins and Helen Mirren drive down Ludgate Hill in *The Long Good Friday*.

Tower of London, Tower Hill

© 0870.756.6060
website: www.hrp.org.uk
opening times: 1 November-28 February, Tuesday-Saturday, 9.00-17.00, Sunday-Monday, 10.00-17.00, 1 March-31 October, Monday-Saturday, 9.00-18.00, Sunday, 10.00-18.00, admission charge
tube: Tower Hill (District and Circle lines)
DLR: Tower Gateway

The unmistakable outline of one of London's most familiar tourist attractions is often seen as little more than an establishing shot in the movies to signal either "Hey, let's steal the Crown Jewels!" (in caper movies) or "Bugger, we've just insulted the Queen!" (in comedies). The real Tower rarely features as an actual location, partly because the proximity of the fabulous Crown Jewels would induce anxiety attacks in any insurance company, but also because the intrusive skyline of the modern capital means that period costume dramas tend to be filmed elsewhere. You would think the guardians of the Tower would be unlikely to welcome jewel heist movies in particular, but, back in the days when he still seemed to care about his movies, Michael Winner did manage to persuade the authorities. (He also snatched documentary-style footage before official permission had been granted, just to be on the safe side). Winner's cheerfully anarchic 1966 caper *The Jokers* sees rascally brothers Oliver Reed and Michael Crawford lift the famous jewels, for a laugh. Apart from this, the Tower is generally relegated to the level of a touristy backdrop, as it is in *Alfie*.

WEST LONDON
FITZROVIA TO HATTON GARDEN
British Museum, Great Russell Street
© *020.7323.8299*
website: www.thebritishmuseum.ac.uk
opening times: Galleries: Saturday-Wednesday, 10.00-17.30, Thursday-Friday, 10.00-20.30; Great Court: Sunday-Wednesday, 9.00-18.00, Thursday-Saturday, 9.00-23.00; Round Reading Room: Saturday, Wednesday, Friday, 10.00-17.30, Thursday, 10.00-20.30
tube: Russell Square (Piccadilly line)
In Hitchcock's first talkie, *Blackmail*, the blackmailer (Donald Calthrop) stops at the drinking fountain at the museum's entrance, though the chase through the museum's galleries used giant photographic blow-ups. It's the real McCoy in the Merchant-Ivory film of EM Forster's novel *Maurice*, when James Wilby bumps into his old teacher, Simon Callow, in front of the Assyrian statues. Hywel Bennett meets up with his nurse in the sculpture court in the 1971 penis-transplant comedy *Percy*. Vanessa Redgrave is entranced by the Elgin marbles in *Isadora*, just as, years later, Jane Horrocks is in David Kane's *Born Romantic*. For Hindi smash *Kabhi Khushi Kabhie Gham...*, the museum's newly-roofed sparkling white Great Court became the college interior in the 'Deewana Hai Dekho' number. The Round Reading Room, where Karl Marx used to grapple with the problems of Capitalism, is where the assassin Edward Fox consults French daily newspaper *Le Figaro* in *The Day of the Jackal*. The first film to shoot extensively in the museum during public opening hours, and in non-public areas, too, was Neil LaBute's adaptation of AS Byatt's Booker Prize-winning novel *Possession*.

SOUTHEAST LONDON
Old Royal Naval College, Greenwich
© *020. 8269.4747*
website: www.greenwichfoundation.org.uk
opening times: grounds: 08.00-18.00; Painted Hall and chapel: 10.00-17.00
rail/DLR: Greenwich
rail: Maze Hill
Established in 1694 as Greenwich Hospital, serving seamen and their dependants, this dramatic site was planned by Sir Christopher Wren and completed over the course of fifty years by a veritable army of archi-

tects, including Hawksmoor and Vanbrugh. Home to the Royal Naval College from 1873 until 1998, a charitable trust, the Greenwich Foundation, now runs the site. The University of Greenwich and Trinity College of Music are now housed in some of the buildings, but the two great spaces, the astonishing Painted Hall, with its *trompe-l'œil* pillars and drapery, and the Royal Naval College Chapel, King William Walk, remain open to the public.

The chapel became the Catholic 'St Mary of the Fields, Cripplegate, EC2' for 'Wedding II (Bernard and Lydia)' in *Four Weddings and a Funeral*.

The Painted Hall is extremely popular with filmmakers. In Michael Winner's 1983 remake of *The Wicked Lady*, it's the 'Duke's Theatre', where Lady Skelton (Faye Dunaway) meets Charles II (Mark Burns). It's also used for the wonderful bellringing concert in *The Madness of King George*, the meeting of world leaders addressed by August de Wynter (Sean Connery) in *The Avengers*, the 'Palace of Versailles' in *Quills* and the interior of the 'Venice' church where the council of the Illuminati meet in *Lara Croft: Tomb Raider*. Oddly, the hall was recreated in the studio for the formal banquet addressed by Cary Grant in Stanley Donen's *Indiscreet*.

The college exterior has proved equally adaptable. It became the 'Pentagon' in the 1992 wartime melodrama *Shining Through*. Bligh (Anthony Hopkins) arrives at the college for his court martial in Roger Donaldson's 1984 film *The Bounty*. It's also the exterior of 'Buckingham Palace' in *King Ralph*. Most bizarrely though, like Jeremy Irons in *Dead Ringers*, the college plays opposite itself in Phillip Noyce's geographically hilarious *Patriot Games*. It's both the 'Royal Naval College, Greenwich', where Jack Ryan (Harrison Ford) is lecturing, and 'Buckingham Palace', where he foils an IRA attack. In the film's plot, the college and the palace are adjacent to each other, despite being a considerable distance apart in reality. The complex of college buildings, criss-crossed by red buses, stand in for wartime London streets at the beginning of Gillian Armstrong's *Charlotte Gray*, and the creepy soldier mummies scuttle across the college's pillars during the bus chase in *The Mummy Returns*. More recently, it made another appearance as itself, along with the chapel, in the 2002 remake of *The Four Feathers*, and the complex became the bustling area around 'Charing Cross', where Jackie Chan and Owen Wilson arrive in London in *Shanghai Knights*.

Eltham Palace and Courtauld House, Court Yard, Eltham
© *020. 8294.2548*
opening times: April-September, Wednesday-

Friday and Sunday, 10.00-18.00, October,
Wednesday-Friday and Sunday, 10.00-17.00,
November-December and February-March,
Wednesday-Friday and Sunday, 10.00-16.00,
admission charge
rail: Eltham
There has been a royal residence on the site since
1311, but the Medieval manor house was deserted
and almost derelict when it was bought and restored
by the Courtauld family in the 1930s. Which is why
the Tudor building contains not only a Great Hall
with original hammerbeam roof, but a series of glorious art deco rooms. A gift to film-makers, it became
King Richard's private cinema for *Richard III*, and
is the home of slightly fey gangster Michael Gambon
in *High Heels and Low Lifes* (although some of the
more extravagant rooms are sets). It can also be seen
in the film of Dodie Smith's novel *I Capture the
Castle*.

SOUTHWEST LONDON
Leighton House, 12 Holland Park Road
✆ 020.7602.3316
website: www.rbkc.gov.uk/leightonhousemuseum
opening times: Wednesday-Monday, 11.00-17.30
*tube: High Street Kensington (District and Circle
lines)*
Located north of the western reaches of Kensington
High Street, this former home and studio of painter
and Royal Academician Frederick, Lord Leighton, is
full of Pre-Raphaelite delights and infused with his
love of the Middle East. The Arab Hall, with its gen-
tly spattering fountain, and camped up with copies of
Michelangelo's David in its alcoves, became the setting for Katherine Helmond's facial surgery in Terry
Gilliam's *Brazil*. Decorated in gilt and blue Islamic
tiles, the hall is part of the Leighton House Museum,
which contains more restored Victorian interiors and
paintings by Leighton himself, along with his con-
temporaries, Burne-Jones, Millais and Watts.

Linley Sambourne House, 18 Stafford Terrace
website: www.rbkc.gov.uk/linleysambournehouse
*tube: High Street Kensington (District and Circle
Lines)*
A perfectly preserved Victorian townhouse, built in
1874, with almost all its original furniture and fittings intact. Originally home to cartoonist Edward
Linley Sambourne, it is now owned and maintained
by the Royal Borough of Kensington and Chelsea.
The house has been closed for major renovation work,
but re-opened in April 2003. It can be seen in two
Merchant-Ivory productions: in *A Room with a View*,
as the "well-appointed" London home of Daniel Day-
Lewis, and as Hugh Grant's residence in *Maurice*.

Natural History Museum, Cromwell Road
✆ 020.7942.5011
website: www.nhm.ac.uk
opening times: Monday-Saturday, 10.00-17.50,
Sunday, 11.00-17.50, admission charge
*tube: South Kensington (District, Circle and
Piccadilly lines)*
The Natural History Museum has been extensively
revamped to appeal to kids (with animatronic
dinosaurs and the insect galleries redubbed 'Creepy
Crawlies') since it appeared in the Boulting brothers'
1950 thriller *Seven Days to Noon*. Tarzan (Christopher
Lambert) is, unwisely, invited to the opening of the
'Greystoke Wing' of the museum in Hugh Hudson's
Greystoke: The Legend of Tarzan, Lord of the Apes.
Ted Danson relents on his plan to reveal the exis-
tence of the Loch Ness monster to the world's press
here in *Loch Ness*.

Victoria and Albert Museum, Cromwell
Gardens
✆ 020.7942.2000
website: www.vam.ac.uk
opening times: Thursday-Tuesday, 10.00-17.45,
Wednesday, 10.00-22.00, admission charge
*tube: South Kensington (District, Circle and
Piccadilly lines)*
The national museum of art and design is part of the
complex of cultural institutions established by Prince
Albert in South Kensington. In the Cast Court,Michael
Crawford and Oliver Reed contemplate pulling off a
spectacular caper – "Can't be something petty. It's got
to be a real challenge" – in *The Jokers*. Sidney Poitier
takes the kids on a school outing to the V&A in the
stills montage sequence of *To Sir, With Love*.

FAR WEST LONDON
Chiswick House, Burlington Lane
✆ 020.8995.0508
*opening times: April-September, Wednesday-
Friday and Sunday, 10.00-18.00, Saturday, 10.00-
14.00, October, Wednesday-Friday and Sunday,
10.00-17.00, Saturday, 10.00-14.00, admission
charge*
tube: Turnham Green (District and Piccadilly lines)
Built in 1725 for the Earl of Burlington, the house, mod-
elled after the Villa Rotonda in Vicenza, Italy, is one of
the finest Palladian villas in the country. It's set in formal gardens populated with classical statuary, obelisks
and sphinxes. It is the home of aristocrat James Fox's
parents in Joseph Losey's *The Servant*. The rear of the
house is used for the glitzy video promo shoot directed by Jerry Devine (Eddie Izzard) in *Velvet Goldmine*.

Osterley Park House, Jersey Road, Isleworth

© 020.8232.5050
website: www.osterleypark.org.uk
opening times: park: 09.00-19.30 or sunset;
house: March, Saturday and Sunday, April-2
November, Wednesday-Sunday, 13.00-16.30,
admission charge
tube: Osterley (Piccadilly Line)
rail: Isleworth

An Elizabethan mansion transformed into a neo-Classical villa by Robert Adam between 1760 and 1780, it's now a National Trust property. It became the Earl of Rhyall's stately home in *The Grass Is Greener* (originally a hit West End play), which pairs Cary Grant and Deborah Kerr, and has Noël Coward writing the songs. In 1965 it became the ancestral pile of Lord Carfax (John Fraser) in James Hill's Sherlock Holmes versus Jack the Ripper shocker *A Study in Terror* (which was subsequently adapted into a novel by Ellery Queen). In 2001, Osterley was used for the school concert where Krishi is supposed to sing 'Do Re Mi', in Karan Johar's Hindi smash *Kabhi Khushi Kabhie Gham....*

Syon House, Syon Park, Brentford

© 020. 8560.0881
website: www.syonpark.co.uk
opening times: gardens: 10.30-17.30 or sunset,
admission charge; house: 26 March-2 November,
Wednesday, Thursday and Sunday, 11.00-17.00,
admission charge
tube: Gunnersbury (District Line)
rail: Kew Bridge

The family seat of the Dukes of Northumberland for over 400 years, the house was built on the site of a Medieval abbey (and named after Mount Zion). The stunning interiors, glass-domed Great Conservatory and the grounds, landscaped by 'Capability' Brown, are perenially popular with film-makers. The bizarre 'football game' in Harold Pinter's adaptation of *Accident* was shot in the classical grandeur of Robert Adams' Great Hall, and must still give the film's insurers nightmares. The rough and tumble includes Dirk Bogarde keeping goal in front of a bronze copy of the cast of a Dying Gladiator which, even in 1773, cost a cool £300. The hall was also used for the opening party of *The Wings of the Dove*, where Helena Bonham Carter meets cynical aristo Alex Jennings, some of the 'Buckingham Palace' interiors for *King Ralph* and the conference of giant teddy bears in the disastrous film of *The Avengers* (though it's supposed to be within the Lloyds Building in the City). Syon House also featured in Dick Clement's 1983 Bulldog Drummond spoof *Bullshot*, Carol Reed's 1971 film *Follow Me*, with Mia Farrow and Topol, and more

recently Robert Altman's *Gosford Park*. You can see more of Syon's elegant rooms and corridors in *The Madness of King George*, as the 'Long Gallery', in which the King meets Prime Minister Pitt. The Great Conservatory became 'Heaven' for the ending of Stanley Donen's original 1967 film of *Bedazzled* (vastly superior to the recent remake with Brendan Fraser), where Dudley Moore and devil Peter Cook are supposed to meet God.

FAR NORTHWEST LONDON

London Zoo, Outer Circle, Regent's Park

© 020.7722.3333
website: www.londonzoo.co.uk
opening times: 17 February-9 March, 10.00-16.30, 10 March-26 October, 10.00-17.30, 27 October onwards, 10.00-16.00, admission charge
tube: Camden Town (Northern line)

The world's first scientific zoo, which opened in 1828, but didn't open to the public for another nineteen years, has a long and varied history as a film location. In *The Fallen Idol*, the film adaptation of Graham Greene's story 'The Basement Room', the day out was filmed at the old refreshment stall in front of the Mappin Terraces. Pranksters Michael Crawford and Oliver Reed stage a bomb hoax at the lion enclosure in the 1966 film *The Jokers*. Gregory Peck and Sophia Loren escape from villain Alan Badel's palatial house through the zoo in Stanley Donen's *Arabesque*. Ben Kingsley and Glenda Jackson take it upon themselves to liberate one of the zoo's denizens (guess which) in the Harold Pinter-scripted *Turtle Diary*. David Naughton wakes up naked in the zoo after a bloody night as an American Werewolf in London. Harry Potter learns he is a Parsel-tongue (he can talk to serpents) and liberates the boa constrictor in the Reptile House, in *Harry Potter and the Philosopher's Stone*. Hugh Grant and Nicholas Hoult have a man-to-man chat alongside the famous Penguin Pool in *About a Boy*. One of the zoo's better kept secrets, though, must be its ballroom, the Prince Albert Suite (there's also a Raffles Suite, named after founder Sir Stamford Raffles), the venue for the boisterous Jewish wedding reception in Gary Sinyor and Vadim Jean's quirky comedy *Leon the Pig Farmer*. You can hold your wedding here, too (© 020. 7449.6374).

Central London: Leicester Square to Blackfriars

Don a plastic Union Jack bowler hat, collect a postcard of Prince William and join the throng of bewildered backpackers and sightseers in the tourism centre of the capital. This walk will take you through a neighbourhood whose most famous screen appearance was faked in Burbank, past a deserted underground tunnel and along the 'Street of Shame', to end at a turn-of-the-century folly.

Starting Point: Leicester Square

Leicester Square (**1**), a fashionable residential address in the 18th century, metamorphosed into a centre of entertainments, both educational and exploitational, during the 19th century. During the 1850s, one of its most extraordinary features was the Great Globe, a vast hollow sphere containing a map of the world, viewed from staircases and galleries inside. By the mid-1860s the Globe had gone and the present gardens were laid out, where a rather small, bronze statue of one of Britain's greatest cinema talents, Charlie Chaplin, was erected in 1981. A fitting place, as the theatres which once filled the square have been remodelled as cinemas, including the **UCI Empire Leicester Square** (see **Entertainment: Cinemas**, p24), the interior of which can be seen in *Notting*

Hill, and the exterior in *Kabhi Khushi Kabhie Gham....*

Just east of the square is the multi-screen **Warner Village West End, 3 Cranbourn Street** (see **Entertainment: Cinemas**, p24).

North of the square, between the Empire and the Warner, runs Leicester Place. Another great sideshow once stood here: the Barker-Burford Panorama, displaying elaborate cityscapes and famous battles. The street is now home to the **Prince Charles Cinema, 7 Leicester Place** (see **Entertainment: Cinemas**, p24), a repertory house with a different rota of films every day.

On the eastern side of the square, the Moorish-style Royal Panopticon of Science and Art was erected in the mid-1850s. A typically uplifting Victorian project to exhibit the latest developments in science and industry, the Panopticon was a financial disaster and was soon replaced by the much more popular Alhambra Music Hall. Theatre scenes for the *Othello*-inspired 1936 backstage melodrama *Men Are Not Gods*, with Miriam Hopkins, Gertrude Lawrence and Rex Harrison, were filmed in the Alhambra which, in turn, was demolished to make way for the **Odeon Leicester Square** (see **Entertainment: Cinemas**, p24), the exterior of which can be seen in *Frenzy*.

On the south side of Panton Street, southwest of the square, stands a little bit of film history. The **Odeon Panton Street** (© *0870.5050.007*) opened its doors in 1969 as the Cinecenta, with the near-forgotten *Wonderwall* (soundtrack by George Harrison). Specialising in arthouse releases, this innovative 4-screen venue was the country's first small-scale multiplex. It's now part of the mainstream Odeon chain.

The tour proper starts at **Leicester Square tube station**. Richard Attenborough slips out of the station after picking up the kidnap ransom in *Séance on a Wet Afternoon*. Posters for the original stage production of Lionel Bart's musical *Oliver!* which ran at the Albery Theatre for 2618 performances, can be seen displayed on its sister theatre, the **Wyndhams Theatre, Charing Cross Road** (© *020.7369.1731*), in the background. Wyndhams also features in the glum little drama *Connecting Rooms*, when Michael Redgrave arrives in the West End to uncover Bette Davis' little secret. You can also glimpse the old Talk of the Town nightclub – now the **Hippodrome** – where Judy Garland was notoriously heckled during one of her more wobbly later appearances. Wyndhams was transformed into the 'Windsor Theatre', where Redgrave discovers that Davis, rather than playing the cello in concert, is scraping catgut for small change by the theatre's stage door in **St Martin's Court**. And how they love their in-jokes – the 'Windsor' is apparently playing *Remembrance* starring Margo Channing, Davis' grand dame actress character in *All About Eve*. Wyndhams saw the West End débuts of both Diana Rigg and the outrageous star of Hitchcock's *Lifeboat*, Tallulah Bankhead ("My father warned me about men and booze – but he never said anything about women and cocaine.").

The narrow court connecting the Wyndhams and the Albery Theatres was a traditional haunt of buskers (street performers) entertaining the pre-show queues. The 1938 backstage melodrama *St Martin's Lane* gives a fascinating glimpse of this pre-television era, when the tradition of street entertainment was already on the wane. In the film, St Martin's Court bustles with accordionists and tap-dancers. Theatre-goers, waiting outside the New Theatre (now the Albery), certainly seem to be getting value for their coppers with a quartet including theatrical legend Tyrone Guthrie, Charles Laughton (who co-wrote the script, in the year before his classic Hollywood performance as *The Hunchback of Notre Dame*) and Vivien Leigh (in her last film role before gaining iconic status as Scarlett O'Hara in *Gone With the Wind*). The film's US title, *Sidewalks of London*, blithely ignores the fact that the British term is 'pavement'.

Cecil Court, the other narrow thoroughfare linking Charing Cross Road to St Martin's Lane, lined with antiquarian bookshops, seems hardly touched by the passage of time. If you want to splash out, you might search through the old postcards and Victorian

prints for classic, authenticated – if pricy – Hollywood autographs.

Victim: the West End bar: The Salisbury, St Martin's Lane

Bookseller Frank Doel (Anthony Hopkins), though, is more interested in the dusty volumes lined up outside in the film of *84 Charing Cross Road*. One of the nervous homosexuals blackmailed in 1961's *Victim* ran a bookshop here. The British film industry grew up in the court during the early years of the 20th century, earning it the nickname 'Flicker Alley', before moving to its present base around Wardour Street in Soho.

On the southeast corner of St Martin's Court the splendid Victorian **Salisbury, 90 St Martin's Lane** (see **Bars & Restaurants**, p12), which can be seen in *Victim* and *Travels With My Aunt*. Opposite the Salisbury runs the narrow alleyway of **New Row**, where the fictitious 'Silver Fox' nightclub was situated in the 1950 film *Night and the City*.

Turn left into Garrick Street. Charles Dickens was among the luminaries frequenting **The Garrick Club, 15 Garrick Street** (**2**), where he became embroiled in a notorious feud with fellow scribe William Makepeace Thackeray. One of the most famous of the city's exclusive gentlemen's clubs, unless you're the guest of a member there's little chance of you getting to see the club's interior. Founded in 1831 as a civilised retreat for actors and literary types, the club moved to its present building in 1864. It's now frequented by journalists and barristers, and is the gentlemanly retreat of top cop Richard Attenborough, where he lunches with rough, tough Chicago cop John Wayne – who naturally has to be given a tie ("club rule"), in *Brannigan*.

The tiny alleyway of Rose Street runs off Garrick Street, where you'll find **The Lamb and Flag, 33 Rose Street** (see **Bars & Restaurants**, p12), which can be seen in *Travels With My Aunt*. Don't get carried away, though, there are more

Brannigan: Richard Attenborough's exclusive club: The Garrick Club, Garrick Street

Frenzy: flat of the 'Necktie Strangler': Henrietta Street

pubs to come.

Continue south on Bedford Street and turn into Maiden Lane. The exterior of **Rules Restaurant, 35 Maiden Lane** (**3**; see **Bars & Restaurants**, p12), London's oldest restaurant, can supposedly be seen in Neil Jordan's film of *The End of the Affair*, though to be honest, I can't see it.

Turn left into Southampton Street and continue on to the famous Piazza of Covent Garden, in front of the chunky pillars of St Paul's. **3 Henrietta Street** was the flat of the 'Necktie Strangler' Robert Rusk (Barry Foster) in *Frenzy*, where Hitch pulls off the eerie silent tracking shot down the stairs and into the street (watch for the craftily disguised cut from the stairwell, which was a studio set, to the real doorway, as the porter carrying a sack of potatoes passes in front of the camera).

Covent Garden (**4**) (the name is a corrupted reference to the old convent garden which once occupied the area) was once one of the capital's three great produce markets: Billingsgate for fish, Smithfield for meat and Covent Garden for fruit, veg and flowers. It was a world in itself; one of the few places where the country's stringent licensing laws were officially relaxed, allowing porters to down a pint at the civilised hour of six in the morning – if you didn't look too much like a tourist, chances were you could join them. Lindsay Anderson kicked off his cinematic career here in 1957, as part of the Free Cinema movement, with a documentary about the market porters, *Every Day Except Christmas*. In 1973, though, the whole operation moved to a soulless new facility at Nine Elms, south of the Thames near Vauxhall, and the old market buildings were titivated to become terrace cafés and boutiques stocked with designer clothes and scented candles. By 1992, Richard Attenborough was obliged to use the meat market at Smithfield as a stand-in for the Garden in his biopic *Chaplin*. The real fruit and veg business market was still in full swing in 1972 though, when Alfred Hitchcock used it as the setting for *Frenzy*. Hitch's first film in London since the 1950 *Stage Fright*, *Frenzy* is an adaptation of Arthur La Bern's novel *Goodbye Piccadilly, Farewell Leicester Square* scripted by

Frenzy: Jon Finch is sacked from the pub: The Globe, Bow Street

Anthony Shaffer, the writer of *Sleuth* and cult horror flick *The Wicker Man*. Hitchcock seemed oblivious to the social changes in London since his move to LA in 1940, and the whole film is infused with a strangely musty air. Despite the director's inevitably audacious set-pieces, it's hard to believe *Frenzy* was made a year after *The French Connection*. Shaffer's blackly witty screenplay collided horribly with Hitchcock's virulent misogyny, previously kept in check by production codes but now given free reign by seventies permissiveness. Nevertheless the great moments occur against an excellent use of setting.

A Kiss Before Dying: Philadelphia Central Police HQ: First National Bank of Chicago, Long Acre

Stop off for a pint in **The Globe, 37 Bow Street** (see **Bars & Restaurants**, p12), which can be seen in *Frenzy*.

The second film adaptation of Ira Levin's novel *A Kiss Before Dying*, with James Dearden directing Matt Dillon as the charming psychopath, was set in the USA, but filmed in the UK, which is why the **First National Bank of Chicago, First Chicago House, 90 Long Acre**, is passed off as the 'Philadelphia Central Police HQ'.

The interior of Freemasons Hall (more properly, **United Grand Lodge of England Freemasons Hall**), **60 Great Queen Street** (**6**), is another screen regular. It can be seen in *The Saint*, *Fairy Tale: A True Story*, *The Wings of the Dove*, Dodie Smith's *I Capture the Castle* and *Miranda* with Christina Ricci. Both the exterior and interior is Rowan Atkinson's 'MI7 HQ' in *Johnny English*.

Johnny English: the MI7 HQ: Freemasons Hall, Great Queen Street

The wood-panelled luxury of the **New Connaught Rooms, 61-65 Great Queen Street** (**7**; © 020.7405.7811; website: www.newconnaughtrooms.co.uk), became the luxury hotel where Peter Falk, Ben Gazzara and John Cassavetes spend their lost weekend in *Husbands*. Ben Kingsley and Jeremy Irons spar

Husbands: losing a weekend: New Connaught Rooms, Great Queen Street

Frenzy: the city gents:
Nell of Old Drury,
Catherine Street

over lunch here in the film of Harold Pinter's play *Betrayal*. Apart from the market, Covent Garden's other great landmark is the **Royal Opera House** (**5**; © *020.7304.4000; website: www.royal opera.org*), the theatrical backdrop to the London scenes of Michael Powell and Emeric Pressburger's *The Red Shoes*, also seen in six-ties international espionage thriller *Where the Spies Are*, starring David Niven. While closed for the re-cent radical renovation, it became the 'Fhloston Paradise' opera house, where the blue alien diva performs, in Luc Besson's *The Fifth Element*.

There's another strangely alien performance at the **Theatre Royal Drury Lane, Catherine Street** (© *020.7494.5000*), when Amyl Nitrite (Jordan) sings a punk version of 'Rule Britannia' in Derek Jarman's *Jubilee*. In the 1989 comedy *The Tall Guy*, Jeff Goldblum deserts his job as straight-man to egoma-niac comic Rowan Atkinson to take on the title role in a musical version of *The Elephant Man* here.

Opposite the theatre is **Nell of Old Drury, 29 Catherine Street** (see **Bars & Restaurants**, p12), which can be glimpsed in *Frenzy*.

Jenny Seagrove disrupts a meal behind the the-atre at **Sarastro, 126 Drury Lane** (**8**; see **Bars & Restaurants**, p12) at Kemble Street, in *Don't Go Breaking My Heart*.

The branch of **Café Rouge** on **Wellington Street** (**9**; see **Bars & Restaurants**, p12) used to be the Dome, where Andie MacDowell gives a quick run-down of her sexual history in *Four Weddings and a Funeral*.

The **Aldwych Theatre, Aldwych** at Drury Lane (**10**; © *020.7379.3367; website: www.aldwych-theatre.-com*), is the lobby and exterior of the the-atre where Harry Houdini (Harvey Keitel) performs in the whimsical *Fairy Tale: A True Story*. Vivien Leigh triumphed as Blanche Dubois at the Aldwych in *A Streetcar Named Desire* before the film version. The theatre, though, is probably most famous for two totally contrast-ing seasons: the Aldwych Farces by Ben Travers (several of which, such as *Rookery Nook, Plunder* and *A Cuckoo in the Nest*, were sub-

Don't Go Breaking My Heart: Jenny Seagrove disrupts the evening: Sarastro, Drury Lane

sequently filmed) during the twenties and thirties, and the Royal Shakespeare Company from 1960 until the company moved to the Barbican in 1982.

Matthew Rhys, under the bad influence of transvestite DJ Jason Donovan, manages to leap onto a moving bus on the crescent of the **Aldwych**, outside the Waldorf Hotel in *Sorted*.

The Long Good Friday: Bob Hoskins is abducted: Savoy Hotel, Strand

The **Lyceum Theatre, Wellington Street** (**11**; © *0870.243.9000*), once managed by theatrical legend Henry Irving (whose stage manager was Bram Stoker, author of *Dracula*), was used for the theatre interi-ors in *St Martin's Lane*.

The **Savoy Hotel, 1 Savoy Hill, Strand** (**12**; see **Hotels**, p8), is where Bob Hoskins is dumped by the US mobsters at the end of *The Long Good Friday*. It also appears in *The French Lieutenant's Woman* and *Entrapment*. The hotel is actually an addition to the Savoy Theatre, once home to the Gilbert and Sullivan operettas, but since given a delicious thir-ties deco makeover (now painstakingly restored after a disastrous fire in 1990), which meant that when Mike Leigh came to make *Topsy-Turvy*, he had to use the unchanged Richmond Theatre as a substitute.

On a traffic island in the Strand stands James Gibbs' 1717 church **St Mary-le-Strand**, which can be glimpsed in Michael Winner's *West 11*. As you might guess from the title, this 1963 slice-of-life is centred around Notting Hill, but the central charac-ter, Alfred Lynch, works in a gents outfitters on the Strand before chucking the job to live a life of petty

The Criminal: the final twist: Savoy Hotel, Strand

Howards End: "So thoroughly old English": Simpson's-in-the-Strand, strand

crime.

Behind the Savoy, at the foot of the steps down from the Strand, is the site of the final revelations and the tying up of loose ends in Julian Simpson's neat 1999 thriller *The Criminal*.

Simpson's-in-the-Strand, 100 Strand (see **Bars & Restaurants**, p13), is a world-famous institution. Its interior can be seen in *Howards End*, but it was recreated in the studio for *Sabotage*.

Adelphi Terrace was an ambitious, but financially shaky, 18th-century riverside development by Robert and John Adam (*adelphi* is Greek for 'brothers'). It was demolished in 1936, but its name lives on in the Adelphi Theatre on the Strand, and in the **Adelphi Building, 1-11 John Adam Street (13)**, south of the Strand. This is the deco hotel to which Tom Jericho (Dougray Scott) is led by the mysterious phone call in Michael Apted's film of Robert Harris' novel *Enigma*. It's behind the Adelphi that Joseph Fiennes reveals a sinister violent streak after catching a mugger in Chen Kaige's erotic thriller *Killing Me Softly*. A door on **John Adam Street** stood in for No. 10 Downing Street, the Prime Minister's London residence, in *Johnny English*.

Turn down Villiers Street to **Heaven (14**; website: *www.heaven-london.com*). This vast gay complex under the arches at Charing Cross was the disco in the opening of Tony Scott's stylish, but empty, vampire saga *The Hunger*.

On the pedestrian walkway of **Hungerford Bridge (15)**, Nina Beckman (Greta Scacchi) reveals the beginnings of the government cover-up to investigative journo Nick Mullen (Gabriel Byrne) in David Drury's 1985 paranoia thriller *Defence of the Realm*. The narrow walkway, which ran along the eastern side of the railway bridge, has recently been demolished, to be replaced by a pair of swanky new pedestrian bridges.

Head east down **Northumberland Avenue**, the site of the diamond heist in Peter Yates' 1967 film *Robbery*. At the foot of the avenue is the **Playhouse Theatre (16)**, which was used for the recreation by Gary Oldman of Sid Vicious' notorious trashing of 'My Way' in Alex Cox's *Sid and Nancy*.

Enigma: the mysterious hotel: Adelphi Building, John Adam Street

The elegant wood-panelled rooms of the **National Liberal Club, 1 Whitehall Court** at Whitehall Place, now incorporated into the Royal Horseguards Hotel, have been seen in several films. They became the office of Carr Gomm (John Gielgud) in David Lynch's *The Elephant Man*, and feature in two Russell Mulcahy films: *Blue Ice*, as the gentlemen's club where Michael Caine confronts Ian Holm, and the far more successful *Highlander*, as the 'New York library' where Roxanne Hart figures out 'Russell Nash's' deathless signature. The club also supplied sumptuous interiors for period dramas such as *Wilde* and *The Wings of the Dove*, and, with its striking oval staircase (destroyed by bombs in 1941 but reconstructed in the fifties), stood in for Whitehall's corridors of power in *Who Dares Wins*. The club's **Billiard Room** became Katherine Helmond's cluttered home in Terry Gilliam's *Brazil*.

A little way along Whitehall Court, you might recognise **4 Whitehall Court** at Horseguards Avenue as the entrance to the fictitious 'Baltic Hotel', where Okwe (Chiwetel Ejiofor) discovers nasty goings-on in London's subculture in Stephen Frears' *Dirty Pretty Things*.

Follow the Victoria Embankment along the north bank of the Thames to **Shell Mex House**. The address is actually **80 Strand**, but it's the towering river frontage you want to see. Another of the wittily imaginative locations for *Richard III*, it's in front of the deco clock face high above the river that the doomed Buckingham (Jim Broadbent) realises he's fallen out of favour with the king (Ian McKellen).

At the foot of **Cleopatra's Needle (17)**, just along the Embankment, Cary Grant and Ingrid Bergman are disturbed by autograph hunters during a quiet moment together in Stanley Donen's *Indiscreet*. Return to the

Sid and Nancy: 'My Way' at the Paris theatre: Playhouse Theatre, Northumberland Avenue

The Elephant Man: John Gielgud's office: the National Liberal Club, Whitehall Court

Dirty Pretty Things: the exterior of the sinister Baltic Hotel: Whitehall Court

GoldenEye: St Petersburg: Somerset House, Strand

Strand and continue east to **Somerset House** (**18**), on the south side, which used to be the registry of births, marriages and deaths. Edward Fox collects his false birth certificate here in Fred Zinnemann's 1973 film *The Day of the Jackal*. The facility subsequently relocated to St Catherine's House, at which point the handsome central courtyard was relegated to the role of car park. During this time it saw frequent service as a movie backdrop, featuring in two Pierce Brosnan Bond movies. In *GoldenEye*, the courtyard is the 'St Petersburg square' where Jack Wade (Joe Don Baker) uses a sledgehammer to fix his car after picking up James Bond (Pierce Brosnan) from the airport, and it subsequently reappears as the 'Ministry of Defence' in *Tomorrow Never Dies*. In Billy Wilder's superb *The Private Life of Sherlock Holmes*, Somerset House provides the exterior of 'The Diogenes Club', where Sherlock's smarter older brother Mycroft is a member. It's also the exterior of 'Pratt's Club', where Viggo Mortensen calls on Nicole Kidman, in Jane Campion's *The Portrait of a Lady*. In *Wilde* it appears as the exterior of the writer's West End apartment. In Tim Burton's *Sleepy Hollow* it passes for turn-of-the-century 'New York'. Sandra Goldbacher's *The Governess* uses the building as a backdrop. It's also where, with a bit of prompting from Owen Wilson, Jackie Chan invents the kung fu movie at the end of *Shanghai Knights*.

Further on, at the junction with Surrey Street, is the entrance to the disused **Aldwych tube station** (**19**). A sad little one-stop spur of the Piccadilly Line, running back and forth to Holborn, this little-used station finally closed its doors to the public in 1994. The lack of disruption to the rest of the tube system, plus the station's generously proportioned lifts, meant that Aldwych was London Transport's venue for shooting scenes on the Underground. The station has a lengthy roster of credits, including *An American Werewolf in London* (where it was used for some of the 'Tottenham Court Road' sequence), *Nil by Mouth*, *Sliding Doors*, *Death Line* (as 'Russell Square' station), *Superman IV* and *This Year's*

An American Werewolf in London: the deserted tube: Aldwych tube station, the Strand

Harry Potter and the Philosopher's Stone: Gringott's Bank: Australia House, Strand

Love. Londoners cheer themselves up on its platforms during the Blitz in *The Krays*, and Joe Orton (Gary Oldman) picks up rough trade on its stairwell in *Prick Up Your Ears*. The studio sets used for 'Vauxhall Cross' station in *Die Another Day* and the gorgeous period underground station in *The Wings of the Dove* were based on the design of Aldwych Underground Station.

At the eastern end of the traffic island where Aldwych meets the Strand stands the home of the Australian High Commission since 1918, on land once covered by notorious slums, mentioned by Charles Dickens in *Bleak House*. The imposing **Exhibition Hall** of **Australia House** (**20**), with its chandeliers and columns of Australian marble, became 'Gringott's Bank', the wizard bank staffed by clever – if unfriendly – goblins where Harry is taken by Hagrid to make a withdrawal, in *Harry Potter and the Philosopher's Stone*. It is not generally open to the public, but there are daily tours.

Just behind, at the junction of Aldwych and Kingsway, stands **St Catherine's House, 10 Kingsway** (**21**). This is the Office of Population Censuses and Surveys, the place to visit if you need to track down a birth, marriage or death certificate. Marianne Jean-Baptiste discovers her true mother's identity here in Mike Leigh's *Secrets & Lies*.

At the start of the Strand, on the north side, stands a startling burst of Victorian mock-gothicism, the **Royal Courts of Justice, Strand** (**22**), where civil cases are decided. John Gregson works as a barrister at the courts in *Genevieve*, and it's outside on the Strand that the eponymous Darracq is first seen. Bridget covers an extradition case here for TV show *Sit Up Britain* in *Bridget Jones's*

Genevieve: first glimpse of the Darracq: Royal Courts of Justice, Strand

Brothers in Law: Ian Carmichael is called to the bar: King's Bench Walk, Inner Temple

Diary, but the view of the building in Alfred Hitchcock's 1936 film *Sabotage* (a backdrop to the Lord Mayor's Show) was an enormous photographic blow-up. By the way, if you want to grab a packet of fags like Bridget, the newsagent is **BK News, 212 Strand** at Essex Street.

Turn right into Middle Temple Lane. **Middle Temple (23)** was used for the law court scenes in *Wilde* and can also be seen in *Shakespeare in Love*. As tradition has it that Shakespeare's *Twelfth Night* was first performed in Middle Temple Hall, it seems fitting that a quote from *Henry VI, Part 2* kicks off the Boulting brothers' 1957 film *Brothers in Law*, set in the leafy courts of the Temple: "The first thing we do, let's kill all the lawyers". Even if the film never quite aims for the savagery of Shakespeare, it's still an enjoyable reminder of the gentle satire of the period. Newly called to the bar, Roger Thursby (played by the quintessentially innocent everyman Ian Carmichael) learns the tricks of the legal trade as pupil of scatty Miles Malleson in his chambers at **6 King's Bench Walk, Inner Temple**. The only perceptible change in the location since the film was shot, and probably in the last two hundred years, is the glow of computer screens from the windows. Following the flustered Malleson to the courts, Carmichael emerges onto the Strand, alongside the venerable **George Inn**, from **Devereux Court** – named after Robert Devereux, the Earl of Essex and favourite

of Elizabeth I, whose house once stood on the narrow lane. Essex, who lost his head after falling out of favour with the Queen, was played by Errol Flynn in Hollywood's, no doubt historically precise, *The Private Lives of Elizabeth and Essex*.

Return to the Strand as it becomes **Fleet Street (24)**, for many years the heart of the newspaper industry (and consequently dubbed the 'Street of Shame'). Gradually, one by one, the papers left the street, though many of the buildings retain the names of their former occupants. Drunken journo Denholm Elliott is poured into a cab here after the trashing of his friend Ian Bannen in the conspiracy thriller *Defence of the Realm*. Jack Hawkins and his band of misfits drive down the street, past the Daily Express and the Daily Telegraph buildings, to the ill-fated robbery in the 1960 heist thriller *The League of Gentlemen*.

By far the most impressive building on the street is the black glass deco box of the **Daily Express Building**, which was the setting for Val Guest's excellent semi-documentary style sixties sci-fi movie *The Day the Earth Caught Fire*, which really was filmed in the newspaper's offices, with Arthur Christiansen playing the paper's chief editor, a job that he had previously done for real. Across the road stood Harry's, the real bar (now gone) where the journalists gather as the effects of nuclear tests crank up the UK's temperature.

At Ludgate Circus, pausing to take in a glimpse of St Paul's Cathedral (don't worry, that's covered in **The City of London**, p89, and **Historic Sites**, p30), turn right into New Bridge Street. On the bend of Queen Victoria Street, alongside Blackfriars Station, stood the 'Unity Domestic Bureau', where Vera Miles tries to trace the mysterious Janet the nursemaid in Henry Hathaway's glossy Hitchcockian mystery *23 Paces to Baker Street*. The building has since been redeveloped.

Stop at the lone flatiron building alongside the railway line opposite Blackfriars Station. **The Black Friar, 174 Queen Victoria Street (25**; see **Bars & Restaurants**, p12) is the pub where Lord Risley is arrested in *Maurice*. Unless it's a weekend – when the pub, like most of those in the City of London area, will be closed – relax with a pint and admire the friezes of industrious monks, admonishing the drinkers with severe warnings.

Maurice: trouble with a guardsman: The Black Friar, Queen Victoria Street

The Day the Earth Caught Fire: the newspaper office: Daily Express Building, Fleet Street

Central London: Oxford Street to Cambridge Circus

A push through the crowds in the heart of London's West End. Traditionally, the borough of Westminster has not been as film-friendly as, say, New York or Los Angeles, in terms of closing down the centre of the city for filming – although the astonishing opening scenes of *28 Days Later* indicate that this may now be changing. There are few major set-pieces or classic moments here, but plenty of odd, snatched scenes in the West End's shops, bars and restaurants.

Starting Point: Tottenham Court Road Underground Station

Tottenham Court Road tube station (1) itself is notable for its depressingly grubby mosaics, a design disaster by sculptor Eduardo Paolozzi. Tube station

scenes are traditionally filmed in the bowels of the permanently-closed Aldwych Station (see **Central London: Leicester Square**, p39) to avoid disruption, but for once Tottenham Court Road really is where Gerald Bringsley, the city gent (played by Michael Carter – familiar as Bib Fortuna in *Return of the Jedi*), gets chomped by *An American Werewolf in London* (in some of the shots, at least).

Above the station, the first thing you'll notice is the huge frontage of the **Dominion Theatre** (℗ *020.7413.1713*), home to lavish musicals. It's in front of the Dominion that Janet Suzman meets up with on-the-run agent-husband Michael Caine, who's trying to track down their kidnapped son, in Don Siegel's 1974 thriller *The Black Windmill*.

If you like, pop south to check out the guitar shops of **Denmark Street**, the centre of the music biz in the fifties and sixties, earning it the nickname 'Tin Pan Alley'. It featured, naturally enough, as the backdrop to the 1951 documentary *Tin Pan Alley*.

Now one of the entrances to the vast Virgin Megastore, **3 Tottenham Court Road** was one of the chain of famous Lyons Corner Houses until 1968, when it became a casino – the Sportsman Club – its walls adorned with cut-out metal sporting motifs, designed to attract laddish and loaded sportsmen. One person it did attract was the fiercely independent maverick film-maker John Cassavetes. In Cassavetes' 1970 film *Husbands*, Peter Falk, Ben Gazzara and Cassavetes himself played three New Yorkers, shaken up by the sudden death of their friend, who spontaneously decide to lose a weekend in London. The Sportsman was the club where the three play craps and, with varying degrees of success, hit on women. The casino has since moved to 40 Bryanston Street, W1, where it now sports a riverboat theme.

Turn west into Oxford Street, a tiresomely crowded shopping hell, which offers little more than you'd find on the average high street, only in bigger shops. It's far too crowded for filming and it would be hellishly expensive to close down on a weekday, or open up on a Sunday, so it's rarely been seen on screen. However, there is the briefest glimpse under the opening credits of *Sorted* when Matthew Rhys arrives in the capital from Yorkshire.

Take a look at the building on the southeast corner of Wardour Street. The elaborate wrought-iron frontage above **119 Oxford Street (2)** is the last remaining trace of the arched passageway that once ran south from Oxford Street. Down this narrow passage stood 'The Blaney Bureau', the marriage agency run by Barbara Leigh-Hunt, and site of the very nasty strangling in Alfred Hitchcock's queasily misogynistic *Frenzy*. It's outside, on the passageway, that Hitchcock holds the camera still far longer than you would believe possible until we hear the scream of Jean Marsh that indicates she's found the body.

At **Oxford Circus (3)** stood department store Littlewood's, where Shirley Valentine gets the passport photo that allows her escape to Mykonos, in the film of Willie Russell's stage play.

Take a small detour north on Regent Street, until the vast, lop-sided ocean liner of **Broadcasting House (4)** looms into view at **Portland Place**. Headquarters of BBC radio, the Portland stone-clad landmark was enormously controversial when it was opened in 1932, as much for its severe lines (which now look so classically deco) as for the Eric Gill carving of Prospero presenting a naked Ariel to the world (an apocryphal story has Gill being obliged to trim the rather too-well endowed Ariel down to a more acceptable size). While still a novelty, the building was the setting for 1934's *Death at Broadcasting House*, a whodunnit with inspector Ian Hunter investigating the murder of broadcaster Donald Wolfit live on air – though the studio

GoldenEye: St Petersburg's Grand Hotel Europe: Langham Hilton, Portland Place

Sense and Sensibility: the Dashwoods' London home: Chandos House, Queen Anne Street

interiors were recreated in the old Wembley Studio. Radio producer Val Gielgud (the older brother of theatre knight Sir John) wrote the script, which featured a musical number from Elisabeth Welch, whose lengthy career, amazingly, went on to include an appearance in Derek Jarman's 1980 film of *The Tempest*.

Cross the road to the **Langham Hilton, 1c Portland Place (5**; see **Hotels**, p8), which appears as a 'Russian' hotel in *GoldenEye*.

Continue to Chandos Street. At the northern end stands **Chandos House, 2 Queen Anne Street (6)**, which was used for the 'Greenwich Village' party where Jack Reed (Warren Beatty) cuts a rug with Louise Bryant (Diane Keaton) in Beatty's Oscar-winning film *Reds*. The house also became the London home of the Dashwoods in Ang Lee's *Sense and Sensibility*. After years of neglect, this Grade I-listed Robert Adam mansion, dating from 1769, was compulsorily purchased from the investment company which owned it and is currently being restored to its original splendour.

Continue along Queen Anne Street to **Harley Street (7)**, its name synonymous with expensive private medicine. In films, a brief shot of the street sign usually signifies a visit to an overpriced quack. Mr Bridger (Noël Coward) takes a break from

Maurice: the concert: Wigmore Hall, Wigmore Street

Frenzy: site of the Blaney Bureau: Oxford Street

Darling: Laurence Harvey's apartment: Wimpole Street

the rigours of Wormwood Scrubs to enjoy a luxury check up here in *The Italian Job*.

Turn left and immediately right into Wigmore Street. **Wigmore Hall, 36 Wigmore Street** (**8**), is where a jittery Clive Durham (Hugh Grant) and Maurice Hall (James Wilby) attend a concert after the arrest of their friend Lord Risley for 'immorality' in the Merchant-Ivory film of EM Forster's *Maurice*. The hall, originally called Bechstein Hall, was built in 1901 by the famous piano manufacturer, alongside their showroom. Its alabaster and marble interior (by Thomas Collcutt, who also designed the Palace Theatre on Cambridge Circus and the Savoy Hotel on the Strand) is famed for its acoustics and attracted the highest calibre musicians, but the name Bechstein became a distinct drawback during WWI and the hall was sold to Debenham's department store in 1916 (℗ *box office: 020.7935.2141; website: www.wigmore-hall.org.uk*).

Crossing Wigmore Street is **Wimpole Street**, made famous by Katherine Cornell's play *The Barretts of Wimpole Street*, about the romance between Elizabeth Barrett and Robert Browning. It's been filmed twice in Hollywood, in 1934 and 1957, both versions directed by Sidney Franklin, and providing star roles for first Charles Laughton and then John Gielgud as the overbearing paterfamilias Barrett. Famous residents included surgeon Sir Frederick Treves, the benefactor of *The Elephant Man*, played by Anthony Hopkins in the David Lynch film, who lived at **number 6**. **40-41 Wimpole Street** (**9**) was the pad of Laurence Harvey in *Darling*. **2 Upper Wimpole Street** was home to Sherlock Holmes' creator Sir Arthur Conan Doyle.

If you're hungry, grab a bite at Italian restaurant **Its, 56-60 Wigmore Street** (**10**; see **Bars & Restaurants**, p13) alongside Easley's Mews – though Derek Thompson has a less pleasant dining experience here in *The Long Good Friday*.

Heading west along Wigmore Street brings you to the famed Wallace Collection, home of Franz Hals' Laughing Cavalier, among many other famous paintings, in **Hertford**

The Long Good Friday: the pavement cafe: Its, Wigmore Street

House, Manchester Square (**11**; ℗ *020.7563.9551; website: www.wallacecollection.org*). Bizarrely, Hertford House was transformed into the lavish 'Majestic Hotel', where Chris Rea holes up, for Michael Winner's disastrous movie *Parting Shots*.

Cross Wigmore Street into Marylebone Lane and then cross Oxford Street to Bond Street. World-famous auction house **Sotheby's, 34 New Bond Street** (**12**; ℗ *020.7293.5000*) is where the Fabergé egg is put on sale in *Octopussy* (though the interior was recreated in the studio), and also where anarchic billionaire Sir Guy Grand (Peter Sellers) buys the nose – just the nose, mind you – of an old master, to the horror of supercilious dealer Mr Dougdale (John Cleese) in the sixties satire *The Magic Christian*.

Another London institution, **Asprey, 165-169 New Bond Street**, is the jewellers where the Beatles try unsuccessfully to get the sacrificial ring removed from Ringo's finger in Richard Lester's *Help!*

The Halcyon Gallery, 29 Bruton Street (**13**) is the art gallery in Alex Jovy's *Sorted*.

Turn left into Conduit Street. The **Mayfair Westbury Hotel, Conduit Street** (**14**; see **Hotels**, p8) at Bond Street, can be seen in the Jerry Lee Lewis biopic *Great Balls of Fire!*

Continue to Savile Row, home of the classic tailored suit. Although, when the Beatles opened their Apple Corps office on the row, it was lawsuits that were the order of the day. The doomed philanthropic venture, created to launch innovative new talent, rapidly turned into a free-for-all for any dingbat freeloader. It was on the roof of the office at **3 Savile Row** that the Beatles performed what turned out to be their last-ever gig, before the law turned up and pulled the plug, as recorded in Michael Lindsay-Hogg's gloomy 1970 documentary *Let It Be*.

Savile Row

Octopussy: the Fabergé egg: Sotheby's, New Bond Street

Great Balls of Fire!: Jerry Lee Lewis' hotel: Mayfair Westbury Hotel, Conduit Street

Sorted: the art gallery: The Halcyon Gallery, Bruton Street

runs south to Piccadilly. Ronald Neame's 1955 fact-based wartime drama *The Man Who Never Was* has the British top brass, led by Clifton Webb,

The Man Who Never Was: Stephen Boyd checks out the fictitious major: The Naval and Military Club, Piccadilly

planting fake ID and misleading intelligence on a corpse, which is then dumped at sea to wash up on the Spanish coast. The idea is to dupe the Nazis, who – in the fictional version – duly send an agent to check up on the credibility of 'Major Martin'. **The Naval and Military Club, Egremont House, 94 Piccadilly** (**15**), known ocally as the 'In and Out' because of its unsubtle gateposts, is where German-sympathising Irish spy Stephen Boyd tries to check out the fictitious military background of the corpse.

The hilarious liberties taken with London's geography by Phillip Noyce in *Patriot Games* suggest that the movie was primarily aimed at an American market. The intimidatingly formal **Burlington Arcade** (**16**), full of jewellers and gentlemen's outfitters you probably won't dare set foot in and fiercely monitored by costumed beadles (no whistling, running, opening umbrellas...), is where the IRA has its London HQ, in a dusty little antiquarian bookshop. When the villains hotfoot it from here, the nearest tube station they can find is not Green Park or Piccadilly Circus, but Aldwych, on the Strand. Equally unlikely is Jeff Daniels whizzing through the arcade as he's dragged from Trafalgar Square to St James's Park in *101 Dalmatians*. More credibly, John Standing and Oliver Ford Davies windowshop here in Marleen Gorris's *Mrs Dalloway*.

Alongside the arcade is the **Royal Academy, Burlington House** (*© 020.7300.8000; website: www.royalacademy.org.uk*). An art school founded by Gainsborough and Joshua Reynolds, and home of traditional academic values, the academy now divides its time between blockbuster exhibitions and headline-grabbing shock tactics. Miriam Hopkins sits entranced before the portrait of Edmund Davey as Othello, in the melodrama *Men Are Not Gods*.

Fortnum and Mason, 181 Piccadilly (*website: www.fortnumandmason.com*), is the lavish emporium decked out with seasonal decorations, where Emma

Patriot Games: the IRA bookshop: Burlington Arcade, Piccadilly

Thompson demonstrates "the scientific approach to Christmas shopping – a list", to Vanessa Redgrave in *Howards End*. Julie Christie and swinging photographer Roland Curram shoplift a bagful of luxury foods here in John Schlesinger's Swinging London-set *Darling*.

Darling ends on the steps of the statue of Eros in **Piccadilly Circus** (**17**), after Julie Christie has returned with her Italian prince to virtual exile in Rome, with an old woman singing 'Santa Lucia'. Since 1986, when the need to ease traffic congestion meant sidelining the famous statue from its central island to the pedestrianised area in front of the Criterion Theatre, the Circus has lost much of its visual impact. Truth be told, though, it was never as familiar a cinematic backdrop as New York's Times Square. The muffed postal drop in John Wayne's only UK movie, *Brannigan*, centres around an unlikely postbox situated on a traffic island, beneath which the villains manage to vanish into the sewers. Another Wayne, Wayne Campbell (Mike Myers), with his pal Garth (Dana Carvey) – and certainly not a pair of cheap lookalikes filmed by a second unit – fetch up here, searching for the legendary roadie in *Wayne's World 2*. The Circus' trademark illuminated signs flash up diary entries in *Bridget Jones's Diary*.

Most memorably perhaps, it took the unstoppable gung-ho enthusiasm of John Landis to stage mayhem in the heart of the capital. Part of the building now housing ubiquitous clothes store Gap, on the corner of **Shaftesbury Avenue**, used to be the Eros News Cinema, where David Naughton is nagged by his undead victims in *An American Werewolf in London*. As the werewolf tears through the cinema's security doors at the movie's climax, major traffic chaos ensues. For the first time ever, Piccadilly Circus was closed for filming on two successive nights, albeit in the wee, small hours. Nevertheless, much of the complex sequence was shot on a backlot recreation of the Circus at Twickenham Studios (look for the wobbly street sign!).

Before its current incarnation as **Tower Records**,

Maurice: saying *bon voyage* to Clive: Café Royal, Regent Street

Bridget Jones's Diary: Bridget gets advice from her friends: Momo, Heddon Street

the building to the west of the Circus between Piccadilly and Regent Street was the sedate department store Swan and Edgar, where Alastair Sim deliberately tries to get himself arrested for shoplifting (in order to satisfy the conditions of a mischievous will) in the 1951 comedy *Laughter in Paradise*. Outside the shop, Julie Christie buys up a pile of *Evening Standards* after her little publicity coup in *Darling*.

Take a short detour east along Coventry Street towards Leicester Square. Positively oozing gilded and mirrored glamour is the **Café de Paris, 3 Coventry Street** (see **Bars & Restaurants**, p13), an exclusive nightclub opened in 1924, which can be seen in *King Ralph*, *Absolute Beginners*, *Scandal* and *The Krays*.

Planet Hollywood, 13 Coventry Street (see **Bars & Restaurants**, p13), is the central London branch of the überstars' vanity project. Crowded and touristy, it's still a great place to gawp at movie memorabilia.

Return to Regent Street. There's more traditional luxury at the famous **Café Royal, 68 Regent Street**. It once numbered Oscar Wilde and George Bernard Shaw among its patrons, and is now a conference and banqueting centre. Jack Hawkins assembles his team of reprobates here to form The League of Gentlemen, Rupert Graves celebrates his new post in the **Grill Room** in Louis Malle's *Damage*, and there's another family meal here, before Clive departs for foreign parts, in *Maurice*.

The building on **Regent Street** at New Burlington Street was the Iberian Airline office where George Segal books tickets for what turns out to be a disastrous holiday in Malaga with Glenda Jackson in *A Touch of Class*.

Eyes Wide Shut: the reconciliation: Hamley's toystore, Regent Street

Tucked away in a tiny side-alley off Regent Street is Maghreb restaurant **Momo, 25 Heddon Street** (**18**; see **Bars &**

Restaurants, p13), where Bridget is given dating advice by her friends in *Bridget Jones's Diary*. But if there is an eerie familiarity to Heddon Street, that might be because this is famously the darkly ominous alley on the cover of David Bowie's 1972 album *The Rise and Fall of Ziggy Stardust and the Spiders from Mars*.

The 39 Steps: shooting Mr Memory: the London Palladium, Argyll Street

Hamley's, Regent Street (**1**), claimed to be the biggest toyshop in the world, is the 'New York' store where Tom Cruise and Nicole Kidman come to some kind of a reconciliation at the end of Kubrick's *Eyes Wide Shut*. A little further on, the venerable department store **Dickens and Jones, 224 Regent Street** (**20**), is where Bridget's mum works, demonstrating the strangely erotic egg peeler, in *Bridget Jones's Diary*.

Argyll Street, running east of Regent Street, is home to the **London Palladium** (**21**; *©️ 020.7494.5020*). This 2,286-seat theatre, specialising in big, bright, crowd-pleasing musicals, became something of a national institution during the fifties and sixties, when the entire nation would round off the weekend huddled in front of their black and white TV sets to watch variety show *Sunday Night at the London Palladium*. Robert Donat and Madeleine Carroll finally end up at the Palladium, where the unfortunate Mr Memory is shot, at the end of Hitchcock's original 1935 film *The 39 Steps*. And in an uncannily convincing scene, a coolly professional Dirk Bogarde persuades a quiveringly neurotic, and very drunk, Judy Garland to go onstage and belt out the title number of *I Could Go on Singing*, her final film. In 1970, Richard Attenborough unveiled a plaque in the theatre, commemorating the legendary singer's appearances.

Head south to **Carnaby Street**, for a brief time the heart of the Swinging Sixties London phenomenon when it was lined with the new breed of boutiques. Naturally enough, this is where Yvonne (Lynn Redgrave) goes to find fame in 1967's *Smashing Time* and hooks up with fashion photographer Tom Wabe (Michael York). At sports superstore **Soccer Scene, 46 Carnaby Street** (**22**), Jess (Parminder K Nagra) gets her boots in *Bend It Like Beckham*.

Smashing Time: Sixties Swinging London: Carnaby Street

Bend It Like Beckham: Jess gets her boots: Soccer Scene, Carnaby Street

Naked: Johnny meets the Scots drifter: Lina Stores, Brewer Street

Continue on into Soho, to Brewer Street. In the doorway of **Lina Stores, 18 Brewer Street (23)**, David Thewlis bumps into twitchy Scots drifter Ewen Bremner in Mike Leigh's *Naked*. A few doors away, **Madame Jo-Jo's, Brewer Street**, became 'Club Sonata', the 'New York' jazz club where Tom Cruise winkles the password to the orgy out of his old pal the pianist in *Eyes Wide Shut*. The rather sleazy little passageway alongside Madame Jo-Jo's is **Walker's Court**, where you'll find soft-core porn baron Paul Raymond's long-established **Raymond Revuebar**, which doubled as the strip club of Mortwell (Michael Caine) in *Mona Lisa*.

Walker's Court leads to **Berwick Street** fruit and veg market, a colourful place to pass time in the West End. Richard Attenborough buys fruit here in *Séance on a Wet Afternoon*, and Sid Vicious (Gary Oldman) and pal Wally (Graham Fletcher-Cook) stroll through the market in *Sid and Nancy*. Behind the well-stacked fruit and veg stalls are a clutch of specialist record stores where Carl (Matthew Rhys) tries to find out about his late brother in *Sorted*.

The **Windmill Theatre, Great Windmill Street**, a training ground for many of the great British comics, is currently dark – which is ironic, since 'We never closed' was its proud boast at the end of WWII. Its other motto, 'If it moves, it's rude', stems from the theatre's trademark tableaux vivants, which could be passed off as artistic displays just so long as the nude

Mona Lisa: Michael Caine's club: Raymond Revuebar, Walker's Court

Brannigan: John Wayne eats out: Lupo, Dean Street

models held frozen poses. In 1949, Val Guest made the minor mystery *Murder at the Windmill* here.

The nearest thing that London has to a semi-official red-light district (though relentless efforts to gentrify the area have tempered the real sleaze which once characterised it), **Soho** is an enticingly confusing jumble of the seedy and the stylish, and home to disparate communities – film companies around Wardour Street, the gay village of Old Compton Street and Chinatown centred around Gerrard Street to the south. The real Soho provided a backdrop for scenes in *Melody*, *Nuns on the Run* and *Rancid Aluminium*. However, for *Absolute Beginners*, a colourful fifties take on the neighbourhood was created entirely in the studio.

Love Is the Devil: Bohemian watering hole: the Colony Room Club, Dean Street

Classy Italian restaurant **Lupo, 50 Dean Street (24**; see **Bars & Restaurants**, p13), used to be the legendary Mario and Franco's Terrazza, which can be seen in *Brannigan*.

The **Colony Room Club, 41 Dean Street (25**), has been the centre of that peculiarly alluring blend of hard drinking, rudeness and sexual unorthodoxy typified by Francis Bacon and his artistic clique since 1948. The club's cluttered, smoky atmosphere was conjured up in the studio for John Maybury's *Love Is the Devil*, with Derek Jacobi as the bibulous genius and Tilda Swinton as the fearsome founder and longtime proprietor Muriel Belcher.

The **Pitcher and Piano, 69 Dean Street** (see **Bars & Restaurants**, p13), can be seen at the opening of *Wonderland*.

In *Expresso Bongo*, Val Guest's 1959 satire on the burgeoning music biz, **Old Compton Street** provides cutting-edge decadence: strip joints and coffee bars – a suitable backdrop for Laurence Harvey (taking over from Paul Scofield who played the role on stage) as the unscrupulous promoter and Cliff Richard as his protégé, the fabulously-named Bongo Herbert. Over forty years later, only the style has changed. It's on the same street, now packed with gay bars sporting rainbow flags, that Jason Donovan (trying to regain some cred as a transvestite DJ) introduces naïve northerner Matthew Rhys to

Wonderland: Gina McKee's blind date: The Pitcher and Piano, Dean Street

Wonderland: the café where Gina McKee works: Duke's Bar, Old Compton Street

Bend It Like Beckham: Jess celebrates in the West End: The Three Greyhounds, Greek Street

the joys of speed in Alex Jovy's drug-fuelled film *Sorted*. **Duke's Bar, 27 Old Compton Street**, is the snack bar where Gina Mc-Kee works in *Wonderland*.

Opposite the Prince Edward Theatre, **The Three Greyhounds, 25 Greek Street (26**; see **Bars & Restaurants**, p14), can be seen in *Bend It Like Beckham*. **Ronnie Scott's Club, 47 Frith Street** (see **Bars & Restaurants**, p13), a legendary jazz venue since 1965, is the easy-listening club where Craig Ferguson turns on the charm in *Born Romantic*.

Film industry screening rooms abound: Warner Bros has its office on **Wardour Street**, 20th Century Fox is on the southwest corner of **Soho Square (27)** itself, and 3 Soho Square is home to the British Board of Film Classification. This tiny pocket of green, with its half-timbered mock-Tudor folly (actually a ventilation shaft for the underground), is where Anthony Hopkins watches the bright young things trot off to Carnaby Street in *84 Charing Cross Road* and, more recently, where Carl walks with Sunny (Sienna Guillory) in *Sorted*.

Shaftesbury Avenue, London's theatreland, slices through Soho from Piccadilly Circus to Charing Cross Road. It's outside the **Queens Theatre, Shaftesbury Avenue**, that Glenda Jackson spies George Segal and his wife leaving the preview of a new Harold Pinter play (she thought he was working late) in the dated romantic comedy *A Touch of Class*. The couple's

seedy lovenest can be found just to the south, in Chinatown. Running between Shaftesbury Avenue and Gerrard Street, with its stage-set scarlet gates and kitschy oriental phone boxes, is Macclesfield Street. Squashed between restaurants, **3 Macclesfield Street (28)** is the flat where Jackson (winning her second Oscar) and Segal attempt to conduct their illicit affair.

Sid and Nancy: Sid Vicious up west: The Spice of Life, Moor Street

Shaftesbury Avenue leads east into **Cambridge Circus (29)**. Jittery hairdresser Henry (Charles Lloyd-Pack) keels over from a heart attack after being threatened by sinister blackmailer Derren Nesbitt, in his barber shop at **2 Earlham Street**, on the south side of the Circus alongside the Marquis of Granby pub, in *Victim*. The shop is now a newsagents.

The stretch of Charing Cross Road immediately to the south is famous for its cluttered, independent little bookshops (though they're slowly being eased out), while the giants such as Foyle's and the big chains can be found to the north. No longer a bookshop, the building on the northeast corner of Cambridge Circus has an address you're bound to recognise: **84 Charing Cross Road**. It's hard to visualise this smart restaurant as Marks & Co, the dusty little business made famous by Helene Hanff's book. The area has changed so much that for the 1986 film, starring Anthony Hopkins as the staid Brit bookseller and Anne Bancroft as the American bookworm with whom he conducts a transatlantic correspondence, the shop – and a stretch of Charing Cross Road – had to be recreated in the studio.

Dominating the Circus is the huge red brick and faience frontage of the **Palace Theatre**. Built in 1890 as an opera house for Richard D'Oyly Carte, it's traditionally the home of long-running musicals (the illuminated signs for *Flower Drum Song* can be seen in *Victim*) and currently houses *Les Misérables*. It was temporarily transformed into the exterior of the 'St James Theatre', where *Lady Windermere's Fan* premières, in *Wilde*.

Now it's time to relax with the tourists waiting to see, or having just seen, *Les Mis*, in **The Spice of Life, 6 Moor Street** (see **Bars & Restaurants**, p14), alongside the theatre, the exterior of which can be glimpsed in *Sid and Nancy*.

A Touch of Class: Glenda Jackson's Chinatown flat: Macclesfield Street

Central London: Westminster to Pimlico

With a concentration of government buildings, the HQ of the Metropolitan Police and the monied enclave of Belgravia, it's not surprising to find satire, crime and big, big money. Less obviously, there are massed fascists, Russian revolutionaries and Nazi stormtroopers…

Starting Point: Westminster Station

Emerging from Westminster Station, you're immediately overwhelmed by the sheer visual overkill of Charles Barry's Palace of Westminster and Big Ben (actually St Stephen's Clocktower – Ben is the bell hanging inside), but before we come to that, first take a walk, left along Bridge Street to **Westminster Bridge (1)**. The Boulting twins John and Roy – best known for their amiable satires – produced a tense thriller in 1950: *Seven Days to Noon*, one of the few films of the period to use real locations around the capital. It is also one of the first to exploit the oft-copied plot of conscience-riddled boffin threatening to detonate a lethal weapon unless the government

halts the arms race. It's on the deserted Westminster Bridge that slightly faded actress Goldie hears the all-clear siren, and realises that London is safe from Professor Willingdon's superbomb. Jerry Lee Lewis (Dennis Quaid) reads the news placards while travelling over the bridge in Jim McBride's underrated comic-strip biopic *Great Balls of Fire!* More bizarrely, Cruella De Vil has spotty hallucinations here after the chimes of Big Ben undo her aversion therapy in *102 Dalmatians*. Coming full circle, the bridge is desolate again as Cillian Murphy wanders the city after waking up in *28 Days Later*.

In *The Accidental Tourist*, William Hurt's travels take him to Europe, where he likes his meals fast, bland and international – at the Yankee Delight on the Embankment by Westminster Bridge, now replaced by the New Parliamentary Building development.

Turn left onto Victoria Embankment and walk a little way along to **Derby Gate** to see the familiar round corner towers of the 'old' New Scotland Yard building. The street **Great Scotland Yard** is actually a couple of blocks north, running between Whitehall and Northumberland Avenue. It was here that the first headquarters of the Metropolitan Police was built in 1829 (though the address was actually 4

Whitehall). In 1867, the police moved to Norman Shaw's horizontally-striped red brick HQ at Derby Gate but kept the name, hence New Scotland Yard – the familiar building seen in countless crime movies and TV shows until the late sixties. After one hundred years of occupation, the police upped and moved to the third, 'new' New Scotland Yard, the current HQ on Victoria Street. Oddly, when Harry Palmer (Michael Caine) consults his cop pal for the low-down on "Grantby – a right master criminal" in *The Ipcress File*, it's the original Great Scotland Yard address he goes to.

Inspector George Gideon (Jack Hawkins), however, works in the old Derby Gate building in *Gideon's Day*, a 1958 oddity from the master of Westerns, John Ford, which follows one fraught day in the career of a top London cop. Among countless appearances, 'old' New Scotland Yard can be seen in Fred Zinnemann's *The Day of the Jackal* (made in 1973, but set ten years earlier). There's obviously a greater visual impact to the Parliament Street entrance though, which is where Hugh Cross and Sheila Manahan emerge to hail a cab in *Seven Days to Noon*. There's no access through Derby Gate, so return via Bridge Street.

Flanked by government ministries, Whitehall is hardly likely to be closed down to host massive crowd scenes or frantic car chases. If it's seen on screen, it is usually glimpsed through a car window as government agents are briefed on the latest impending crisis. But when Mike Myers and Elizabeth Hurley drive down Whitehall, it's courtesy of rear projection in *Austin Powers: International Man of Mystery*, made entirely in the US.

Before MI6 went public with its attention-grabbing Vauxhall Cross HQ, the movies saw the secretive organisation operate out of various buildings around Westminster, where the prime requirement for the intelligence services seemed to be a clear view of Nelson's Column. 007's HQ is the **Old War Office Building, Whitehall** (**2**), in three films, *A View to a Kill*, *Octopussy* and *Licence to Kill*, all directed by James Bond regular John Glen.

10 Downing Street (**3**), the London residence of the Prime Minister, is another location you can reasonably assume is reproduced in the studio, particularly since gates were erected to cordon off the street during the turbulent Thatcher administration. However, in the more sedate – or naïve – fifties, Professor Willingdon (Barry Jones), carrying his doomsday bomb, is able to lurk in the crowd outside the famous door in *Seven Days to Noon*.

Continue down Whitehall to **Parliament Square** (**4**). In the 1978 adaptation of John Buchan's novel *The Thirty-Nine Steps* (the first to use Buchan's plot),

crowds in the square watch Richard Hannay (Robert Powell) hanging from the hands of St Stephen's clockface (which was, of course, recreated in the studio), a stunt repeated by Owen Wilson and Jackie Chan in the comedy actioner *Shanghai Knights*. In Mel Smith's 2001 comedy thriller *High Heels and Low Lifes*, gang boss Kerrigan (Michael Gambon) is embarrassed by a 40-foot poster exhibited in the square. These scenes are rare, though. The Houses of Parliament and Big Ben are usually relegated to a grainy shot, yanked out of the stock library, as a visual shorthand to indicate London. In *Konga* (the UK's 1961 micro-budget, monkey suit spin on *King Kong*), although villain Michael Gough appears to be alongside the famous clocktower, clutched in the paw of the overgrown ape, the seething crowds below (numbering well into double figures) are cowering on the streets of Croydon, South London. On the east side of the square, a party of worthies sets out from the gates of the Houses of Parliament to investigate the sinister government facility in Val Guest's superbly atmospheric sci-fi sequel *Quatermass 2*.

In the same film, Professor Quatermass (Brian Donlevy) meets up with the investigative MP in a scene actually shot in the formal grandeur of the foyer of the **House of Lords**. However, the Lords is rarely treated with such reverence in British cinema. The unelected chamber has a more familiar image as a repository for the feckless, brainless and chinless. Cured of his dangerously radical Christ delusions, and happily believing himself to be Jack the Ripper, the 14th Earl of Gurney (Peter O'Toole) arrives at **St Stephen's Entrance** to take his seat in the Lords in the savagest of satires, *The Ruling Class*. Ursula Andress races through the same entrance, fetching dim aristo David Warner ("He went there to sulk.") to pull the bank job in Peter Hall's *Perfect Friday* .

In 1981, Warren Beatty walked off with the Best Director Oscar for his epic story of American radicals Jack Reed (Beatty) – the only non-Russian to have been interred in the Kremlin – and Louise Bryant (Diane Keaton). The 'Liberal Club, Portland,

Reds: the Liberal Club, Oregon: Institute of Civil Engineers, Great George Street

Reds: the St Petersburg post office: Central Hall Westminster, Storey's Gate

Oregon', where wannabe journo Bryant first claps eyes on the charismatic Reed, is actually the **Institute of Civil Engineers, 1 Great George Street**. It is now used as a conference and banquet centre – you can get married here, too (*website: www.onegreatgeorgestreet.com*).

Great George Street continues into **Birdcage Walk**, along the southern border of St James's Park, where Dalby and Ross, Harry Palmer's superiors, plot their devious strategies in *The Ipcress File*. On the south side of the walk, at **Wellington Barracks**, the Scots Guards parade at the beginning of Michael Anderson's globetrotting extravaganza *Around the World in Eighty Days*. The scene was supposedly filmed clandestinely, with a camera hidden in a vegetable stall. So that's a widescreen Todd-AO camera hidden in a vegetable stall on the guards' parade ground, then? Hmm.

Return to Parliament Square. On the west side is **Central Hall Westminster, Storey's Gate** (*© 020.7222.8010; website: www.c-h-w.com*), opposite the entrance to Westminster Abbey, where members of the SS lounge in the 1966 film of life under Nazi occupation, *It Happened Here*. The 'St Petersburg post office' in *Reds*, where Warren Beatty sends increasingly frantic telegrams, is the interior of the Hall and, yes, there are guided tours of the building daily.

The blobby alien in 1955's *The Quatermass Xperiment* is finally cornered in **Westminster Abbey** (see **Historic Sites**, p29), though the interior is actually a set.

In 1969, *The Magic Christian*, a novel by Terry Southern (the American satirist who co-wrote the screenplays for *Dr Strangelove* and *Easy Rider*) was loosely adapted for the screen, taking little more than the book's basic conceit: a mischievous multi-millionaire uses his vast wealth to subvert cherished institutions. The inaccessible **Little Dean's Yard** is

Without a Clue: 221b Baker Street: Barton Street

home to the faux-innocent Sir Guy Grand (played in a wonderfully beady eyed manner by Peter Sellers), constantly feigning surprise at the mayhem he's caused. You can see the entrance to **Dean's Yard**, where Sir Guy drives his Roller, just to the right of Westminster Abbey.

Indiana Jones and the Last Crusade: Berlin Airport: New Royal Horticultural Hall, Greycoat Street

Off Great College Street, to the south, is Barton Street. **9 Barton Street (5)**, off Millbank, became the fictitious '221b Baker Street', where the brilliant Dr Watson (Ben Kingsley) hires drunken actor Michael Caine to bring to life his fictitious creation Sherlock Holmes in the 1988 Conan Doyle spoof *Without a Clue*. A few doors away, at **14 Barton Street**, you can see the real home of TE Lawrence, better known as Lawrence of Arabia.

Continue south to Great Peter Street and turn west onto Greycoat Street. On the corner of Greycoat Street and Elverton Street is the twenties deco lettering of the **New Royal Horticultural Hall, Greycoat Street (6)**. If there's an exhibition, take the opportunity to look inside at the brutalist concrete arches, a gift for location scouts needing a backdrop for fascist rallies. Unsurprisingly then, it's here that rockstar Pink performs for ranks of ugly skinheads in Alan Parker's film of *Pink Floyd: The Wall*, and that Richard III addresses a jackbooted mob in Richard Loncraine's thirties-set version of Shakespeare's play. The hall has twice stood in for 'Berlin Airport': in another thirties-set film, *Indiana Jones and the Last Crusade*, and in the present as the "cosy transit lounge" of 'Templehof', where Simon Templar (Val Kilmer, improvising most of his lines), in the guise of fey Bruno, meets up with Boris the Spider, in Phillip Noyce's 1997 film of *The Saint*. The hall was also transformed into the severe museum of art where Frank (Rufus Sewell) tries to prove to Martha (Monica Potter) that art galleries are no more than pick-up joints for pretentious phonies, in the 1998 romcom *Martha Meet Frank, Daniel & Laurence*.

Turn down Regency Street and left into Page Street. You might be forgiven for thinking that the shops are sporting period dressing for a film shoot but, no, they've just been left mercifully

Buster: Buster Edwards hides out: Abady House, Page Street

Shooting Fish: demonstrating the computer: Horseferry Road

Mona Lisa: Bob Hoskins' flash new suit: Jolly St Ermin's, Caxton Street

unmodernised. **Abady House, Page Street (7)**, on the Grosvenor Estate, became the flat of Sheila Hancock, mother-in-law of train robber Buster Edwards (Phil Collins) in the cutesily sentimentalised *Buster*.

Return north on Horseferry Road. **124 Horseferry Road (8)** at Chadwick Street, Channel 4's gleaming new HQ designed by Richard Rogers (architect of the Lloyds Building), is where con artists Dan Futterman and Stuart Townsend demonstrate their "sixth-generation voice recognition" computer in *Shooting Fish*.

Return north on Horseferry Road, and cross Victoria Street into Broadway, to Caxton Street on the left. The **Jolly St Ermin's, 2 Caxton Street (9**; see **Hotels**, p8), can be seen in *Mona Lisa*. The interior features in *Reds*, and the ballroom was transformed into the dining room of the Savoy for 2002's *The Importance of Being Earnest*. Gunplay between Nancy Spungen and Sid Vicious was filmed on the

Howards End: Anthony Hopkins' London house: 51 Buckingham Gate

roof of the hotel for *Sid and Nancy* – a risky thing to do when the hotel overlooks **New Scotland Yard (10)**, the current home of the Metropolitan Police. "All of a sudden, about twenty armed police appeared on the roof", says the film's location manager Paul Raphael. The anti-terrorist squad takes a keen interest weapons brandished on central London rooftops...

New Scotland Yard's famous revolving sign can be seen in countless thrillers, including *The File of the Golden Goose*, Hitchcock's *Frenzy* and *Sweeney!*

Continue along Caxton Street to Buckingham Gate, and another prestigious lodging, **51 Buckingham Gate (11**; see **Hotels**, p8), which can be seen in *Howards End*.

Turn right onto Victoria Street to Palace Street. On the right of the street is the Westminster City School. 1958's *The Inn of the Sixth Happiness* tells the story of missionary Gladys Aylward famously marching 100 children through the mountains of China (actually, North Wales) to the tune of 'This Old Man'. The small gatehouse at the right of **Westminster City School, Palace Street (12)**, is the exterior of the 'China Missionary Office', where Aylward (Ingrid Bergman) first applies, unsuccessfully, to become a missionary.

Hemmed in by bland shops and office blocks, is the exotically Byzantine **Westminster Cathedral (13**; see **Historic Sites**, p29), the exterior of which appears in *Foreign Correspondent* and *Jubilee*.

The **Victoria Palace Theatre, Victoria Street (14**; ℡ *020.7834.1317)*, was home for many years to the bizarre, and now thankfully defunct, Black and White Minstrel Show. It's at the Palace that Bongo Herbert (Cliff Richard) gets his break on The Dixie Collins Show in *Expresso Bongo*. "It's not generally known that I'm a deeply religious boy", intones Herbert, in Wolf Mankowitz's

The Inn of the Sixth Happiness: the China Missionary Office: Westminster City School, Palace Street

Foreign Correspondent: Rowley falls to his death: Westminster Cathedral

Expresso Bongo: big break for Bongo Herbert: Victoria Palace Theatre, Victoria Street

The Ipcress File: the Dalby Domestic Employment Bureau: Grosvenor Gardens

sharply cynical script, before serenading his Mum with the disturbingly saccharine 'The Shrine on the Second Floor'. How times do change. At the Palace's stage door on **Allington Street** he accepts an invitation to go back to Dixie's place for drinks, which turns into an extended stay at the Dorchester.

Victoria Railway Station (**15**), traditional point of departure for that frisky weekend on the south coast, is where Stanley Baker arrives in Peter Yates' 1967 film *Robbery*, a detailed – yet fictionalised – account of the Great Train Robbery (there's a great car chase, too, from the director whose next film was *Bullitt*). Minnie Driver and Mary McCormack board a train at Victoria, in an attempt to outwit the bankrobbers, in Mel Smith's *High Heels and Low Lifes*.

Further down Buckingham Palace Road is the deco-ish **Victoria Coach Station**, Rita Tushingham's point of arrival at the beginning of *The Knack*.

From Victoria Railway Station, turn right into Buckingham Palace Gardens and Grosvenor Gardens. Ebury Street crosses the centre of the 'bow tie' created by the two triangular gardens. Look at the ornate building at the southern tip of the northerly triangle. **30 Grosvenor Gardens** (**16**) at Ebury Street, is the 'Dalby Domestic Employment

Howards End: the home of the Schlegel sisters: Victoria Square

Bureau', the staffing agency used as a front for Major Dalby's outfit in *The Ipcress File*, to which Harry Palmer gets transferred. Much of the movie was shot within the building, which was entirely taken over for the production.

As you continue north and Ebury Street becomes Beeston Place, you come to Victoria Square, a quiet enclosed haven in the bustle of Victoria. '6 Wickham Place', home of the Schlegel sisters (Emma Thompson and Helena Bonham Carter) in *Howards End*, was **6 Victoria Square** (**17**). In the 1956 cameo-infested extravaganza *Around the World in Eighty Days*, Passepartout (Mexican star Cantinflas) arrives in Victoria Square by penny-farthing bicycle. His destination is **5 Lower Grosvenor Place**,

Around the World in Eighty Days: Hesketh-Baggott's Employment Office': Lower Grosvenor Place

The Stud: Fontaine Khaled's place: Eaton Square

the pepperpot-shaped building at the end of the narrow road leading out of the northeastern side of the square, which currently houses a stockbroking company. This was 'Hesketh-Baggott's Employment Office', where Mr Foster (John Gielgud) complains to his boss Hesketh-Baggott (Noël Coward), and Passepartout gets the job as gentleman's gentleman to Phileas Fogg (David Niven).

The route to Eaton Square takes in blue plaques marking the homes of two writers whose creations became long-running screen legends. **22 Ebury Street** was the home of James Bond creator Ian Fleming, and at **24 Chester Square** lived *Frankenstein* author Mary Shelley. This seems to be the neighbourhood for writers – a few blocks from the 'employment office' lived Hesketh Baggott's alter-ego Noël Coward, at **17 Gerald Road**.

On to the jaw-droppingly expensive Eaton Square. Where else would you expect to find Fontaine Khaled (Joan Collins)? **11 Eaton Square** (**18**), on the south side of the gardens near Lower Belgrave Street, is the luxury pad

The Tamarind Seed: the home of Julie Andrews: South Eaton Place

Around the World in Eighty Days: the home of Phileas Fogg: Belgrave Square

The Million Pound Note: the home of the Montpelier brothers: Belgrave Square

where she notoriously makes out with toyboy Tony Blake (Oliver Tobias) in the lift, in seventies disco-trashfest *The Stud*. A little to the west, number **53 Eaton Square** was the home of Vivien Leigh.

13 South Eaton Place (19) is home to Judith Farrow (Julie Andrews) in Blake Edwards' 1974 glossy international romance *The Tamarind Seed*.

Belgrave Square gives its name to the whole unwelcoming area of Belgravia – barely distinguishable cream streets and squares of intimidatingly grand, soulless houses, many of which bristle with security devices and video surveillance, and sport pompous embassy plaques. **17 Belgrave Square (20)** (now the Royal College of Psychiatrists) is the home of globetrotting Phileas Fogg in *Around the World in Eighty Days*.

Ronald Neame's 1954 comedy *The Million Pound Note* stars Gregory Peck as Henry Adams, a penurious American given the titular note by fabulously wealthy brothers Roderick and Oliver Montpelier (Wilfrid Hyde-White and Ronald Squire). The joke – although he's loaded with cash, no one can change the note, so he gets things for free – came from a Mark Twain story, and was pretty much recycled by John Landis in 1983 as *Trading Places*. **47 Belgrave Square** is the home of the Montpelier brothers. Peck chases the wind-borne note across Belgrave Square and around the corner to **Montrose Place**.

4 Cadogan Lane was the last home of Judy Garland. She lived here with her fifth husband Mickey

Hanover Street: the home of Lesley-Ann Down: Wilton Crescent

Deans (aka Michael de Vinko), who discovered her dead in the bathroom on the morning of 22 June 1969, her bloodstream awash with barbiturates.

Perfect Friday: the bank robbery: Grosvenor Place

To Wilton Crescent. **4 Wilton Crescent (21)**, north of Belgrave Square, was the home of Margaret Sellinger (Lesley-Anne Down), where she lived with husband Paul (Christopher Plummer) and daughter Sarah (a very young Patsy Kensit), until falling for dashing US airman David Halloran (Harrison Ford) in Peter Hyams' 1979 WWII romance *Hanover Street*. Down the road at **23 Wilton Crescent**, lives villainous Martha Hyer in Alvin Rakoff's lightweight sixties spy caper *Crossplot*.

Perfect Friday: the flat: Grosvenor Crescent

12 Grosvenor Crescent (22) is the flat provided by mousy bank manager Stanley Baker for accomplices David Warner and Ursula Andress in Peter Hall's sprightly caper *Perfect Friday*. On the corner, the modern block at **1 Grosvenor Place** became the 'National Metropolitan Bank', where Baker works and sets up his neat little scheme to relieve the company of its cash.

Rotten Row (23), the riding path running along the southern perimeter of Hyde Park, is where the elegant Victorians stroll at the opening of *Around the World in Eighty Days*. George Segal plays baseball here, when he first bumps into Glenda Jackson in the Oscar winning, but dated, comedy *A Touch of Class*. T108, the bench used for clandestine meetings in *The Ipcress File*, stood on Rotten Row.

Lowndes Square, towered over by the cylindrical London Casino Hotel, and with Harvey Nichols as its corner shop, hardly seems to be the place to find a squalid hippie retreat, yet although the retreat of Turner Purple (Mick Jagger) in *Performance* was supposed to be in Notting Hill (and, indeed, exteriors were filmed there), the unlikely interior was the apartment block at **23 Lowndes Square (24)**.

A few years before the undeniably landmark film

Performance: the Notting Hill interiors: Lowndes Square

The Servant: the restaurant: Lowndes Street

The Fourth Protocol: Anton Rodgers' house: Chesham House, Chesham Place

The Long Good Friday: Harold Shand's nightclub: the Villa Elephant on the River, Grosvenor Road

Performance, *The Servant* challenged the dutiful naturalism of British cinema. Joseph Losey's film drips with baroque embellishment: when toff James Fox meets his fiancée Wendy Craig in a Knightsbridge restaurant, the camera drifts in and out of surrounding conversations, including a louche Harold Pinter (who wrote the screenplay) as Society Man, and Patrick Magee and writer Alun Owen (who scripted the Beatles' *A Hard Day's Night*) as a pair of disturbingly worldly priests. The restaurant stood on **Lowndes Street**, just to the south at Motcomb Street. It's now a shop, but the street itself is pretty much unchanged.

Chesham House, 30-31 Chesham Place (25), was Anton Rodgers' house in *The Fourth Protocol*, the strangely dated 1987 spy thriller adapted from Frederick Forsyth's novel and directed by John Mackenzie (who made the far superior *The Long Good Friday*). The striking glass-domed entrance seen in the movie is **Chesham Close** around the corner in **Lyall Street**. The 'discreet knocking shop', where the IRA carries out a bloodily bungled attack on a judge in *The Crying Game*, is **100 Eaton Place**. Just opposite, at 37 Chesham Street, stood the Lowndes Arms, the pub Jaye Davidson follows Stephen Rea to in the same film. Sadly, it is now a private house.

The Crying Game: the attack on the judge: Eaton Place

If you want, you can take a quick detour down toward the river. In Pimlico you'll find **Dolphin Square (26)**.

The Sorcerers: the midnight swim: Dolphin Square

The swimming pool in the Dolphin Square complex is where mind controllers Boris Karloff and Catherine Lacey send Ian Ogilvy in *The Sorcerers*. Dirk Bogarde meets blackmailer Derren Nesbitt on the Embankment south of the square in *Victim*.

Opposite Dolphin Square, Italian restaurant **Villa Elephant on the River, 135 Grosvenor Road (27**; see **Bars & Restaurants**, p14; © *020.7834.1621*) is Harold Shand's casino in *The Long Good Friday*.

Central London: Trafalgar Square to Mayfair

From the scruffy, bustling, pigeon-infested open space at the heart of the city, take a walk through the expensive, if rather cold and impersonal, centre of London, dominated by gentlemen's clubs and exclusive hotels... though, in all probability, you won't get to see many of the interiors. All this money and property seems to attract the dark side; there's corruption, conspiracy and gangsterism aplenty, subverted by just a touch of sixties anarchy.

Starting Point: Trafalgar Square

Trafalgar Square (1) isn't the most elegant of European city squares – it sprawls too much, and is constantly overwhelmed by the swirl of traffic. This could soon change though, with the pedestrianisation of the square's North Terrace, to be completed in the summer of 2003, linking it to the National Gallery with a central staircase. The hygiene-conscious powers, who want to turn the entire city into a squeaky-clean, family-friendly theme park, are also bent on driving out the ubiquitous scruffy pigeons – you can't buy corn to feed them any more.

Big enough to accommodate filming without disrupting traffic, the square is one of the few central London landmarks to feature regularly in movies. Sylvia Sidney meets with undercover cop John Loder in Trafalgar Square in *Sabotage*, Alfred Hitchcock's

1936 adaptation of Joseph Conrad's *The Secret Agent.* Fourteen years later, Jules Dassin shot wannabe-wrestling promoter Richard Widmark meeting up with club owner Francis L Sullivan here in the excellent film noir *Night and the City*. During the opening of *The Inn of the Sixth Happiness,* Ingrid Bergman gazes up at Edwin Landseer's enormous bronze lions. Sophia Loren picks up on-the-run Gregory Peck in the square in Stanley Donen's convoluted 1966 comedy thriller *Arabesque.* A fraught David Naughton tries to get himself arrested here in *An American Werewolf in London*. Jeff Daniels is – naturally – dragged through Trafalgar Square by Pongo the dog during the geographically bizarre chase near the beginning of *101 Dalmatians*. In David A Stewart's legendary turkey *Honest*, Nicole Appleton and Peter Facinelli trip out in the fountains. In 1961's *The Day the Earth Caught Fire* the square is filled with CND protesters. In another sci-fi movie, Brian Donlevy sees something suspicious being driven through the square, past Admiralty Arch, in *Quatermass 2.* Most incongruously, the square is decked out with swastikas for the fascist rally in Kevin Brownlow and Andrew Mollo's fake documentary of life under Nazi occupation, *It Happened Here.* In *The Living Daylights*, James Bond's 'MI6 HQ' is on the south-west corner of the square, in **Malaysia House, 57 Trafalgar Square**, the office of Malaysian Tourism.

Admiralty Arch itself, the entrance to the Mall at the southwest corner of Trafalgar Square, is the backdrop for the 'money shot' in *Howards End,* which seems to use every existing horse-drawn vehicle in

The Ipcress File: Harry Palmer is summoned to the office of Colonel Ross: Foreign and Commonwealth Office Building

London.

At the square's northeast corner stands **St Martin-in-the-Fields**, where Dougray Scott waits on the steps for Kate Winslet at the end of *Enigma*.

The huge **Trafalgar Square Post Office**, opposite the northeast corner, is where Richard Attenborough makes phone calls in Bryan Forbes' 1964 psychological thriller *Séance on a Wet Afternoon*. In 1975, he's back as a police commander in *Brannigan*, watching scooter messenger Tony Robinson pick up a package after the money drop.

To the northwest of the square, at the **Haymarket Theatre Royal, Haymarket** (**2**; ✆ *0870.901.3356*), the grown-up Billy's father proudly attends his ballet performance at the end of *Billy Elliot*.

Behind Haymarket once stood the Buckstone, a famous old actor-laddies' club, seen in the 1964 drama *The Comedy Man*, with Kenneth More. (It was in the Buckstone that British TV comedy duo the Two Ronnies, Corbett and Barker, first met, while Corbett was working as a barman.)

Exit Trafalgar Square through Admiralty Arch. To your left, gleaming and much-cleaned up, stands the **Foreign and Commonwealth Office Building** (**3**), the old Admiralty Building, which became the 'Ministry of Defence' building where Harry Palmer is summoned to the office of Colonel Ross to be transferred to Major Dalby's outfit in *The Ipcress File*.

Further along the Mall, on the north side, are the cream, pillared porticos of **Nash House, Carlton House Terrace**, home to the **Institute of Contemporary Arts** (**4**; ✆ *020.7930.3647; website: www.ica.org.uk*), the incongruously conservative home of provocative avant garde exhibitions and performances, housing a 2-screen

Bridget Jones's Diary: launching Kafka's Motorbike: the ICA, the Mall

cinema (see **Entertainment: Cinemas**, p25), a bookshop (see **Shopping**, p23) and an excellent Italian café. The literary party for the launch of *Kafka's Motorbike*, attended by Salman Rushdie, Lord Archer *et al*, in *Bridget Jones's Diary*, is held at the ICA. **The Stables, Carlton House Terrace**, a three-story stable with sloping ramps, can also be seen in 1950's *The Elusive Pimpernel*.

You can carry on along the Mall, if you want, to the Queen's London residence – although Her Maj seems rarely to be in, and is even more rarely to be seen. The exterior of **Buckingham Palace** (**5**; see **Historic Sites**, p29) can be glimpsed on screen in *The Knack*, *The Jokers*, *Austin Powers in Goldmember*, *Die Another Day* and *Ooh, You Are Awful*, the latter of which also features the Queen's Picture Gallery.

You can take time out to relax in **St James's Park** (**6**). It used to be said that if you stood on the the bridge over the lake in the centre of the park, sooner or later you'd see everyone in London (though nowadays Piccadilly Circus would seem to be a likelier bet). It's here that Sir Guy Grand (Peter Sellers) picks up the homeless young man who will become Youngman Grand Esq (Ringo Starr), his adopted son, in *The Magic Christian*. Jeff Daniels careers through the park on his bike and plunges into the lake in *101 Dalmatians*.

If you traipsed up the Mall to see the palace, return to Carlton House Terrace. Alongside the ICA are the **Duke of York's Steps**. At the opening of *The Inn of the Sixth Happiness*, wannabe-missionary Gladys Aylward (Ingrid Bergman) walks along by the ICA and up these often-seen steps to the Duke of York's Column. Jeff Daniels is dragged down the steps in *101 Dalmatians*. John Vernon and crooked lawyer Mel Ferrer discuss offing Chicago cop John Wayne here in *Brannigan*. The titular Clarissa Dalloway (Vanessa Redgrave) looks up from the steps at the new fangled aeroplane in Marleen Gorris' film of the Virginia Woolf novel *Mrs Dalloway*. The chap on the top of the column, by the way, is Frederick, Duke of York, second son of the famously mad George III.

At the top of the steps, on the immediate right, **10 Carlton House Terrace** is home to Helena Bonham Carter in Iain Softley's Henry James adaptation of *The Wings of the Dove*, and also to Italian Prince Amerigo (Jeremy Northam) in another James adaptation, *The Golden Bowl* (although this time the interior was

The Wings of the Dove: Helena Bonham Carter's house: Carlton House Terrace

Around the World in Eighty Days: the Reform Club: Institute of Directors Club

filmed at Syon House).

The open square, usually taken up with parked cars, is **Waterloo Place (7)**. Halfway along the east side, wrapped up in his polar gear, is a statue of explorer Robert Falcon Scott, immortalised in *Scott of the Antarctic*.

On the northeast corner of the square stands the **Institute of Directors Club, 116 Pall Mall**, the first of several exclusive gentlemen's clubs we'll be passing in the area (but probably not entering). The exterior of the institute stands in for the Reform Club, from which Phileas Fogg (David Niven) sets off in *Around the World in Eighty Days*. Founded as the United Service Club (aka the Senior), catering to the upper echelons of the military – it was the Duke of Wellington's favourite club – it began to lose its identity after mergers with various other clubs and simply fizzled out, before the building was taken over by the Institute of Directors. It is the interior of 'Claridges Hotel', where Mrs Cheveley (Julianne Moore) and Lord Goring (Rupert Everett) reminisce in Oliver Parker's 1999 adaptation of Oscar Wilde's *An Ideal Husband*. It can also be seen in *Gandhi, Keep the Aspidistra Flying, Enigma* and 2003's *I Capture the Castle*, the film adaptation of a novel by Dodie Smith, author of *101 Dalmatians*. Most surprisingly, its dining room was transformed into the lowlife café where DI Walker (Bernard Hill) hassles rentboy Jonny (Daniel Brocklebank) near the beginning of *The Criminal*. "One of the most exclusive dining rooms in London," said director Julian Simpson, "and we dressed it up to look like a greasy spoon. The joke is that we actually didn't have to do very much."

Facing the Institute of Directors, on the square's northwest corner, you can see the **Athenaeum Club**, with its Grecian-style frieze, copied from the Parthenon. Founded in 1824, the Athenaeum is one of the more staid and severe of the London gentlemen's clubs, offering virtually automatic membership to the Speaker of the House of Commons, cabinet ministers, bishops, judges and other such pillars of the establishment. As such, cinematic appearances of the Athenaeum tend to imply mysterious high-ranking conspiracies. Malcolm McDowell is dropped off at the club to pick up his sinister orders in the second of Lindsay Anderson's trilogy featuring McDowell as Mick Travis, the freewheeling *O Lucky Man!* The Athenaeum becomes 'Banque Generale', where Mr Malik transfers funds to the sinister Peoples Lobby organisation in the 1982 SAS thriller *Who*

Dares Wins. Newshound Nick Mullen (Gabriel Byrne) is picked up by government spooks here after trying to contact shadowy informant Anthony Clegg (Oliver Ford Davies) in David

O Lucky Man!: Malcolm McDowell picks up orders: the Athenaeum Club

Drury's 1985 paranoia thriller *Defence of the Realm*. The club also provided period interiors for *Wilde*.

Just around the corner from the Athenaeum, on the south side of Pall Mall, stands the **Reform Club, 104 Pall Mall**. Its stark grey-block exterior contrasts with its lavish, Italianate interior. As its name implies, the Reform, founded in 1836, was intended to be the home of more radical opinions than establishments like the Athenaeum – though it stands in for the interior of the 'Athenaeum' in *O Lucky Man!* – and still has a distinctly Liberal membership. The Reform was Phileas Fogg's setting-off point in Jules Verne's novel *Around the World in 80 Days*. The interior can be seen in Roger Donaldson's 1984 version of *The Bounty*, when Lieutenant Bligh (Anthony Hopkins) invites Fletcher Christian (Mel Gibson) to join him on the fateful voyage. With all that broken glass and swords plunged into wood-panelled walls, it's clear that 'Blades', the club where Gustav Graves (Toby Stephens) challenges Bond to cross blades in the twentieth Bond movie, *Die Another Day*, is a studio set. However, the central section of the fight, and the lobby in which Bond receives a mysterious key, are the Reform Club. More recently, the Reform's pillared interior is the site of the grand party in he 2002 version of *The Four Feathers*.

It's in the pillared library of the **Travellers' Club, 106 Pall Mall (8)**, that Susan (Meryl Streep) sorts out the problems of the Coronation Committee in Fred Schepisi's film of David Hare's play *Plenty*. Intended to be a gathering place for intrepid voyagers, the membership requirement of having travelled 500

Die Another Day: Bond duels with Gustav Graves in Blades: the Reform Club, Pall Mall

Brannigan: John Vernon gets kidnapped: the RAC Club, Pall Mall

miles from London has never been increased, and would now seem to include the Club 18-30 crowd. Despite its reputation as one of the duller clubs, it does have the distinction of hosting one of the raunchier scenes shot in a gentlemen's club, as Streep and the tentative father of her child (Sting) make out in the library while the coronation of Her Majesty is broadcast on TV. It's rumoured that Princess Margaret mischievously arranged a screening of the movie for the Royal Family. HM was not amused.

Further west, opposite St James's Square, is the **Royal Automobile Club (RAC), 89 Pall Mall**, one of the later clubs, founded in 1897 for 'the Protection, Encouragement and Development of Automobilism', and one of the most lavish. You can see it as the gentlemen's club from which villain John Vernon (remember him as the Mayor in *Dirty Harry*?) gets kidnapped in *Brannigan*. The film showcases the RAC's famously extravagant swimming pool.

At the end of Pall Mall, past two royal residences, St James's Palace and Clarence House, stands **Lancaster House (9)**. Although conferences are held here, the breathtaking interior is rarely open to the general public. Lancaster House became the Tsar's 'St Petersburg Winter Palace' in Warren Beatty's historical epic *Reds*. "Kerensky's some Socialist, huh?" observes John Reed (Beatty) wryly to Louise Bryant (Diane Keaton) as they make their way up the opulent staircase to interview the revolutionary leader in his newly-acquired office. The same interior appears as itself for the Lancaster House costume ball, where Fanny Assingham (Anjelica Huston) is shocked by Charlotte Stant (Uma Thurman) turning up accompanied by her son-in-law Prince Amerigo (Jeremy Northam), in the Merchant-Ivory film of Henry James' novel *The Golden Bowl*. It's also Lady Bracknell's improbably lavish home in Oliver Parker's *The Importance of Being Earnest*.

Return north on St James's Street. On the east side, immediately north of Ryder Street, is **Economist Plaza (10)**, a hidden courtyard housing the tower block of the *Economist* magazine offices, which featured in two iconic scenes of

Reds: the St Petersburg Winter Palace: Lancaster House

Blowup: the white-face students: Economist Plaza, St James's Street

Sixties cinema. In Michael Winner's 1967 satire *I'll Never Forget What's 'is Name*, advertising exec Andrew Quint (Oliver Reed) famously quits the rat race by taking an axe to his desk in the **Economist Building, 25 St James's Street**. The plaza appears deceptively large, as the rather creepy white-face students career around the tiny space in a truck at the beginning of Michelangelo Antonioni's *Blowup*.

Continuing toward Piccadilly, turn off to take a look at Jermyn Street, one of the last vestiges of the old order. "I got it from a little man in Jermyn Street", hisses insinuating gentleman's gentleman Dirk Bogarde, as he proffers a mysterious bottle to dissolute aristo James Fox in *The Servant*. This street of exclusive shops caters to a class who expect everything to be hand-made, from the shirts of Turnbull & Asser to the cigars of Davidoff. **Tramp** nightclub, **40 Jermyn Street (11)**, was featured in Michael Winner's 1966 film *The Jokers*, in the days when it was Society Restaurant.

The very name of **The Ritz, 150 Piccadilly (12**; see **Hotels**, p9), has become a byword for luxury. It's the site of the press interview in *Notting Hill*, another hangout for working girl Cathy Tyson in *Mona Lisa*, and can be seen in *Modesty Blaise*.

Walk north on Berkeley Street. On Curzon Street stands the **Curzon Mayfair, 38 Curzon Street** (see **Entertainment: Cinemas**, p24), the original Curzon Cinema (there's now a Soho branch), specialising in first-run arthouse movies, where,

I'll Never Forget What's 'is Name: axing the desk: Economist Building, St James's Street

Notting Hill: the press junket: The Ritz, Piccadilly

Performance: Harry Flowers' office: Mount Street

in the seventies, you could catch the latest Bergman, Buñuel or Pasolini.

Continuing north brings you to **Berkeley Square (13)**. The army lorries career recklessly through the square on their way to the war game at the opening of *The Life and Death of Colonel Blimp*. The square features in another attention-grabbing opening sequence, as Oliver Reed makes his first appearance, carrying the axe he uses to smash up his desk, during the credits of *I'll Never Forget What's 'is Name*.

Leave the square by the northwest corner into Mount Street. On your left, at Mount Street Mews, is **115 Mount Street (14)**, the office of gangster boss Harry Flowers (Johnny Shannon) in *Performance*. It's now the Goedhuis art gallery. Incidentally,

The Life and Death of Colonel Blimp: "War starts at midnight!": North Row

44 Mount Street was home to suave song-and-dance man Jack Buchanan, best remembered from Vincente Minnelli's 1953 musical *The Band Wagon*.

Walk north to Grosvenor Square, dominated on the west side by the giant eagle of the **American Embassy, Grosvenor Square (15)**, where crazed priest Patrick Troughton (the second Doctor

in the cult BBC series *Doctor Who*) hounds US Ambassador Gregory Peck in *The Omen*. In the last of the *Omen* trilogy, *The Final Conflict*, Damien Thorn (Sam Neill) takes over as US Ambassador here after the previous incumbent blows his brains out.

If you walk east to Broadbent Street, you'll see the blue plaque at **21 Grosvenor Street**, on the north side, which records that this was the office of Hungarian-born film director and producer Sir Alexander Korda – responsible for such British classics as *The Private Life of Henry VIII*, *The Four Feathers* and *The Thief of Bagdad* in the thirties and forties – from 1932 to 1936.

Head north to North Row and west to Park Lane. Lorries screech round the corner of **Park Lane and North Row** in Michael Powell and Emeric Pressburger's classic film *The Life and Death of Colonel Blimp* (139 Park Lane is not the entrance to the 'Home Guard HQ' though, which is clearly a studio set).

Continue on to Marble Arch. The northern end of Park Lane begins at this undisciplined traffic free-for-all. The arch itself, originally designed as the ceremonial entrance to Buckingham Palace, is now forlornly stranded on a traffic island. A nearby plaque records the spot of the notorious Tyburn gallows, London's popular public execution spot, where tens of thousands met their deaths. In the late 18th century, the show moved to Newgate Gaol in the City, and a different form of mass entertainment is now provided by the **Odeon Marble Arch (16; ©︎ 0870.5050.007)** on the northern side. Once boasting the largest screen in London, this used to be *the* place to catch a Hollywood blockbuster in the eye-popping way it was meant to be seen. In 1996, however, the Odeon was shamefully chopped up to become just another 5-screen multiplex.

Opposite the entrance to the Odeon, across Edgware Road, is the tiny cul-de-sac Connaught Place, with its row of pillared porticos. Don't be fooled by the slightly scuffed exteriors; elegant chandeliers gleam behind the net curtains. The first house bears a blue plaque commemorating Winston's father, Lord Randolph Churchill, but the movie location here is **7 Connaught Place**, the home of manipulative shrink Richard Attenborough in the 1971 film of Iris Murdoch's civilised satire *A Severed Head*.

Cross back to Hyde Park, and visit **Speaker's Corner** at the park's northeast corner where, if

A Severed Head: shrink Richard Attenborough's home: Connaught Place

Morgan – A Suitable Case For Treatment: Morgan disrupts the reception: Dorchester Hotel

Wilde: the Cadogan Hotel: South Audley Street

it's a Sunday afternoon, you can witness the limits of free speech regularly being tested to breaking point by all manner of political and religious – or just plain wacko – zealots. With **Marble Arch** in the background, Robert Newton and Celia Johnson ignore the creepy fascist blackshirt mouthing off in David Lean's 1944 film of Noël Coward's *This Happy Breed*. Relax here a moment before facing the dusty wastes of Park Lane itself.

Herbert Wilcox's frothy 1948 film *Spring in Park Lane* (actually shot on studio sets) harks back to an age when the classy thoroughfare bounding Hyde Park's eastern border was lined with elegant townhouses. Now the mansions are long gone, replaced by exclusive hotels and car showrooms.

Like The Ritz, another name that reeks of unattainable glamour is the **Dorchester Hotel, 53 Park Lane** (**18**; see **Hotels**, p8). *Brannigan* villain Ben Larkin (John Vernon) stays at the Dorchester, as do Bongo Herbert and Dixie Collins in *Expresso Bongo*, while its roof terrace features in *Morgan – A Suitable Case For Treatment*.

Turn into Curzon Street, to the effusive red-brick Victorian fantasies of South Audley

Gangster No. 1: Freddie Mays' club: Hill Street

Sorted: Tim Curry's luxury pad: English Speaking Union, Charles Street

Street. When Oscar Wilde was arrested in April 1895 for gross indecency, following the collapse of his ill-advised libel action against the Marquis of Queensberry, he was staying at the Cadogan Hotel in South Kensington. Although the hotel still survives, modernisation meant that

Notting Hill: confrontation over the sushi: Nobu, Park Lane

Sexy Beast: Ray Winstone's London stay: Le Meridien Grosvenor House Hotel, Park Lane

it couldn't be used for Brian Gilbert's 1998 biopic *Wilde*. Instead, the house at **2 South Audley Street** (**19**) was dressed to provide a photogenically ornate 'Cadogan'. During the 1970s, the house was the office of James Bond film producer Cubby Broccoli's Eon Productions.

Turn right into Hill Street. With all this money and luxury, Mayfair seems to have more than its fair share of movie gangsterism. **38 Hill Street (20)** at Waverton Street is the upscale club outside which Freddie Mays (David Thewlis), 'the Butcher of Mayfair', is bloodily gunned down in Paul McGuigan's sharp-as-a-spike *Gangster No. 1*. On nearby Charles Street, the **English Speaking Union, Dartmouth House, 37 Charles Street**, is the classy pad of villain Damian (Tim Curry) in clubbing thriller *Sorted*.

Head back to Park Lane, and move from fussy Victoriana to the squat concrete and glass minimalism of the **Metropolitan Hotel, 19 Old Park Lane** (**22**; see **Hotels**, p9), which houses the dizzyingly expensive **Nobu** restaurant (see **Bars & Restaurants**, p14), which can be seen in *Notting Hill*. The fashionably low-key entrance is on the corner of Hertford Street.

More gangsters: it's at **Le Méridien Grosvenor House Hotel, Park Lane** (**17**; see **Hotels**, p9), that Ray Winstone stays in *Sexy Beast*.

The **Sheraton Park Lane Hotel, Piccadilly** (**24**; see **Hotels**, p9), makes an appearance in

The End of the Affair: the Café Royal: Sheraton Park Lane Hotel, Piccadilly

Dr. No: "The name's Bond... James Bond": Les Ambassadeurs, Hamilton Place

Mona Lisa, and you can admire its luxurious toilets in *Gangster No. 1*. The hotel also stands in for the 'Café Royal' in *The End of the Affair*.

The construction of the towering Hilton Hotel, now the **London Hilton, 22 Park Lane** (**21**; see **Hotels**, p9), meant the destruction of two famous Hitchcock filming locations: Park Lane House, the 'Embassy' where Doris Day entertains the party in Hitchcock's 1956 remake of his own 1934 film *The Man Who Knew Too Much*, and 78 Hertford Street, the house of glamorous actress Charlotte Inwood (Marlene Dietrich), and the site of the murder, in *Stage Fright*. The Hilton itself went on to become a Hitchcock filming site in 1972, when the director made *Frenzy*. The exterior of the hotel can also be glimpsed in *Mona Lisa*.

Take a look south of the Hilton, at **Les Ambassadeurs, Hamilton Place** (**23**), where two enduring sixties icons were launched onto the screen. In 1962, James Bond – in the person of Sean Connery – made his first screen appearance, in *Dr. No*, at the *chemin-de-fer* table in the Ambassadeurs' Le Cercle Club, with the words "The name's Bond... James Bond." OK, the gaming room was duplicated in the studio at Pinewood, but in 1964 it was the real Ambassadeurs, the **Garrison Room** to be precise, when the Beatles escape from their hotel suite to bop the night away in their first feature film, *A Hard Day's Night*.

Wind down and drink to classic film locations that are no longer with us at a *Stage Fright* location which remains virtually unchanged, **Shepherd's Tavern, 50 Hertford Street** (**25**; see **Bars & Restaurants**, p14). Cheers!

Stage Fright: Jane Wyman downs a brandy: Shepherd's Tavern, Hertford Street

North-Central London: King's Cross to Camden

A wander through some of the grittier streets of North London, often used as the backdrop to doomed romance, from naïve George's dogged pursuit of classy prostitute Simone in *Mona Lisa*, to the confused couplings of David Kane's dark comedy romance *This Year's Love*, by way of post-war Bethnal Green and 19th century Moscow.

Starting Point: St Pancras Station

Although the area is called King's Cross, it is dominated by that station's more flamboyant and, surprisingly, younger sister, **St Pancras Station (1)**. Serving Derby and Sheffield, the station is hidden away behind **St Pancras Chambers**, originally Sir George Gilbert Scott's Midland Grand Hotel, a lavish palace of luxury for Victorian travellers. The last word in comfort when it opened in 1873, the hotel was soon overtaken by changing demands. Ironically, the building's solid construction proved its downfall.

Richard III: the Royal Palace: St Pancras Station

Chaplin and Spider: Charlie and Spider arrive at Waterloo Station, Charlie from Southampton and Spider from the institution: St Pancras Station

Unable to accommodate such modern improvements as en-suite bathrooms and central heating, the hotel inevitably closed down. Its ceilings were boarded over, its lavish rooms divided up into offices, and in the sixties the wildly unfashionable extravaganza came close to being demolished. Grade I listing finally ensured its survival and radical restoration means that it will soon function as a luxury hotel again.

This most photogenic of stations is the cinema's traditional arrival point for visitors from the North. Smarmily sinister gentleman's gentleman Dirk Bogarde collects his slutty 'sister' Vera (Sarah Miles) from here when she arrives from Bolton in Joseph Losey's 1963 film *The Servant*, while northern lasses Brenda and Yvonne (Lynn Redgrave and Rita Tushingham, cheekily given the pet names of HM the Queen and the late Princess Margaret in George Melly's self-consciously camp script) arrive to take 1967 Swinging London by storm in Desmond Davis' messy but likeable *Smashing Time*. An obvious inspiration for the *Austin Powers* films, the movie features Basil Exposition himself, Michael York, as the inevitable white-jeaned photographer. Eight years later, crooked lawyer Mel Ferrer swaps cars here on the way to pay a ransom in the John Wayne vehicle *Brannigan*.

Despite the fact that trains from St Pancras run north, the station's façade is visible from the front door of Mrs Wilberforce's house in fifties Ealing classic *The Ladykillers*, which would put her lopsided home to the south of the station in **Argylle Street**. This is odd, since the house clearly backs onto the tracks. In fact, the geography of the area was shamelessly manipulated for picturesque effect, and the cul-de-sac where Alec Guinness'

Howards End: Vanessa Redgrave buys tickets to Hilton: St Pancras ticket hall

gang of crooks hides out is about a mile to the north of King's Cross, as we'll see later. The terminus can also be seen in Agnieszka

Mona Lisa: Bob Hoskins buys the ice cream sundae: Pancras Road

Holland's 1993 version of the classic children's story *The Secret Garden*. Its snow-covered appearance in *Bridget Jones's Diary* was consigned to the cutting-room floor (you can catch it among the DVD's deleted scenes). However, the most imaginative use of St Pancras' flashy polychrome exterior must be Richard Loncraine's 1995 film *Richard III*, which digitally transports the building to the banks of the Thames and transforms it into the Royal Palace.

In the movies, St Pancras is often mysteriously able to accommodate trains from the South. It has twice stood in for 'Waterloo Station': Charlie Chaplin (Robert Downey Jr) is mobbed here when he arrives from Southampton on a fleeting visit from the US, in the Richard Attenborough biopic *Chaplin*, and – underscoring the film's gasometer motif – it's also where Spider (Ralph Fiennes) gets his first taste of freedom at the opening of the sombre David Cronenberg movie. Cruella De Vil (Glenn Close) and Le Pelt (Gérard Depardieu) even manage to board the Orient Express (which actually runs out of Victoria) from St Pancras in *102 Dalmatians*.

The long-disused interior of St Pancras Chambers became the 'Cane Hill Asylum', where Charlie's mother (Geraldine Chaplin) is confined after her mental breakdown in *Chaplin*. It also appears in the 1976 WWII melodrama *Voyage of the Damned*, and in Robert Bierman's 1997 film of George Orwell's *Keep the Aspidistra Flying*, with Richard E Grant. There is, at last, free access to at least some of the old hotel's ground floor areas (if there's no filming in progress), Monday to Friday, 11.30-15.30 (© 020.7304.3900 for details of guided tours). You might recognise the elaborate stairwell from the first Spice Girls video, *Wannabe*.

The station's beautifully restored wood-panelled ticket office, by the western entrance, is where Emma Thompson and Vanessa Redgrave buy tickets to the fictitious village of 'Hilton' to visit the titular cottage in *Howards End*.

Take a look along Pancras Road, running alongside the eastern border of the station. Until recently the brick arches housed a series of junk shops. **Arches 65, 67** and **69** (**2**), just past Cheney Road, were the now closed Railway Café, where George (Bob Hoskins) buys an ice cream sundae for the young

Shadowlands: Anthony Hopkins and Debra Winger marry: Hastings Street

hooker (Sammi Davis) who quickly does a runner before she can eat it, in that defining film of the King's Cross district *Mona Lisa*.

Facing St Pancras, across the busy Euston Road, stands the grey bulk of **Camden Town Hall (3)**, which is itself occasionally featured in films. The interior of the council offices became the 'US Embassy' in 'Moscow' for Phillip Noyce's big screen version of *The Saint*, with Val Kilmer. It's also where buttoned-up British writer CS Lewis (Anthony Hopkins) marries brash American Joy Gresham (Debra Winger) in Richard Attenborough's film of William Nicholson's play *Shadowlands*.

Cross Euston Road, walk a little way down Judd Street past the town hall entrance, and turn right into Hastings Street. The door from which Lewis and his new wife emerge into the rain is not the Town Hall at all, but the rear entrance of the **BT Office, Hastings Street (4)**, opposite Thanet Street.

Return to Judd Street and turn right on Euston Road, past the ghastly seventies extension to Camden Town Hall, where Stephen Rea works in the planning office in Les Blair's 1993 comedy *Bad Behaviour*.

If you want more of *Mona Lisa*'s melancholy sleaziness, this is a good point to take a detour down the east side of the dusty, unlovely stretch of Gray's Inn Road, past the Eastman Dental Hospital and St Andrew's Gardens, where you'll find a striking, newly-restored blue and white art deco apartment block. **Trinity Court, Grays Inn Road (5**: off the map) is home to hooker Simone, the impossible object

Harry Potter and the Philosopher's Stone: Platform 9 ¾, to Hogwarts: King's Cross Station

of George's affection in *Mona Lisa*. Director Neil Jordan wanted the exterior of the place where she lived to have "a kind of Middle European quali-

ty to the architecture", as well as a pair of parallel, open cage lifts, in order to stage the claustrophobic shootout with Anderson.

Returning to King's Cross, take a moment to check out the scruffy doorway on Pentonville Road beneath the domed cupola at the junction with Gray's Inn Road. **297 Pentonville Road (6)** are the seedy digs of that sixties antidote to James Bond, agent Harry Palmer (Michael Caine), in *Billion Dollar Brain*, the second sequel to *The Ipcress File*, which was unwisely entrusted to the unsuitable talents of wayward genius Ken Russell. Palmer's cornflakes spilled all over the carpet are a long, long way from 007's Caribbean cocktails.

And back to **King's Cross Station (7)** itself, the London terminus of the Great North Eastern Railway serving Leeds, York and the Northeast, thirteen years older than St Pancras. In recent years the name King's Cross has become synonymous with drugs and prostitution, though the abiding image of prostitutes hanging out on the girdered railway bridge in *Mona Lisa* was actually shot near Liverpool Street Station (despite the director's inexplicable assertion on the DVD commentary that the scene was filmed behind Waterloo). Unless you needed to check the time from its clocktower, it's unlikely you'd notice the portion of the original handsome Italianate station building peeking over the extensive modern forecourt. There's no character left, and little to compete visually with its more extrovert neighbour. Katrin Cartlidge meets her old college friend Lynda Steadman at King's Cross in Mike Leigh's *Career Girls*, but the station finally got its moment of cinematic glory in *Harry Potter and the Philosopher's Stone*, when the **arched wall between platforms 4 and 5** became the magical entrance to 'Platform 9 ¾', from which young Harry catches the Hogwarts Express. Stardom, though, seems to have been undermined by the sequel, *Harry Potter and the Chamber of Secrets*, which reveals the station exterior to be St Pancras.

Walk northeast to the corner of **Caledonian Road and Twyford Street (8)**. This is the street corner where Johnny (David Thewlis) gets a kicking from the bill-poster, who drives off with his bag, at the end of Mike Leigh's raw, sour *Naked*.

Continue north on Caledonian Road to **Frederica Street**, facing Pentonville Prison. This bland modern cul-de-sac is where Mrs Wilberforce's house was built for *The Ladykillers*. The

The Ladykillers: dumping the bodies: Copenhagen Tunnel

Alfie: "I suppose you think you're goin' to see the bleedin' titles now": Camley Street

quirky set, constructed without a single right-angle, filled the western end of the road, which has since been completely redeveloped. There's little to see unless you walk around to the private car park at the end of **Vale Royal (9)**, another cul-de-sac running east from York Way, which gives you a view of the arched brick entrance to the **Copenhagen Tunnel**, the spot behind Mrs Wilberforce's house where Alec Guinness' ill-assorted gang of crooks dumped bodies onto passing railway trucks.

Return south on York Way and turn right into **Goods Way**. This small enclave of Victorian industrial buildings and cobbled streets, dominated by the unique group of linked gasometers, has been a favourite cinematic backdrop since the bullion robbery at the opening of *The Ladykillers* was filmed on Goods Way in 1955. However, the area was earmarked for the Channel Tunnel link and, disgracefully, a whole district of Grade II listed buildings has been demolished. As well as the buildings, the splendid iron-frame Victorian gasometers have gone, and with them an irreplaceable part of Britain's film heritage.

Turn right again into **Camley Street (11)**, used for the opening scene of *Alfie* – "I suppose you think you're goin' to see the bleedin' titles now" – Lewis Gilbert's 1966 film of Bill Naughton's stage play, which audaciously uses the device of straight-to-camera address.

The industrial buildings where Alfie's steamed-up car is parked have gone, and the site is currently **Camley Street Natural Park**, a wildlife preserve.

Michael Caine and his mate Murray Melvin walk alongside the **Grand Union Canal** by the Lock-Keeper's cottage in *Alfie*. Dreadlocked Roedean dropout Jennifer Ehle keeps her houseboat moored on the canal in *This Year's Love*. While Samantha Mathis spends time sitting glumly by the canalside in *Jack & Sarah* after Richard E Grant turfs her out of his house.

Stanley Buildings, half demolished, half to be redeveloped as 'luxury flats', is the home Ruth Sheen and Philip Davis shared with their cactus Maggie ("a pain in the

High Hopes: Davis and Sheen's flat: Stanley Buildings

bum...") in Mike Leigh's terminally glum *High Hopes*. It was also Michael Palin's 'dockland' mission to fallen women in *The Missionary*, and home to "fat bird" Kathy Burke in *This Year's Love*. On its roof, among the pigeon cotes, the Duke of Gloucester (Ian McKellen) procured Tyrrell to murder the two princes in 1995's thirties-set *Richard III*. While Christian Bale got it together with bisexual rockstar Ewan McGregor in *Velvet Goldmine* – gamely humping away long after the camera, on a nearby roof, had ceased turning.

Shirley Valentine walked the cobbled **Battle Bridge Road (10)** before escaping to Mykonos, and Robbie Coltrane and Eric Idle flounced their habits here in *Nuns on the Run*. The ageing rockers of re-formed seventies stadium band Strange Fruit boarded their tour bus here in *Still Crazy*.

The 1904 **German Gymnasium** (named for the continental city workers who used it), on **Cheney Street**, became Liverpool's 'Anchor' pub, where Stuart Sutcliffe (Stephen Dorff), one of the original Beatles line-up, and John Lennon (Ian Hart) get into a fight at the beginning of *Backbeat*. In fact, as we'll see, much of Iain Softley's account of the early days of the legendary sixties supergroup – largely set in Hamburg – was filmed around North London.

In 1992, a gigantic set, constructed over 4 months around the cobbled junction of **Cheney Street and Battle Bridge Road**, turned the area into the 'Lambeth' neighbourhood of Charlie Chaplin (Robert Downey Jr) in Richard Attenborough's *Chaplin*.

Before the area was called King's Cross, it was known as Battle Bridge, supposedly named for the village of Battle Bridge where Queen Boadicea faced her last battle with the Romans. Rather than be taken prisoner, she took poison – and legend has it that she is buried beneath Platform 10 of King's Cross Station.

Head north on Pancras Road. On the right you come to a church alongside a small, peaceful graveyard. **St Pancras Old Church (12)**, in St Pancras Gardens, is where Douglas Henshall marries Catherine McCormack at the opening of the Camden-set comedy *This*

Chaplin: Chaplin's Lambeth home: Cheney Street

This Year's Love: the doomed wedding: St Pancras Old Church, Pancras Road

The Gentle Gunman: the IRA hideout: Mornington Place

Year's Love. In the churchyard of this 11th-century church (which was substantially renovated in the 14th, 17th and 19th centuries) rested Mary Wollestonecraft, early feminist and the mother of the woman who wrote *Frankenstein*, until she was whisked off to the family plot. Still in place is Sir John Soane, architect, whose odd grave, which he designed himself, is covered by a stone canopy. This grave was the inspiration for Gilbert Scott, when he designed the old red London phone box.

Continue into Crowndale Road and over to **Mornington Place (13)**, at the corner of Mornington Crescent. This is the flat of the IRA cell raided by the police in Basil Dearden's *The Gentle Gunman.*

Famous music venue **Camden Palace, 1a Camden High Street**, was once known as the Music Machine and, as such, starred as the disco in, yes, *The Music Machine*, a 1979 pale British imitation of *Saturday Night Fever.*

Turn right into **Plender Street (14)**. The set-back building became 'Pricks and Chicks', the women-only tattoo parlour of heartbroken Douglas Henshall in *This Year's Love.* At the time of writing, the building is still decorated with tattoo designs.

Continue east on Plender Street to **Royal College Street (15)**, the site of 'Ambrose Chapel', the taxidermist where James Stewart follows a red herring in Hitchcock's 1956 remake of his own *The Man Who Knew Too Much.* The taxidermist was real and, unusually for Hitch, was used for both exteriors and interiors. Gerrard Family Taxidermists supplied stuffed animals to Hollywood studios. **8 Royal College Street**, seen in the background as Stewart gets out of the taxi, was, in 1873, home to poets Arthur Rimbaud and Paul Verlaine, played by Leonardo DiCaprio and David Thewlis in Agnieszka Holland's 1995 film of

This Year's Love: Pricks and Chicks tattoo parlour: Plender Street

The Man Who Knew Too Much: Stewart looks for Ambrose Chapel: Plender Street

Christopher Hampton's play *Total Eclipse.*

On the other side of Camden High Street, **106 Arlington Road (16)** provided the oddly peaked interior of the Stables Market flat shared by comic-book dealer Liam (Ian Hart) and scruffy, would-be painter Cameron (Dougray Scott) in *This Year's Love.*

Head back to Camden High Street itself. Look at the door to the office block over the supermarket at **125-133 Camden High Street. Bedford House** now stands on the site of the old Bedford Music Hall, where Marie Lloyd and Charlie Chaplin once performed. The music hall was recreated in the studio for the colourful backstage romance *Trottie True* in 1949. Two years later, in the real Bedford Music Hall – though it is supposedly a 'Dublin' theatre – Audrey Hepburn's film career kicked off with a role in Thorold Dickinson's spy drama *The Secret People.* However, the music hall didn't survive the coming of cinema and went into decline after WWII, finally being demolished in 1969.

Parkway (17) runs from Camden up to Regent's Park, to the old wolf enclosure (though the wolves are long gone) where Richard E Grant recites Shakespeare at the end of *Withnail & I.* Parkway was also the supposed site of the coffee bar in Jez Butterworth's fifties-set music-biz drama *Mojo* (though it was really Alfredo's in Islington).

The smartly refurbished **Camden Odeon (18)**, once the Parkway Cinema, stood closed and empty and close to being demolished in the nineties, but a heroic campaign by local residents, who included celebs like Michael Palin, saved it. It subsequently became a film location itself, appearing as the interior of the 'Hamburg' cinema, where Stuart Sutcliffe (Stephen Dorff) and Astrid Kirchherr (Sheryl Lee) watch Jean Cocteau's *Les Enfants Terribles*, in *Backbeat.*

The old Camden Plaza, which stood around the corner on Camden High Street, was not so lucky. Ironically, even the cut-price video and DVD store, which opened on the site, has now closed.

Turn right on Camden Road and continue past Camden Road Railway Station. Just under the railway bridge, turn right into Rousden Street and continue toward Randolph Street. In Mike Leigh's *Career Girls*, northerner Annie (Lynda Steadman), a twitchy bundle of low self-esteem and dermatitis, endures the embarrassing hell that is student life with cocky southerner Hannah (Katrin Cartlidge) in scruffy digs at **40 Rousden Street (19)**. The flat on the corner of Randolph Street, now substantially renovated, was transformed into the Chinese takeaway, where Ricky (Mark Benton) pigs out on curry and chips. (Do you think Lo Hung Lee was a real name?)

Continue north on Camden High Street to Inverness Street, once the modest local vegetable market, though the fruit and veg stalls are gradually but inexorably being edged out by tacky souvenir stalls. Walk through the market to the quiet, residential Gloucester Crescent, home to many of North London's literati. In the eighties you could have seen the yellow van immortalised in Alan Bennett's book and subsequent play *The Lady in the Van*, parked outside his home in the crescent. **24 Gloucester Crescent (20)** was the True family home in the colourful turn-of-the-century backstage drama *Trottie True*. Just around the corner, **46 Inverness Street** was the family's photographic studio.

The cast-iron footbridge over the Regent's Canal at **Hampstead Road Lock (21)** (by Camden Lock Market) can be seen in the Sherlock Holmes spoof *Without a Clue*, while Dougray Scott picks out more personal ads on the bridge in *This Year's Love*. Jack (Richard E Grant) sits beneath it with Amy (Samantha Mathis) and baby Sarah after browsing the market in *Jack & Sarah*.

Go north to **Stables Market (22)**, where Steven Mackintosh ran a sadly low-security dope business in *Lock, Stock and Two Smoking Barrels*. Just inside the Chalk Farm Road entrance, on the left, you can see the metal staircase up to the dope den, where the lads took an unfortunate traffic warden along for the ride. The den itself is another warehouse opposite. Ian Hart's flat is in Stables Market in *This Year's Love*. Take a break in the café where he sank a couple of bottles of wine

Lock, Stock and Two Smoking Barrels: the dope factory: Stables Market

with Sophie (Jennifer Ehle).

Across Chalk Farm Road is **Hartland Road (23)**. Walk up toward the railway bridge. This section of the road, overshadowed by the truncated spire of **Most Holy Trinity With St Barnabas**, became 'Coronet Grove, Bethnal Green', home to Googie Withers (we never actually see which house she's supposed to live in), where she hides old flame and Dartmoor escapee John McCallum, in Robert Hamer's 1947 film *It Always Rains on Sunday*. Just on the right, **60 Hawley Road** was home to weaselly fence Mr Neesley. Maybe artificial by the standards we're used to from the likes of Ken Loach, this sad, downbeat melodrama, from the Ealing Studios, was one of the first attempts to put working-class life centre-screen, with its petty shysters and Yiddish slang. The novel it's based on was written by Arthur La Bern, the author of *Goodbye Piccadilly, Farewell Leicester Square*, filmed in 1972 by Alfred Hitchcock as *Frenzy*. A little over forty years later, struggling actor Dexter King (Jeff Goldblum) cycles down the same stretch of Hartland Road, after playing the foil to egotistical comic Ron Anderson (Rowan Atkinson) in

Trottie True: the True family home: Gloucester Crescent

Trottie True: the photographic studio: Inverness Street

It Always Rains on Sunday: Bethnal Green: Hartland Road

The Tall Guy: Jeff Goldblum's flat: Hawley Road

The Tall Guy, written by Richard Curtis a few years before he hit paydirt as a one-man Britcom script factory with *Four Weddings and a Funeral* and *Notting Hill*. And Goldblum's home? Why, it's none other than the popular 60 Hawley Road.

At the top of the Stables Market ramp, Kathy Burke spies sleazy charmer Dougray Scott two-timing her on the roof terrace of **Freshh Restaurant, 48 Chalk Farm Road (24)**, in *This Year's Love*.

A little to the north, **Offstage Theatre and Film Bookshop, 37 Chalk Farm Road** (see **Shopping**, p23), predominantly a theatre bookshop, has an excellent film section with a range of technical and professional books.

The Roundhouse (25), a disused railway turning shed which – after many false starts – now functions as a performing arts venue, was used for Michael York's photographic exhibition in Swinging Sixties slapstick movie *Smashing Time*. The Roundhouse has seen many legendary performances, including Pink Floyd and the Soft Machine in 1966, the Doors, and Andy Warhol's bizarre stage production *Pork*. English New Wave director Tony Richardson (*A Taste of Honey*, *Tom Jones*) famously staged an in-the-round production of *Hamlet*, with Nicol Williamson in the title role, Anthony Hopkins as Claudius and Marianne Faithfull as Ophelia, which was filmed here in 1969. Richard Stanley's 1990 sci-fi shocker *Hardware* was also shot here.

Adelaide Road leads to Primrose Hill. Pause on the way to check out **11 St George's Terrace**, Magda's house in *Bridget Jones's Diary*.

Primrose Hill appears in the 1987 spy thriller *The Fourth Protocol*. The view over London is justly famous, but it's not quite as stunning as it appears in Ben Elton's semi-autobiographical *Maybe Baby*. When desperation drives Hugh Laurie and Joely Richardson to attempt conception on a ley line which supposedly crosses the hill, the twinkling night-time view over the city is computer enhanced. You can see the real, untouched daylight vista in

Smashing Time, Hamlet and **Hardware**: the legendary Chalk Farm performance space: The Roundhouse

The Music Lovers: the suicide attempt in Moscow: Gloucester Avenue Bridge, Regent's Canal

Career Girls, when Katrin Cartlidge and Lynda Steadman glimpse their old college pal jogging up the hill.

Regent's Park Road brings you once again to the Regent's Canal. Walk along the canal back to Camden Lock. On the way you'll pass under the **Gloucester Avenue Bridge (26)**, and find yourself in 'Moscow'. This is the site of gay composer Tchaikovsky's tragicomic suicide attempt, after he fails to strangle his naïve, sexually demanding wife Nina in *The Music Lovers*.

Northwest London: Kentish Town to Hampstead

One-time spa, and the last staging-post before leaving London for the North of England, Hampstead remains as exclusive and desirable as ever, thanks to the proximity of the green wilderness of Hampstead Heath and the resistance to wholesale redevelopment. MacDonald's were only permitted to open a branch on Hampstead High Street after agreeing to tone down their distinctive design. By contrast, the scruffy, congested road between Camden and Highgate village, lined with supermarkets and wildly variable eateries, belies the gentrification of the area, as everyone tries to get a bit of Camden's Brit-cool action.

Starting Point: Kentish Town

From Kentish Town tube station, turn left onto Kentish Town Road and head south toward Camden Town. The spirit of Mike Leigh hovers over Les Blair's 1993 film *Bad Behaviour*. Sinead Cusack works at the **Owl Bookshop, 209 Kentish Town Road (1**; see **Shopping**, p23), in this amiable comedy of manners.

Just around the corner, in the old Methodist Church on Prince of Wales Road, is the Drama Centre, where Pierce Brosnan was once a student. Also on Prince of Wales Road, at the corner of Castlehaven Road, stands the tiny **Hope Chapel (2**). You might recognise its neon 'Church of Christ' sign alongside the phone box

Career Girls: Katrin Cartlidge's bachelor-girl flat: Caversham Road

Villain: the East End pub: The Assembly House, Kentish Town Road

where Liam (Ian Hart) phones for help after the well-oiled Sophie (Jennifer Ehle) passes out in *This Year's Love*.

Into Caversham Road. The top floor of **72 Caversham Road** (**3**), at the corner of Bartholomew Road, is the smart flat of no-nonsense Katrin Cartlidge, where a weekend visit from old college pal Lynda Steadman reveals unrealised depths of affection, in Mike Leigh's twitchy *Career Girls*.

Continuing on Caversham Road takes you into Oseney Crescent. Terminally depressed thrift-shop hippy Fiona (Toni Collette) and her son Marcus (Nicholas Hoult) live at **31 Oseney Crescent** (**4**) in *About a Boy*.

Head back to Kentish Town Road. Immediately north of the station, on the corner of Leighton Road, stands the grandly Victorian **Assembly House, 292-294 Kentish Town Road** (**5**; see **Bars & Restaurants**, p14), which can be seen in the 1971 film *Villain*, a thinly-disguised portrait of gay London gangster Ronnie Kray.

An even more elaborate, if slightly shabbier, drinking house stands opposite Tufnell Park Underground Station, the next stop north on the Northern line. **The Boston Arms, 178 Junction Road** (**6**; see **Bars & Restaurants**, p14), houses **The Dome**, which provided another 'Hamburg' location for *Backbeat*.

Walk up Dartmouth Park Hill and turn left into Laurier Road. A few yards down, on the right, is **2 Dartmouth Park Avenue** (**7**), the corner house which is home to Jeremy Irons in the 1982 film of Harold Pinter's inventive reverse-timescale play *Betrayal*, with Irons, Patricia Hodge and Ben Kingsley as the three points of an adulterous triangle.

At the top of the hill, hidden away behind Highgate Village, is **Waterlow Park** (**8**). In the cracking

About a Boy: home of Marcus and his hippy mum: Oseney Crescent

1999 conspiracy thriller *The Criminal*, this quietly discreet green space which looks out over the city is where Eddie Izzard contrives to meet up with innocent man-on-the-run Steven Mackintosh. Writer-director Julian Simpson worked on the film's screenplay in the park, and the covered bench where Izzard explains all about the sinister 'Shackleton Consultancy' is the spot where the scene itself was written.

Highgate itself, a narrow high street of wine shops and estate agents punctuated with fine local pubs, perched at the top of a steep hill, remains one of the few areas of London which can still justify the term village. It provided the backdrop to Anthony Minghella's 1991 ghostly romance *Truly Madly Deeply*, but is probably best known for being home to the city's most famous resting place.

When central London's burial places had filled up in the 19th century, huge cemeteries were opened up on what were then the outskirts of town. Not famous for their quiet modesty in grave styling, the Victorians came up with one of the most gloriously extravagant: **Highgate Cemetery, Swain's Lane** (**9**). The first grandiose monuments were erected in the West Cemetery in 1839, but by 1854 even that was filling up and the East Cemetery, on the other side of Swain's Lane, was opened. However, the expense of maintaining the grounds meant that the already florid Victorian monuments became spectacularly overgrown and the cemetery subsequently provided the ideal Gothic backdrop for films such as Hammer's *Taste The Blood of Dracula* and camp classic *The Abominable Dr Phibes*, in which Dr Phibes and his wife are supposedly laid to rest in the old section of the cemetery.

Cinematic luminaries in the eastern section include William Friese-Greene, interred close to the railings on the Swain's Lane

Backbeat: the Hamburg club: the Boston Arms, Junction Road

Betrayal: Jeremy Irons' house: Dartmouth Park Avenue

Notting Hill: filming the Henry James movie: Kenwood House, Hampstead Lane

side, often credited as the inventor of cinema. The inscription on his tombstone, 'The Inventor of Kinematography', is certainly unequivocal, and even goes on to quote the patent number, for those who might doubt the claim. Friese-Greene, originally a portrait photographer, was certainly a prolific experimenter, but no businessman, and died in poverty in 1921. Thirty years later, during the patriotic frenzy of the Festival of Britain, he was celebrated in John Boulting's dubious biopic *The Magic Box*.

Other notable cinematic figures in this section include German émigré screenwriter Lukas Heller, who adapted the original source novels and plays into the screenplays *Whatever Happened to Baby Jane? Hush... Hush, Sweet Charlotte, The Killing of Sister George* and *The Dirty Dozen* for director Robert Aldrich. Heller's countryman Carl Mayer, who wrote the screenplay for silent German expressionist classic *Das Kabinett des Doktor Caligari*, also lies here. Britain's own Max Wall, the sepulchral-voiced, rubber-limbed music hall performer who reinvented himself as a respected straight actor, appearing in *Chitty Chitty Bang Bang, Jabberwocky, Hanover Street* and, erm, *The Nine Ages of Nakedness* (well, we all have to earn a crust), is another occupant. Theatre knights Sir Ralph Richardson and Sir Michael Redgrave are also buried in Highgate.

The stern visage of Karl Marx, possibly the most famous occupant of the cemetery, tops a bulky plinth in the East Cemetery. Unreconstructed Stalinist Mrs Delt (Irene Handl) takes her son Morgan (David Warner) to pay homage at the grave of Marx in Karel Reisz's 1966 film of David Mercer's play, *Morgan – A Suitable Case for Treatment*. "You know, he wanted to shoot the royal family, abolish marriage and put everybody who'd been to public school in a chain gang," says Handl. "Yes, he was a idealist, your dad." Years later, Philip Davis and Ruth Sheen also pay their respects at Marx's plot in Mike Leigh's *High Hopes*.

In the older, western section lie Patrick Wymark (the stocky character actor who appeared as the predatory Landlord in Roman Polanski's *Repulsion* and as

General Oliver Cromwell in *Matthew Hopkins: Witchfinder General*), Stella Dorothea Webb (who, as Stella Gibbons, wrote *Cold Comfort Farm*, filmed by John Schlesinger) and Adam Worth ('the Napoleon of Crime', the supposed model for Sherlock Holmes' nemesis Professor Moriarty).

Increasing financial demands meant that the West Cemetery closed in 1975. The entire cemetery was subsequently sold, and is now owned and administered by the Friends of Highgate Cemetery (*website: highgate-cemetery.org/index.asp*). The East Cemetery is open to the public every day, admission £2. To view the older West Cemetery you'll need to join a guided tour, which takes about an hour (weekends all year, weekdays March to November, £3).

From the northern end of Highgate Village runs North Road. On the left, the white art deco apartment block, **High Point, North Road** (**10**), stood in for the HQ of Polydor Records in 'Hamburg', where the Beatles get their first record deal, in Iain Softley's *Backbeat*. A little further on, on the right, stands the Wellington service station. This unremarkable little service station stands on the site of the old Wellington pub, where Jimmy and his Mod pals bought dud pills from the hard men in *Quadrophenia*.

South Grove, running southwest from Highgate High Street, leads to Witanhurst Lane. The grand mansion **Witanhurst** (**11**), second largest private home in London, is seen in *Nicholas Nickleby*. It had a busy year in 2002 as the backdrop to TV's acclaimed drama *Tipping the Velvet* and as the BBC's *Fame Academy*.

From the northern end of Highgate High Street, Hampstead Lane leads off towards Hampstead Heath. On the left stands the entrance to **Kenwood House, Hampstead Lane** (**12**; see **Historic Sites**, p29), a mansion remodelled by Robert Adam in the 18th-century, which now houses the Iveagh Bequest of old masters. The exterior can be seen in *Notting Hill*, and the pond appears in *I'll Never Forget What's 'is Name*.

Continue on to the vast, wild green space of **Hampstead Heath** itself, haunted by – mainly fictitious – legends of highwaymen. It's on the fringes of the heath that the body of the murdered music student is found in the 1959 drama *Sapphire*. The victim is discovered to be a pale-skinned – and pregnant – black woman, who'd been passing for white. Coming from the same team who went on to make *Victim* (producer Michael Relph, screenwriter Janet Green and director Basil Dearden), which was released in 1961, *Sapphire* uses a similar police procedural format – liberal older cop, hotheaded and prejudiced younger sidekick – to confront a specific social problem. This time, in the era of the shameful 'colour bar' and the Notting Hill riots, it's race. In 1975, the opening shots – coconut shells and all – of the considerably less weighty film

Bunny Lake Is Missing: Frognall End, Keir Dullea's grand house: Cannon Hall, Cannon Place

Monty Python and the Holy Grail were filmed on the heath, not far from the home of Terry Gilliam.

Behind Jack Straw's Castle (don't be fooled – this ersatz coaching inn was built in the sixties) runs Wildwood Road. **8 Wildwood Road** is the birthplace of Elizabeth Taylor, where the violet-eyed one lived for the first seven years of her life until her family upped sticks and moved to California in 1939, just before the outbreak of WWII.

From Heath Street, turn left into East Heath Road, and then right into Squire's Mount. Discreetly tucked away in this quiet pocket is **Cannon Hall, 14 Cannon Place (13)**, once the home of actor-manager Gerald du Maurier – father of Daphne, author of *Rebecca*, *Jamaica Inn*, 'The Birds' and 'Don't Look Now' – and a major location for Otto Preminger's 1965 off-beat movie *Bunny Lake Is Missing*. Starring Carol Lynley as Ann Lake, the distraught mother searching for her missing, but just possibly imaginary, daughter Bunny, Cannon Hall became 'Frognall End' in *Bunny Lake*, the mansion belonging to Ann's brother (*2001*'s astronaut Keir Dullea), where the mystery is finally unravelled. This almost forgotten gem of a movie fleshes out its sardonic script with a star-studded cast of eccentrics, including detective Laurence Olivier, sadistic landlord Noël Coward and grumpy shop-owner Finlay Currie.

Back across Heath Street, north of Hampstead tube station, are a series of narrow passageways leading from Heath Street to Holly Mount. Take time out to visit **The Holly Bush, 22 Holly Mount (14;** see **Bars & Restaurants,** p14), which can be seen at the beginning of *The Killing of Sister George*. Behind the film's opening credits, June 'George' Buckridge (Beryl Reid) stomps down the narrow stepped passages

The Killing of Sister George: George drinks in the Marquis of Granby: The Holly Bush, Holly Mount

between **Heath Street** and **Hampstead Grove**, before she magically pops out on the other side of London at the Chelsea Embankment.

The Collector: the kidnapping: Mount Vernon

Off Holly Hill is **Mount Vernon**, the tiny lane where unhinged butterfly collector Terence Stamp kidnaps art student Samantha Eggar in William Wyler's disturbing 1965 film of John Fowles' equally disturbing novel *The Collector*.

Damage: Jeremy Irons' London home: Frognall, Hampstead

Continue into Frognal. **94 Frognal (15)**, opposite Oak Hill Park, is the luxurious London home of duplicitous MP Jeremy Irons in Louis Malle's pretentiously overheated Gallic melodrama *Damage*.

Make your way back to Hampstead High Street. Virtually opposite the tube station stands a Hampstead institution, the **Everyman Cinema, 5 Holly Bush Vale** (see **Entertainment: Cinemas,** p25), the UK's oldest repertory cinema, with an informative film bookshop (see **Shopping,** p23).

23 Back Lane (16), at Flask Walk opposite The Flask, is the home of Susannah York, where she's dropped off by playboy cardsharp Warren Beatty, in Jack Smight's flashy 1966 thriller *Kaleidoscope*. **Humla Children's Shop, 13 Flask Walk** is York's trendy 'Angel's' clothes boutique.

Walk down Hampstead High Street to Downshire Hill. Take a quick peek at **Hampstead High Street Police Station, Rosslyn Hill (17)**, on the southeast corner of Downshire Hill, which is the cop-shop where Kevin Sheperd (Ioan Gruffudd) is sprung from his cell by Wad-

Kaleidoscope: Warren Beatty drops off Susannah York: Back Lane

Kaleidoscope: Susannah York's shop: Humla Children's Shop, Flask Walk

102 Dalmatians: Ioan Gruffudd is sprung from jail by a parrot: Hampstead High Street Police Station, Rosslyn Hill

Darling: Dirk Bogarde's house: Jasper House, South End Road

dlesworth the Parrot (voiced by Eric Idle), after being framed for dognapping by Cruella De Vil (Glenn Close), in *102 Dalmatians*.

Now walk down the hill, past some of the capital's most desirable houses. At the foot of the hill, on the right, just before you get to the Heath, is South End Road. Just around the corner is **Jasper House, 106 South End Road (18)**, the home of TV exec Robert Gold (Dirk Bogarde), in John Schlesinger's sixties media satire *Darling*.

Turn right along South End Road to Hampstead Heath station. Alongside the station runs South Hill, where you'll see the plain exterior of **Magdala Tavern, South Hill Park (19)**. In 1955, nightclub hostess Ruth Ellis was hanged for shooting her playboy boyfriend David Blakeley outside the pub – you can still see bullet holes in the brickwork. There was enormous sympathy for Ellis, and the furore surrounding the case contributed to the abolition of capital punishment in Britain. The story was dramatised by Shelagh Delaney (writer of *A Taste of Honey*) in 1985, as *Dance With a Stranger*, directed by Mike Newell. You won't recognise the site from the movie, though, which uses a much more photogenic pub in Clerkenwell (see **Northeast London**, p79). Stop for a drink, read an account of the case in the bar, or sample the excellent restaurant.

Make Mine Mink: Terry-Thomas evades the law: South End Green

South Hill Park leads into **Parliament Hill Fields (20)**, the southeastern section of Hampstead Heath with spectacular views across the city, where American

Bunny Lake Is Missing: Bunny goes missing from The Little People's Garden School: South Hampstead High School, Netherhall Gardens

Ambassador Robert Thorn (Gregory Peck) and his wife (Lee Remick) play happily with young Damien (Harvey Stephens), before extras start dropping like flies in *The Omen*. You might want to stop here, or choose to see the other locations dotted about the area.

If you continue past the station, you'll come to the villagey triangle of **South End Green (21)**. In the 1960 comedy *Make Mine Mink*, Terry-Thomas flees the scene of a robbery disguised as a policeman. The underground gents toilet on the east side is where he jettisons his fake uniform to emerge, in his underwear, as a marathon runner.

Cross the little green, with its marble water fountain, to Pond Street, and walk back up to Rosslyn Hill. Take a detour here, if you like, west toward Finchley Road tube station. **South Hampstead High School, 5 Netherhall Gardens (22)**, was transformed into 'The Little People's Garden School', run by grande dame Martita Hunt, from which Carol Lynley's daughter Bunny apparently disappears, in *Bunny Lake Is Missing*.

Otherwise, turn left into Belsize Park. Close enough to bask in the cachet of Hampstead, but also near to the funkiness of Camden, this is where to move when you make it. Kate Winslet and Sam Mendes recently moved in. Bob Hoskins and Helena Bonham Carter are locals and, of course, Noel Gallagher's previous home, Supernova Heights, blazed briefly on Steeles Road in the late nineties.

Hampstead Town Hall, Rosslyn Hill (23) at Belsize Avenue (which used to house Camden Council's Finance Department but is currently being redeveloped as an arts centre), is the registry office where Charlotte Rampling finally marries Alan Bates at the end of *Georgy Girl*.

Across the main road is Haverstock Hill, where you'll find the local cinema, the **Screen on the Hill, 203 Haverstock Hill**, Belsize Park (✆ *020.7435.3366*).

Georgy Girl: Alan Bates and Charlotte Rampling get married: Hampstead Town Hall, Rosslyn Hill

Sliding Doors: Gwyneth Paltrow stays with her pal: Primrose Gardens

It Happened Here: the doctor's surgery: Belsize Square

Turn down Belsize Grove and left into the narrow oval garden of **Primrose Gardens (24)**. You might recognise this as the street where Helen's friend Anna – who Helen stays with after catching her boyfriend cheating on her – lives in *Sliding Doors*.

Head back to Belsize Grove, turn right into Belsize Park Gardens and continue on to Belsize Park itself. The **Avoca House Hotel, 46 Belsize Park (25**; see **Hotels**, p9), features heavily in *Leon the Pig Farmer*.

Continue on to Belsize Square. "We've fought a war and we've lost it. There's been a terrible lot of suffering on both sides, so why prolong that suffering. The only way to get back to normal is to support law and order" – nurse Pauline (Pauline Murray) rationalises collaboration with the fascist government in Kevin Brownlow and Andrew Mollo's chilling fictional documentary of life under Nazi occupation *It Happened Here*. **14 Belsize Square (26)** is the surgery of anti-fascist Dr Fletcher (played by veteran actor Sebastian Shaw, who went on to become the face of old Anakin Skywalker, the unmasked Darth Vader, in *Return of the Jedi*).

Georgy Girl: James Mason's mansion: Harley Road

Go through the square to Lancaster Drive and Strathray Gardens, which brings you to Eton Avenue, a row of striking red brick mansions, any one of which could provide a suitably gothic Hammer backdrop. And indeed, it's at **53 Eton Avenue (27)**, at King's College Road, that bride-to-be Diana (Jemma Redgrave) gets an attack of the 'Elm Street' blues, slipping in and out of nightmares in Harley Cokeliss' incoherent 1988 shocker *Dream Demon*.

Turn left into Winchester Road, crossing Adelaide Road into Harley Road. The grand house at **7 Harley Road (28)**, once home to opera singer Dame Clara Butt, is James Mason's mansion in that tart slice of sixties cynicism *Georgy Girl*.

Return to Adelaide Road, which will take you to Swiss Cottage. The **Swiss Cottage Hotel** (see **Hotels**, p9) can be seen in *Mike Bassett: England Manager*.

The **Odeon Swiss Cottage, 96 Finchley Road**, now inevitably divided up into multiscreens, was grand enough to number Merle Oberon and Conrad Veidt among the Hollywood celebs at its opening in 1937. You'll also find the **Hampstead Theatre Club** here, where the legendary stage production of *Abigail's Party* was originally devised by Mike Leigh.

Dream Demon: London's answer to Elm Street: Eton Avenue

Northeast London: Islington and Clerkenwell

Famous, or notorious, as home of the liberal intelligentsia so despised by Britain's tabloid press, Islington has become synonymous with minimalist decor, health food and ethnic crafts. In the movies, though, it's laddishness all the way – gangsters, footballers... erm, meat porters...

Starting Point: Islington

A few locations which are a bit off the main walk to begin with. The octagonal **Union Chapel, Compton Terrace (1**; © *020.7226.1686; website: www.unionchapel.org.uk*), near Highbury and Islington tube, a Grade II listed building built in 1877, is now used as a performance space. It became the headquarters of the People's Lobby, the terrorist organisation headed by Judy Davis, in the gung-ho 1982 SAS thriller *Who Dares Wins*, made in the wake of the 1980 Iranian Embassy siege. The chapel's galleried **Studio Theatre** is the Christian sect shelter (supposedly in the Midlands) where Felicia (Elaine Cassidy) discovers, much to the annoyance of the do-gooders, that her money has been stolen in Atom Egoyan's *Felicia's Journey*.

The old **Finsbury Park Astoria, Seven Sisters Road (2**), Finsbury Park, is the theatre where Cliff Richard and chums, in the tradition of those old MGM musicals, put on a show in 1961's *The Young Ones*. Thirteen years later, the theatre's Moorish foyer became the 'Istanbul' restaurant where the passengers meet up at the opening of *Murder on the Orient Express*. Slightly less glamorously, the Astoria is also the dance hall for the fantasy tango sequence between Rigsby (Leonard Rossiter) and Miss Jones (Frances de la Tour) in the big-screen version of classic British TV sitcom *Rising Damp*. Hazel O'Connor breaks down onstage during her concert here, in *Breaking Glass*, made in the same year. The Astoria is now a church.

Highbury Park, Avenell Road (3), is, for the present at least, home to Arsenal Football Club. In 1939 eccentric inspector Leslie Banks investigated the poisoning of a player during a match against the Gunners in *The Arsenal Stadium Mystery*. Although mostly

Who Dares Wins and **Felicia's Journey**: terrorists and cults: Union Chapel, Compton Terrace

shot in the studio, the pitch scenes were filmed at Highbury. In 1997, *Fever Pitch*, Nick Hornby's laddish novel, was filmed with Colin Firth as the Arsenal obsessed fan. This time though the soccer ground scenes were filmed at Craven Cottage in Fulham, where, unlike Highbury, the stand still had old fashioned terraces.

Four Weddings and a Funeral: Hugh Grant's flat: Highbury Terrace

22 Highbury Terrace (4), on the northwest corner of Highbury Fields at Highbury Terrace Mews, is the flat of Hugh Grant, where Andie MacDowell finally turns up in the rain at the end of *Four Weddings and a Funeral*.

The tour proper begins in the cultural epicenter of Islington, home to respected fringe theatres such as the **King's Head, 115 Upper Street** (☎ 020. 7226.1916), the London pub theatre par excellence, and the **Almeida, Almeida Street** (☎ 020.7359.4404; *website: www.almeida.co.uk*). This fringe theatre, housed in the former Literary Institute building, has a reputation formidable enough to have attracted Hollywood heavyweights such as Kevin Spacey, who was electrifying as Hickey in Eugene O'Neill's play *The Iceman Cometh*. Before or after the show, there's a range of restaurants and wine bars to leave you spoiled for choice, though the frequency with which they open, close or just change names, will keep you on your toes. A café you can finally enjoy again after years of being closed and boarded up is the **S&M Café**, previously Alfredo's, **4-6 Essex Road (5)**, just north of Angel tube station. The period look of Alfredo's made it ideal for the sixties London hangout of Jimmy and the Mods in *Quadrophenia*. It also played a similar role as 'Luigi's' coffee bar in the well-cast, but disappointingly stagey, adaptation of Jez Butterworth's fifties-set play *Mojo*. Incidentally, the S&M stands for Sausage and Mash…

Also in the centre of Islington, and now reopened after a facelift, is **The Angelic, 57 Liverpool Road** (**6**; see **Bars & Restaurants**, p14). It appears in Brit-gangster movie *Love, Honour and Obey* in its previous incarnation as the Moriarty Bar.

Behind Angel Underground Station, **26 Danbury Street** (**7**), by the Grand Union Canal, can be seen in the film of Dodie Smith's novel *I*

Quadrophenia: the Mods' London hangout: S&M Café, Essex Road

Love, Honour and Obey: Brit gangster hangout: The Angelic, Liverpool Road

Capture the Castle.

25 Noel Road was home to Joe Orton (a plaque marks the house), author of *Loot* and *Entertaining Mr Sloane*, where he was murdered by partner Kenneth Halliwell in 1967.

You can take a detour further east if you like to **Poole Street** at New North Road, alongside the Regent's Canal, site of the old Gainsborough Studios. This one-time power station converted into film studios was bought by the Gainsborough corporation in 1924, and is where Alfred Hitchcock got his start in the film business, designing title cards for silent movies. He later made *The Lodger* and *The Lady Vanishes* at the studio. The old buildings still exist, redeveloped as luxury flats.

Head south across Pentonville Road into St John Street, then turn right into Chadwell Street, which will lead you into Myddleton Square, a large, elegant and beautifully preserved development dating from 1827. **63-65 Myddleton Square (8)**, on the west side at Inglebert Street, is the home of Father Smythe (Jason Isaacs), the priestly confidant of Sarah Miles (Julianne Moore), in Neil Jordan's adaptation of Graham Greene's novel *The End of the Affair*. The elegant square is made to look weedy and grubby in Jordan's film, which manages to conjure an austere poetry from the exhausted shabbiness of the forties. Across the street is **St Mark's Church**, where Moore finds the investigator's boy asleep in the doorway.

Just past Exmouth Market you can see the massed postal vans of London's postal hub, the **Mount Pleasant Sorting**

The End of the Affair: the priest's house: Myddleton Square

The End of the Affair: the church: St Mark's Church, Myddleton Square

Love, Honour and Obey: pink champagne: Mint 182, St John Street

Sliding Doors: Jeanne Tripplehorn's loft apartment: Pattern House, St John Street

Office. Until recently, the largely unknown Post Office underground railway, **Mail Rail**, rattled beneath the streets of London. Fully automated (the trains have no drivers), this unique but expensive system has now been taken out of service and is awaiting a buyer. It stands in for the 'Vatican railway' in Michael Lehmann's movie *Hudson Hawk*, the doomed Bruce Willis vanity project.

Return to St John Street, which runs all the way from Islington to Clerkenwell (and how trendy is that?), an odd mix of offices and cooler-than-cool drinking spots. **Mint 182, 182-186 St John Street (9**; see **Bars & Restaurants**, p15), can be seen in *Love, Honour and Obey*, in the days when it was Bar Rock.

Pattern House, 223-227 St John Street (10), between Sekforde and Skinner Streets, once the offices of Vogue magazine, now inevitably revamped as loft apartments, is the luxury pad of Bitch-From-Hell Jeanne Tripplehorn, where poor old Gwyneth Paltrow falls down the stairs in *Sliding Doors*, conveniently providing the film with a rather pat ending.

You'll have difficulties tracking down the expansive, glass-fronted bar 'Slammers', where Steven Mackintosh finds Matthew Blackmore dead in the gents, in *The Criminal*. In reality it's Indian restaurant **Café Lazeez, 88 St John Street (11**; see **Bars & Restaurants**, p15).

The Criminal: Slammers bar: Café Lazeez, St John Street

Lock, Stock and Two Smoking Barrels: JD's bar: Vic Naylor, St John Street

Great Sutton Street appears in multi-focus rom-com *Love Actually*, the directorial début of *Four Weddings and a Funeral* writer Richard Curtis, with Prime Minister Hugh Grant falling for tea-lady Martine McCutcheon.

As you approach Smithfield, on the left you'll find **Vic Naylor, 38-40 St John Street (12**; see **Bars & Restaurants**, p15), the bar in *Lock, Stock and Two Smoking Barrels*. If you find Guy Ritchie's movies just a little too – well – *girlie*, you'll prefer a drink at the offshoot next door, **Vic's Bar, 42 St John Street** (see **Bars & Restaurants**, p15), which featurs in *Mean Machine*, starring Vinnie Jones. We're talking serious testosterone territory…

A little further on, **The Gate, 18-20 St John Street** (see **Bars & Restaurants**, p15), can be seen at the beginning of *The Criminal*.

The southern end of St John Street leads into Smithfield. **Smithfield Market (13**) is one of London's famous produce markets: Covent Garden for fruit and veg, Billingsgate for fish and Smithfield for meat. The meat market is where the Dave Clark Five work as porters in *Catch Us If You Can*, John Boorman's début feature film. The famous meat market stood in for the old Covent Garden fruit and vegetable market in Richard Attenborough's biopic *Chaplin*, since the vegetable trade had moved south of the Thames to Nine Elms in the early seventies. In the disused western section of the market, Michael Caine passes on the arcane mysteries of the butcher trade to his son in Fred Schepisi's *Last Orders*.

Within the market, on **East Poultry Avenue** at West Smithfield, you'll find a small unremarkable door which leads down to **The Cock Tavern** (see **Bars & Restaurants**, p15), a market pub with an extended licence which allows the porters to drink at all hours. It can be seen in *Gangster No. 1*.

As old practises are slowly phased out, the market is begining to feel increasingly like an anachronism, and

The Criminal: Jasper meets the mysterious Sarah: The Gate, St John Street

Chaplin and Catch Us If You Can: vegetable market and meat market: Smithfield Market

Gangster No. 1: Saffron Burrows is discovered: The Cock Tavern, East Poultry Avenue

About a Boy: Hugh Grant is tailed: The Comptoir Gascon, Charterhouse Street

indeed there are dark rumours of relocation to Nine Elms. It's not hard to envisage a Covent Garden-style redevelopment, servicing the artsy Clerkenwell enclave. Will (Hugh Grant) lives close by, in brothers Chris and Paul Weitz's film of Nick Hornby's novel *About a Boy*, and shops at **The Comptoir Gascon, 63 Charterhouse Street**, (© *020.7608.0851*), a mouthwatering French deli (an offshoot of restaurant Club Gascon and Cellar Gascon at 57 West Smithfield, alongside the Church of St Bartholomew – see below).

South of the market lies the open space of **Smithfield** itself, notoriously the site of spectacularly gruesome public executions, including that of William Wallace, the real 'Braveheart', who was hung, drawn and quartered here in 1305. A small memorial, usually festooned with flowers and various tartans, can be seen on the south side. The tradition of opening an event by cutting a ribbon originated here, when the Mayor would ceremonially cut the first bolt of material to kick off Smithfield's annual cloth fair.

The Tudor gateway on Smithfield's eastern side leads to the **Church of St Bartholomew the Great** (**14**; see **Historic Sites**, p30). The church has a lengthy list of film credits which include *The End of the Affair*, *Four Weddings and a Funeral*, *Robin Hood: Prince of Thieves* and *Shakespeare in Love*.

Tucked away behind St Bartholomew's is **34-37 Bartholomew Close** at Half Moon Court, currently boarded up. This is the detective's office, where Ralph

Four Weddings and a Funeral: the last wedding: Church of St Bartholomew the Great

Robin Hood: Prince of Thieves: Nottingham Cathedral interior: Church of St Bartholomew the Great

Fiennes hires a PI to tail Julianne Moore, in *The End of the Affair*. The same interior is also Joseph Fiennes' apartment in Chen Kaige's *Killing Me Softly*. It's easy to see why the phrase 'erotic thriller' might get a potential producer drooling, despite the fact that the genre is a guaranteed turkey

generator. But what on earth possessed Kaige, the director of *Farewell My Concubine*, to attempt a *British* erotic thriller? It may yet become a kitsch classic. You can see the entrance to the block (actually the rear of the building), where smitten Heather Graham waits for her enigmatically mean'n'-moody lover, in the small courtyard on **Bartholomew Place**. What would poet Sir John Betjeman, who lived nearby, at **43 Cloth Court**, have made of it all?

Killing Me Softly: Joseph Fiennes' apartment: Bartholomew Close

To the east of Smithfield you can visit the **Barbican Centre (15)**. It is notoriously difficult to navigate this warren of performance spaces, but understandable since it's the largest multi-arts and concert centre in Europe. Apart from the theatres and concert hall, there's the two-cinema **Barbican Screen** (see **Entertainment: Cinemas**, p25), which shows a mix of arthouse and mainstream blockbuster fare, along with special seasons. Step outside and look up at **Shakespeare Tower**, one of the three towers of the complex, where Italian-suited gangster Freddie Mays (David Thewlis) lives until he's ousted by his young nemesis in *Gangster No. 1*. To the north on Goswell Road are the towers of the **Golden Lane Estate**, which can be seen in *Born Romantic*.

Return, if you left it, to Smithfield. On Charterhouse Street alongside the market you'll see the **Port Authority Building** – briefly glimpsed during Vinnie Jones' drunken car ride at the beginning of *Mean Machine*. As you reach Farringdon Road take a quick glance toward **Holborn Viaduct**. On the viaduct, Joe Kirby (Harry Fowler), leader of the boys' gang, buys a copy of *The Trump* comic in *Hue and Cry*. The modern block alongside stands on the site of the office where Jean-Pierre Léaud works, before being sacked, which leads him to hire a hitman in Aki Kaurismäki's seriously odd-ball *I Hired a Contract Killer*.

Turn right into Farringdon Road. Running parallel to the west of Farringdon Road is the

Gangster No. 1: the gangster's luxury pad: Shakespeare Tower

Sorted: the murdered brother's deco apartment block: Ziggurat Building, Saffron Hill

A Fish Called Wanda: disposing of the evidence: St John's Gate, Clerkenwell Road

A Fish Called Wanda: Jamie Lee Curtis in the getaway car: Clerkenwell Green

narrow passageway of Saffron Hill, where a small part of Miami Beach seems to have been transplanted. The stepped terraces of the extraordinary white, art deco **Ziggurat Building, 60-66 Saffron Hill** (**16**), at Saffron Street, a 1930s print works converted into luxury apartments in 1997, is the stylish home of northerner Matthew Rhys' brother, where he stays while investigating the suspicious death in *Sorted*.

Continue north to Clerkenwell Road and turn right again into Clerkenwell proper. Another of those up-and-coming areas that fill the property pages of local papers, Clerkenwell has a fascinating history of radicalism. With a similar history to the East End – a notorious slum area, settling place for immigrants – Clerkenwell was the site of, occasionally violent, demonstrations. In the early years of the 20th century, Lenin edited the Bolshevik newspaper *Iskra* at **37a Clerkenwell Green**, now the **Marx Memorial Library** (you can visit the room where he worked). The *Morning Star*, organ of the Communist Party, had its offices on Farringdon Road. Now it's all loft conversions, and the redistribution of wealth is represented by Jamie Lee Curtis, Kevin Kline and Michael Palin, who relieve Hatton Garden of its surplus diamonds in *A Fish Called Wanda*.

The 16th century **St John's Gate, Clerkenwell Road** (**17**) at St John's Square, is a remnant of the Priory of the Order of St John, which once stood on the site. Michael Palin disposes of evidence here after

the Hatton Garden robbery, while on **Clerkenwell Green** itself, across the street, moustachioed getaway driver Jamie Lee Curtis is spotted by the old lady with the dogs. On the southwest corner at **Farringdon Lane**, Ray Winstone clumsily botches his proposal to Sadie Frost at the opening of *Love, Honour and Obey*.

About a Boy: meeting single mothers at SPATs: Woodbridge Chapel, Haywards Place

A Fish Called Wanda: swapping the getaway car: Roberts Place

Into St James Walk. You probably won't recognise the office building at the corner of Sekforde Street, but **16-18 St James Walk** is Hugh Grant's hi-tech, antiseptic 'island' apartment in *About a Boy*. The striking entrance door was constructed especially for the film at the St James Walk side entrance to the building. **Woodbridge Chapel, Haywards Place**, is where Will (Grant) attends SPATs (Single Parents Alone Together) as a cheesy ploy to meet available single mothers.

Return to Clerkenwell Close. At the top of the close, between the Peabody Trust buildings, is **Roberts Place**, where you'll find the flight of steps alongside which the robbers swap cars after the diamond heist in *A Fish Called Wanda*.

At **St James Clerkenwell, Clerkenwell Close**, Grant almost volunteers for the drop-in centre in *About a Boy*. The cool credentials of Jude (Jude Law) are established by introducing him strolling along Clerkenwell Close, with St James in the background, in *Love, Honour and Obey*. A distraught Ruth Ellis (Miranda Richardson) peers through the railings of the churchyard in Mike Newell's *Dance With a Stranger*. Directly opposite is **The Three Kings** pub, **7 Clerkenwell Close** (see **Bars & Restaurants**, p15), which stands in for the Magdala Tavern in the movie, the Hampstead pub where the real Ruth Ellis shot dead her upper-class boyfriend David Blakeley.

About a Boy: Hugh Grant's hi-tech 'island' apartment: St James Walk

Dance With a Stranger: the shooting at the Magdala Tavern: The Three Kings

The City of London

No matter how well you know the City of London, you can always stumble across one hidden alleyway or an unfamiliar street. The Square Mile is the capital's business district and the historic heart of the original city, as well as being, literally, a law unto itself, with its own police force and ferocious silver dragons guarding its entrances. Ancient inns and courtyards are overlooked by pompous institutions and some, frankly hideous, modern monstrosities.

Starting Point: City Thameslink

The Old Bailey (1), more properly known as the Central Criminal Court, is one of those iconic landmarks often seen in stock shots, to indicate major court cases. As such it can be seen in such courtroom melodramas as Hitchcock's 1947 film *The Paradine Case* and ten years later in Billy Wilder's *Witness for the Prosecution*. In Michael Winner's *The Jokers*, the stolen Crown Jewels are deposited in the scales of justice atop the famed courthouse, and in *Sweeney Two*, Regan (John Thaw) turns up here as a character witness for his corrupt superior Jupp (Denholm Elliott). Regan phones partner Carter (Dennis Waterman), and meets Harry (Johnny Shannon, who played another villainous Harry, fey gang boss Harry Flowers, in *Performance*) in the **Magpie and Stump**

opposite. The old pub, at which crowds once gathered to watch executions, has been completely rebuilt.

Head along Newgate Street to **King Edward Street**. The statue on King Edward Street can be seen apparently overlooking the Barings Bank building during the opening credits of *Rogue Trader*, the dull

The Jokers: Crown Jewels in the scales of justice: The Old Bailey

As 007's base, London regularly features in the Bond series. His first big-screen appearance was supposedly at the *chemin-de-fer* table at Le Cercle in the very exclusive **Les Ambassadeurs, Hamilton Place** (**1**) in *Dr. No*, though the interior was actually a very realistic studio recreation.

Taking over the role briefly in *On Her Majesty's Secret Service*, George Lazenby has to bone up on heraldry at the **College of Arms, Queen Victoria Street** (**2**), in order to pass himself off as Sir Hilary Bray.

The series became more lightweight with the arrival of Roger Moore. In *Octopussy*, the Fabergé egg is put up for sale at world famous auction house **Sotheby's, 35 Bond Street** (**3**). In *A View to a Kill*, MI6 HQ is actually the **Old War Office Building, Whitehall** (**4**), although for the more po-faced Timothy Dalton in *The Living Daylights*, it is **Malaysia House** (**5**) on the southwest corner of Trafalgar Square.

Pierce Brosnan brought back all the old sparkle in the hugely successful *GoldenEye*, which cut a few financial corners by finding exotic locations around the capital. The revamped courtyard of **Somerset House, the Strand** (**6**), was passed off as 'St Petersburg', although in *Tomorrow Never Dies* it masquerades as MI6 HQ. The exterior of the 'Russian' church can be seen in **Brompton Cemetery, Old Brompton Road, Earl's Court** (**7**), and the glitzy 'Hotel Europe' is none other than the **Langham Hilton, Portland Place** (**8**).

Tomorrow Never Dies' remote-controlled BMW demonstrates its capabilities not in Hamburg, but in the multi-storey car park of **Brent Cross Shopping Centre** (**9**).

MI6 finally comes out of the closet in *The World Is Not Enough* – M's command centre is the real HQ, **Vauxhall Cross** (**10**). Most of the stunts for the Thames boat chase were staged on the East End's docks and canals, most notably the **Glengall Bridge** (**11**) and the **Ornamental Canal** (**12**), Tobacco Dock. The entrance to the fictitious 'Vauxhall Cross' station in *Die Another Day* is supposedly beneath the lion at the foot of **Westminster Bridge** (**13**). 'Blades' is the **Reform Club, Pall Mall** (**14**), and the interior of the Cuban cigar factory is **Kingsland House, Stoke Newington Road, Hackney** (**15**).

Four Weddings and a Funeral has transformed London into Europe's most romantic city, with couples stuttering and stumbling their way through the rituals of courtship before declaring love over the theme song. Hugh Grant and Andie MacDowell got the ball rolling in the rain outside his flat at **22 Highbury Terrace (1)** on Highbury Fields.

Some people are never satisfied, and Hugh was soon aiming higher, at megastar Julia Roberts, in *Notting Hill*. The antique mart, used for the ailing bookstore, is now **Gong, 142 Portobello Road (2)**. If you're feeling really flush and want to splash out, impress your date with a meal at **Nobu**, in the **Metropolitan Hotel, Park Lane (3)**, the Japanese restaurant where Roberts gives as good as she gets. **Kenwood House, Hampstead (4)**, is the site of the Henry James movie shoot. David Kane's *This Year's Love* followed a group of twenty-somethings around Camden Town. **St Pancras Old Church, Pancras Road (5)**, is the site of the doomed wedding of Catherine McCormack and Douglas Henshall.

Hugh Grant found himself on the losing side for once in *Bridget Jones's Diary*. Colin Firth wins out, and gets his big clinch with Renée Zellweger in the snow at **Royal Exchange Buildings** on **Cornhill (6)**.

Jack & Sarah put a spin on the theme with widowed Jack (Richard E Grant) struggling to bring up his baby daughter Sarah, while falling for nanny Amy (Samantha Mathis). His house is **22 St James's Gardens (7)** near Holland Park.

Sliding Doors deftly ran two alternative outcomes side-by-side, with Gwyneth Paltrow organising a restaurant launch at **Manor, All Saints Road, Notting Hill (8)**, and drinking with John Hannah at the **Blue Anchor, Lower Mall, Chiswick (9)**.

And it's Hugh Grant again, back centre stage, though minus the floppy locks, learning from young Nicholas Hoult that no man is an island, even if that's Ibiza, in *About a Boy*. The restaurant where Grant gets the brush off from a succession of women is the stylish **Otto Dining Lounge, 215 Sutherland**

Avenue, Maida Vale (10).

Parminder Nagra and Jonathan Rhys-Meyers bring a cross-cultural flirtatiousness to the beautiful game in the feelgood *Bend It Like Beckham*, set in Southall and **Heston (11)**.

Rose Troche rings the changes with the pan-sexual *Bedrooms & Hallways*, which sees James Purefoy cheating on Jennifer Ehle with her gay best friend Kevin McKidd. McKidd's loft apartment has now found fame after becoming Jamie Oliver's **Fifteen Restaurant, 15 Westland Place (12)**.

The guys who are not getting cutely tongue-tied and lovestruck are slipping into sharp suits and packing shooters. Gangster cool is the capital's other current cinematic fashion.

Harold Shand (Bob Hoskins) was the daddy of them all in a film which has been voted the greatest British movie of all time, *The Long Good Friday*. Sink a pint in the **Salisbury, Green Lanes, Harringay (1)**, a great old fashioned pub which became the 'Northern Ireland' bar of the film's opening scenes. Richard Burton is a thinly-disguised Ronnie Kray in *Villain*, which used the **Assembly House, Kentish Town Road (2)**, as a stand-in for an East End boozer.

The Krays immortalises Reggie and Ronnie on film. **Bacchus, Hoxton Street (3)**, stands in for Whitechapel's Blind Beggar, where George Cornell was gunned down, and **Caradoc Street, Greenwich (4)**, is passed off as the Krays' 'Vallance Road' home in the movie.

Guy Ritchie gave the genre a shot in the arm with *Lock, Stock and Two Smoking Barrels*. **Park Street (5)**, alongside Borough Market, provided an ideally characterful backdrop, while the Krays' old hangout, **Repton Boys Club, Cheshire Street (6)**, was used for the poker game.

With *Snatch*, the relentless laddishness was starting to grate, but there's still enough invention to keep it afloat. The 'Drowning Trout', where Vinnie Jones' quiet drink gets rudely interrupted, is actually the **Jolly Gardeners, Black Prince Road (7)**.

Gangster No. 1 is sharp and tough and it's got Malcolm McDowell in his best role for years. Lennie Taylor's East End drinking club is on **Boundary Passage, Shoreditch (8)** (and, no, it's not real), while David Thewlis' luxury penthouse is **Shakespeare Tower (9)** in the **Barbican** complex.

Antonia Bird's *Face* also concentrated on character, without stinting on the action scenes: **Allison Road, Harringay (10)**, was the site of the incendiary shoot-out.

Love, Honour and Obey seemed to many like a home movie for the Brit Pack. **The Queen's Hotel, Broadway Parade, Hornsey (11)**, is where directors Ray Burdis and Dominic Anciano act as bouncers.

More original was Jonathan Glazer's *Sexy Beast*, which crackled with quirky dialogue. Tucked away in the backstreets of South Kensington is **Clock House, Rutland Mews West (12)**, where James Fox is shot.

Hammer Films rarely strayed beyond their studio, until they began to update the storylines. *Dracula AD 1972* saw the Count haunting swinging Chelsea, with Italian restaurant **La Bersagliera, 372 Kings Road** (**1**), as the groovy coffee bar where the trendy young things gather. For *The Satanic Rites of Dracula*, **Queens Gate Lodge, Elvaston Place** (**2**), South Kensington, became the 'Keeley Foundation for Science'.

South Kensington was the site of a very different kind of horror in Roman Polanski's *Repulsion*, but the gloomy apartment block where Catherine Deneuve went murderously loopy was actually in Earl's Court, **Kensington Mansions, Trebovir Road** (**3**).

Newman's Court (**4**), off Oxford Street, was the scene of the opening murder in Michael Powell's once-reviled, now-classic *Peeping Tom*.

Michael Reeves, who went on to direct *Witchfinder General*, made *The Sorcerers* in 1967, with horror legend Boris Karloff. The antique shop of victim Ian Ogilvy still stands at **95 Lisson Grove, Marylebone** (**5**).

All Saints Church, Fulham (**6**), by Putney Bridge, was where the manic priest got spiked by his own lightning conductor in *The Omen*.

The mouth of Hell in Dollis Hill? Naturally. **187 Dollis Hill Lane** (**7**) saw the first appearance of cult funsters Pinhead and the Cenobites in *Hellraiser*.

Tony Scott brought lashings of TV ad style to his vampire flick *The Hunger*. Although set in New York, it was mainly shot in London with the cool deco interior of **Senate House, Malet Street** (**8**), becoming Susan Sarandon's West Side clinic.

More recently, the low budget *Long Time Dead* made excel-

lent use of the darkly Gothic **St Augustine's Vicarage, Lynton Road** (**9**), south of Bermondsey. Now, does this look like a place where *you'd* play with a ouija board?

Balfron Tower, St Leonard's Road, Bow (**10**), is the deserted highrise where Cillian Murphy and Naomie Harris hide out in the scariest British movie in years, Danny Boyle's zombie flick *28 Days Later*.

London seemed like the style centre of the world in the sixties. Julie Christie scooped an Oscar as the ambitious model in John Schlesinger's satire *Darling*. **South End Green, Hampstead** (**1**), is where she spies on Dirk Bogarde and family. David Warner becomes a Marxist in a gorilla suit (how sixties is that?) in *Morgan – A Suitable Case for Treatment*, harassing his ex-wife, Vanessa Redgrave, at **Campden Hill Square, Holland Park** (**2**).

In 1965, Ann Jellicoe's play *The Knack* got the full freewheeling, surreal Richard Lester treatment. The famous White Pad is **1 Melrose Terrace** (**3**), Hammersmith.

Michael Caine was then, as now, the king of British cool. As scriptwriter Bill Naughton's callous womaniser Alfie, he lives in Notting Hill at **22 St Stephen's Gardens** (**4**). As Charlie Croker, organiser of 'The Italian Job', he has a trendy pad off Portobello Road, **18 Denbigh Close** (**5**). And as the seedy,

bespectacled antidote to Bond in the first of the sixties Harry Palmer series, *The Ipcress File*, he works out of the 'Dalby Domestic Employment Bureau', **30 Grosvenor Gardens** (**6**), Victoria.

Michelangelo Antonioni defined the era's sex god as the fashion photographer with his typically enigmatic *Blowup*. The atmospheric **Maryon Park, Woolwich** (**7**), is where David Hemmings might, or might not, have photographed a murder. Tom Courtenay became an even less glamorous agent than Harry Palmer for the spy spoof *Otley*. He gets involved with the world of espionage in the then-trendy **Earl of Lonsdale, Portobello Road** (**8**).

Self-parody reached absurd heights with the primary-coloured *Smashing Time*, a clear inspiration for the *Austin Powers* movies, as northern lasses Lynn Redgrave and Rita Tushingham descend on swinging **Carnaby Street** (**9**).

HITCHCOCK'S LONDON

In his early days, Alfred Hitchcock worked largely in the studio – the Law Courts seen in the Lord Mayor's procession in 1936's *Sabotage* are a giant photographic blow-up – but you can find the water fountain where Donald Calthrop stops in 1929's *Blackmail* at the entrance to the **British Museum, Bloomsbury (1)**.

Richard Hannay's house on Portland Place in *The 39 Steps* is also a set, but as he escapes his pursuers, he leaves the borrowed milk float at **Park Crescent (2)**.

Hitch returned to the same area for his 1947 courtroom drama *The Paradine Case*, with lawyer Gregory Peck living at **60 Portland Place (3)**.

Wartime drama *Foreign Correspondent* sees would-be assassin Edmund Gwenn plummet from the tower of **Westminster Cathedral (4)**.

In 1950's *Stage Fright*, Jane Wyman meets detective Michael Wilding in the **Shepherd's Tavern, Shepherd Street, Mayfair, (5)** after her first visit to the home of chanteuse Marlene Dietrich.

James Stewart follows a red herring to find 'Ambrose Chapel' on **Plender Street, Camden Town (6)**, in Hitchcock's glossy 1956 remake of his own *The Man Who Knew Too Much*.

From 1940's *Rebecca*, Hitchcock worked in the US (many of the London locations in his movies were shot by a second unit), until 1972, when he returned to the UK to make *Frenzy* around the old Covent Garden fruit and vegetable market. **3 Henrietta Street (7)** became 'Necktie Strangler' Barry Foster's home. The **Globe, Bow Street (8)**, is the pub where Jon Finch works, and **Nell of Old Drury, Catherine Street (9)**, is where he overhears city gents drooling over the murders.

Literary adaptations, especially period pieces, have always been a staple of British cinema.

Tony Richardson's 1963 film of Henry Fielding's *Tom Jones* was shot mostly in the West Country, but Albert Finney fights a duel in the vaulted undercroft of the chapel at **Lincoln's Inn Fields (1)**.

Chandos House, Queen Anne Street (2), became the Dashwoods' London home for Ang Lee's film of Jane Austen's *Sense and Sensibility*.

Oliver Parker controversially opened up Oscar Wilde's uncompromisingly theatrical *The Importance of Being Earnest*. **Pitshanger Manor, Ealing (3)**, is the country retreat of Colin Firth where the 'Earnest' confusion is finally unravelled.

The Merchant-Ivory team were on a roll with their trilogy of EM Forster adaptations. The preserved Victorian **Linley Sambourne House, Stafford Terrace (4)**, Kensington, is the 'well appointed home' of Daniel Day-Lewis in *A Room with a View*, as well as Hugh Grant's London house in their film of *Maurice*. The wonderfully art nouveau **Black Friar, Queen Victoria Street (5)**, is the pub where Mark Tandy gets into a spot of bother with a guardsman in *Maurice*. And on **Chiswick Mall (6)**, Anthony Hopkins slips a disastrous bit of insider info to Emma Thompson and Helena Bonham Carter in *Howards End*.

Merchant-Ivory didn't fare so well with Henry James' *The Golden Bowl*, but the locations are as seductive as ever. On **Brushfield Street, Spitalfields (7)**, stood the jeweller shop where Uma Thurman and Jeremy Northam discover the titular gift.

Helena Bonham Carter lives at **10 Carlton House Terrace (8)** in another Henry James adaptation, Iain Softley's *The Wings of the Dove*.

Neil Jordan gave Graham Greene's *The End of the Affair* a gorgeous period look. **Abingdon House, Kew Green (9)**, became Ralph Fiennes' home, supposedly on Clapham Common, and **Myddleton Square, Islington (10)**, was dressed down to provide Jason Isaacs' neighbourhood.

2 St James's Gardens, Holland Park (11), is the London home of Jeremy Irons in Karel Reisz's filming of John Fowles' *The French Lieutenant's Woman*.

Fred Schepisi filmed Graham Swift's Bermondsey-set *Last Orders*, with a top-notch cast, in Peckham. **The Wishing Well, Choumert Road (12)**, became the exterior of the fictitious 'Coach and Horses'.

POPTASTIC METROPOLIS!

In 1959 Cliff Richard starred as Bongo Herbert in *Expresso Bongo*, a cheerful satire on Soho's burgeoning rock'n'roll business, but it's at the **Victoria Palace Theatre, Victoria Street** (**1**), that Bongo gets his big break.

The theatre where the Beatles perform in *A Hard Day's Night* has since been demolished, but opposite the site you can still see the alleyway from which the Fab Four emerge for the climactic concert: **Charlotte Mews, Tottenham Street** (**2**).

A year later, in *Help!* the Beatles found a Beethoven-loving tiger in the cellar of the **City Barge, Strand-on-the-Green, Gunnersbury** (**3**).

The story of the Beatles' early days is told in *Backbeat*, which recreates sixties Germany in North London. The **Dome, Tufnell Park** (**4**), becomes Hamburg's Top Ten Club.

1960s Mod culture is celebrated in The Who's *Quadrophenia*, with the **S&M Cafe, Essex Road, Islington** (**5**), as the Mod hangout.

Todd Haynes' *Velvet Goldmine* takes a fanciful look at the Glam Rock scene of the seventies. **Brixton Academy, Stockwell Road** (**6**), was transformed into the Lyceum Theatre where glitter star Brian Slade fakes his onstage assassination.

Alan Parker's 1982 *Pink Floyd – The Wall* scales the heights of pomposity with Pink's bizarre neo-fascist rally at the **New Royal Horticultural Hall, Westminster** (**7**).

Alex Cox's *Sid and Nancy* celebrates the reaction against pomp rock. Punk's fun couple live and row raucously on **West Lane, Bermondsey** (**8**), while the **Inverness Court Hotel, Inverness Terrace** (**9**) in Bayswater, is the hotel of American star Rock Head.

Remember the Spice Girls phenomenon? The **Broadgate Arena** (**10**) is passed off as Turin for the girls' TV special in *Spiceworld the Movie*.

Sorted grafts a clichéd thriller plot onto a potentially better movie about the London clubbing scene. Its club scenes were filmed at the legendary **Ministry of Sound, Gaunt Street, Elephant and Castle** (**11**). *Spiceworld* filmed there too.

Wilde: intimations of the writer's sexuality: Addle Hill

account of the bank's collapse, which comes across like a made-for-cable true crime reconstruction. Continue south to **St Paul's Cathedral** (**2**; see **Historic Sites**, p30), the dome of which, if we are to believe Hollywood, is visible from every window in the capital. It's certainly visible in David Lean's *Great Expectations* and *Lawrence of Arabia*, and *The Madness of King George*. The night-time, floodlit cathedral can also be seen in *Night and the City* and *The Long Good Friday*. Opposite St Paul's, Jimi Mistry robs a cashpoint customer in *Born Romantic*.

Walking south on Dean's Court and across Carter Lane takes you to **Addle Hill** (**3**), the street where Oscar Wilde (Stephen Fry) first begins to recognise his sexuality as he watches a bunch of working class youths, in *Wilde*. The elaborate Victorian shopfront was added to the undistinguished modern southwest corner, but the highly decorated Venetian-style building on Carter Lane is real enough. Originally the St Paul's Choir School, it's now a YMCA.

Wardrobe leads to **Queen Victoria Street**. Turning left you find the black and gold gates of the **College of Arms** (**4**; see **Historic Sites**, p30), where James Bond gets a crash course in heraldry in *On Her Majesty's Secret Service*.

Queen Victoria Street, in front of the burned out shell of Christopher Wren's **St Nicholas Cole Abbey**, is the site of the bullion robbery in the classic Ealing comedy *The Lavender Hill Mob*. The film was made in 1951, and the ravaged city shows the damage inflicted during the Blitz. The spire of the church has since been restored. Alec Guinness later escapes from the stolen police car by running off down **Cheapside**, past another damaged Wren church, **St Mary-le-Bow**. Yet another bomb-damaged Wren church on

On Her Majesty's Secret Service: Bond's heraldry course: College of Arms, Queen Victoria Street

Queen Victoria Street, **St Andrew-by-the Wardrobe**, can be seen in Douglas McGrath's star-studded Dickens adaptation, *Nicholas Nickleby*.

The Golden Bowl: the Matcham house party: Mansion House, Mansion House Place

Outside the **Guildhall** (**5**), June 'George' Buckridge (Beryl Reid) disgraces herself with a brace of nuns in the back of a black cab ("Out on a mission are we? Ooh, I say, is that what you girls really wear?") in Robert Aldrich's film of *The Killing of Sister George*.

Walk along Victoria Street to **Mansion House, Mansion House Place** (**6**), the official residence of the Lord Mayor of London. Rarely seen on screen, its white and gilt pillars are the backdrop to the 'Matcham' house party, with the exotic dance, in the Merchant-Ivory adaptation of *The Golden Bowl*, and it also appears in the TV movie *RKO 281*, the fictionalised story of the making of *Citizen Kane*. Mansion House isn't generally open to the public, but there are group tours (© *020.7626.2500*).

The **Bank of England, Threadneedle Street**, is rather cheekily used as the exterior of Anthony Hopkins' business in *Howards End*. In front of the pillared portico of the old **Royal Exchange**, George Segal recognises Glenda Jackson on the bus on his way from work in the City in *A Touch of Class*. Apparently timid bank employee Alec Guinness checks his paltry wage packet here – "Eight pounds, fifteen shillings." – in *The Lavender Hill Mob*, and at the end of the movie he evades the police by ducking into **Bank Underground Station** before escaping to Rio.

Walk along Cornhill to the **Royal Exchange Buildings**. You'll probably recognise the quaintly period shops on the southwest corner from the end of *Bridget Jones's Diary*. This is where Mark Darcy (Colin Firth) buys a new diary, and Bridget (Renée Zellweger) finally gets her clinch in the snow – after apparently running all the way from Borough Market in her tiny, stripy pants. The shops were transformed into Nazir's hat boutique 'Le Beau Chapeau' for

Bridget Jones's Diary and **East is East**: Bridget's new diary and Nazir's hat boutique: Royal Exchange Buildings

GoldenEye: the St Petersburg council chamber: Drapers' Hall, Throgmorton Street

northern comedy *East is East*, as well as the flower shop where Clarissa Dalloway (Vanessa Redgrave) briefly glimpses Septimus Warren Smith (Rupert Graves) for the film of Virginia Woolf's novel *Mrs Dalloway*.

Go north to the old **Stock Exchange, Throgmorton Street** at Old Broad Street, which is evacuated after a bomb threat from the fictitious 'Red George' in Michael Winner's *The Jokers*. It's difficult to imagine bomb scares being treated so lightly these days; in 1990 the Stock Exchange really was bombed by the IRA, and as a result of this, the visitors' gallery of the new premises (opened in 1972) is now permanently closed.

The various old trades and guilds of the City own lavish meeting halls, even though there are precious few apothecaries, skinners or tallow-chandlers currently operating in the Square Mile. One such, the **Drapers' Hall, Throgmorton Street (7)**, has twice been seen on screen as the interior of genuine Russian locations. In *GoldenEye* it was the forbidding gilt and wood 'St Petersburg' council chamber, where General Ourumov learns that Natalya has survived the GoldenEye detonation. While in Phillip Noyce's film of *The Saint* it was the 'Tretiak Oil & Gas Industries Moscow HQ', where the billionaire oil magnate stages his televised press conference. The hall isn't generally open to the public.

Head north on Throgmorton Avenue and cross London Wall to Finsbury Circus. More *Rogue Trader*. Even with Ewan McGregor bringing a touch of glamour to the role of Nick Leeson, the trader whose dealings brought down Barings Bank, it proved impossible to make a sympathetic hero out of a crooked commodities dealer and a tragedy out of the collapse of a bank. Just as McGregor is far prettier than Leeson, so **London Wall Buildings**, on the south side of **Finsbury Circus (8)**, is far more striking than the real Barings Bank building.

Walk east along London Wall. It's at the pedestrian crossing outside Caffe Nero that comfortably secure Heather Graham is suddenly smitten by mean, moody mountaineer Joseph Fiennes, sparking off the carnal affair at the heart of Chen Kaige's risible *Killing Me Softly*.

Rogue Trader: Barings Bank: London Wall Buildings, Finsbury Circus

Graham works at **4 London Wall** (actually on Blomfield Street), from where she can peek out across the road to Fiennes in the 'Summit Bookshop', which was travel agency **Austravel, 17 Blomfield Street**.

Return to London Wall and turn right into Broad

Killing Me Softly: Heather Graham meets Joseph Fiennes on the crossing: London Wall at Blomfield Street

Killing Me Softly: Heather Graham's office: London Wall

Street. The bright chrome and glass entrance to **Tower 42, 25 Old Broad Street (9)** – formerly (and better) known as the National Westminster Tower, the tallest building in London – is the 'Cryptonic' building, where Catherine Zeta-Jones spies on Sean Connery riding the escalator in *Entrapment*. Matthew Rhys collects his dead brother's effects from the tower in the initially promising, but ultimately disappointing, clubbing thriller *Sorted*. The tower can also be seen in the 2000 dope-dealing comedy *Saving Grace*.

To the east across Bishopsgate is **St Mary Axe**. The Baltic Exchange stood here until it was destroyed by the IRA bomb attack on the City. The exchange's striking lobby became the bank to which Leonard Bast (Samuel West) applies for a job in *Howards End*. There was talk of using the film as a reference to help the rebuilding of the exchange, but those plans were ultimately dropped and the bizarre Swiss Re building, nicknamed the 'Erotic Gherkin', now occupies the site. Although most of the movie was shot in Melbourne, Australia, some scenes for *Queen of the Damned* – the klutzy follow-up to *Interview with the Vampire*, with Stuart Townsend taking over from Tom Cruise as Lestat, rockstar, up against the late

Entrapment: Zeta-Jones spies on Connery: Tower 42, Old Broad Street

Wilde: the discarded lover: Jamaica Wine House, St Michael's Alley

Aaliyah in the title role of Queen Akasha – were filmed in St Mary Axe.

Go south down Bishopsgate, back to Cornhill. Tucked away in the maze of old streets off Cornhill is the old **Jamaica Wine House, St Michael's Alley** (**10**; see **Bars & Restaurants**, p15). If it's not a weekend (when the deserted City becomes a ghost town and few, if any, pubs open), relax in this odd-looking terracotta pub, originally established as a coffee house in 1652 – making it an appropriate location for its appearance in *Wilde*.

Take a little detour, if you wish, south to the river. Swan Lane leads down to **Fishmongers Hall Wharf** (**11**), below London Bridge, where Epifania Parerga (Sophia Loren) incongruously wanders among the stalls in the title role of Anthony Asquith's adaptation of George Bernard Shaw's play *The Millionairess*, though the surgery of Dr Kabir (Peter Sellers) supposedly on the wharf, is a studio set. The gimmick record 'Goodness Gracious Me' (that's not even a line in the film), put out by Sellers and Loren to publicise the movie, launched that irritating Asian stereotype onto an unsuspecting world.

Head back to Cornhill, if you left it, and east to Leadenhall. On the south side is **Leadenhall Market** (**12**), on the site of an ancient poultry market, though the brightly painted, wrought iron cruciform arcade dates from the 1880s. In *Lara Croft: Tomb Raider*, Lara (Angelina Jolie) zooms through the market on her way back from the auction house. The extremely photogenic market also appears in Nick Willing's thriller *Doctor Sleep*, with Paddy Considine. **Pizza Express** (see **Bars & Restaurants**, p16), on the central hub, was once Thai restaurant Saigon Times, which can be seen in *Proof of Life*. Diagonally opposite, **The Lamb** pub (see **Bars & Restaurants**, p16) is the site of the bar brawl in

Proof of Life: the Thai restaurant: Pizza Express, Leadenhall Market

Brannigan: the pub fight: The Lamb, Leadenhall Market

Harry Potter and the Philosopher's Stone: The Leaky Cauldron: The Glass House, Bull's Head Passage

Brannigan.

Walk down the south arm of the market. On the right runs the tiny **Bull's Head Passage**. Alongside number 42 you'll find a smart new opticians called **The Glass House**. And if the entrance looks familiar, it's because it is the doorway of 'The Leaky Cauldron', which contains the entrance to 'Diagon Alley', where Hagrid takes Harry to buy his wizard school supplies in *Harry Potter and the Philosopher's Stone*.

Towering over the market is Richard Rogers' attention-grabbing metal and glass **Lloyds Building**, with its revolutionary external servicing. Russell Crowe reports back to the insurers here in *Proof of Life*, before descending in one of the exterior glass elevators. The two Emma Peels, one good, one evil (but both Uma Thurman) battle it out on the roof in *The Avengers*. In *Entrapment*, it plays a dual role: it's not only the 'New York' highrise, but its exterior also becomes the entrance to the 'Petronas Towers, Kuala Lumpur'. In *Spy Game*, Tony Scott's trademark speedfreak editing slyly presents the building as the 'US Embassy, Hong Kong', where David

The Avengers: the two Emma Peels battle it out: Lloyds Building

Hemmings is phoned by Robert Redford. It can also be seen in Mike Leigh's *High Hopes*.

Head south across Fenchurch Street to Mincing Lane. **Minster Court, Mincing Lane** (**13**), the vast and extravagantly cod-Gothic monster, was inevitably dubbed 'Munster Court'.

101 Dalmatians: the House of De Vil: Minster Court, Mincing Lane

So what could be more appropriate as the 'House of De Vil', the HQ of Cruella De Vil (Glenn Close) in *101 Dalmatians*?

Continue south, across Great Tower Street, to St Dunstan's Hill. *Village of the Damned*, the excellent 1960 film version of John Wyndham's *The Midwich Cuckoos*, saw the women of Midwich giving birth to sinister blond-haired children. For the 1964 sequel, *Children of the Damned*, however, the kiddies have become a multi-ethnic bunch who use their alien powers for world peace, or some such. **St Dunstan-in-the-East, St Dunstan's Hill** (**14**), north of Lower Thames Street, is the deserted church where they hole up.

Children of the Damned: the alien children: St Dunstan-in-the-East, St Dunstan's Hill

As you head east, Lower Thames Street becomes Byward Street. In John Irvin's boxing drama *Shiner*, Billy 'Shiner' Simpson (Michael Caine) is on the way to his son's big fight, so he's not about to let a bit of traffic hold him up. The one-way street where sidekicks Stoney (Frank Harper) and Mel (Andy Serkis) overturn an inconvenient motor is **Seething Lane** (**15**), running north from Byward Street.

Further east still is Trinity Square Gardens. Looming over the western border of the little park is the vast and elaborate office of insurance company **Willis Faber, 10 Trinity Court** (**16**) (formerly the Port of London Authority building), which has a history as a film location dating back to 1960, when the army escort for the Sultan's diamonds was filmed starting out from here for the Peter Sellers comedy caper *Two Way Stretch*. In 1976, the building became a suitably grand venue for the 'Oil Producers International Conference', where we see British delegate Ian Bannen receive a disturbing phone call, at the opening of *Sweeney!* More recently, its pillared frontage featured as the mansion of the villainous Iain Glen in *Lara Croft: Tomb Raider*. Trinity Court

Lara Croft: Tomb Raider: the mansion of villain Iain Glen: Willis Faber, Trinity Court

also appears in 1998's Liverpool-set music comedy *Swing*, with Hugo Speer and Lisa Stansfield.

The Governor's Office of the old **Royal Mint** building, **Cartwright Street**, a little way to the east, is the 'Horseguards HQ', the office of dotty Lord Raglan (John Gielgud), in Tony Richardson's wryly iconoclastic and hugely underrated 1968 version of *The Charge of the Light Brigade*.

To the south is the unmistakable outline of one of the capital's most familiar tourist attractions, the **Tower of London** (**17**; see **Historic Sites**, p30). Brothers Oliver Reed and Michael Crawford lift the Crown Jewels from here, for a laugh, in *The Jokers*. It is relegated to its more usual film role of touristy backdrop in *Alfie*, when Michael Caine photographs formidable maneater Shelley Winters on its riverside frontage with **Tower Bridge** (**18**) forming a picturesque backdrop.

Tower Bridge also features as a backdrop to the 1939 film *Dark Eyes of London*, with Bela Lugosi running an insurance company whose well-insured clients just keep on drowning. Hitchcock's *Frenzy* – the director's first London-based movie for twenty-two years, since *Stage Fright* in 1950 – opens with a triumphant helicopter shot along the Thames and under the walkway of Tower Bridge, with composer Ron Goodwin's stirring score apparently less concerned with creating atmosphere than with celebrating the Master's return to his birthplace. The bridge's picture postcard Gothicism – created by bogus Medieval cladding which hides a sophisticated metal frame construction, and which infuriated architectural purists of the time who believed that the state-of-the-art technology should speak for itself – is also on display in the spoofy 1986 movie *Biggles* and in *The Mummy Returns*. Angelina Jolie rides over the bridge on her bike on the way to the auction house in *Lara Croft: Tomb Raider*, and Rupert Penry-Jones takes Laura Fraser for a magic carpet ride – sort of – across the bridge in *Virtual Sexuality*. Evacuees board boats at Tower Pier as nuclear disaster looms in the Boulting brothers' excellent 1950 low-key

Brannigan: leaping the bridge: Tower Bridge

The Long Good Friday: mooring the yacht: St Katharine's Dock

chiller *Seven Days to Noon*, and titular boat The Magic Christian, in Joseph McGrath's anarchic adaptation of Terry Southern's novel, remains moored here while its upper-crust passengers are duped into believing they are crossing the Atlantic. But the bridge's most spectacular screen appearance must be in *Brannigan*, as the frantic chase climaxes with John Wayne's car leaping the gap of the raising roadway. You can tour the interior of the towers (© *020.7378.7700; website: www.towerbridge.org.uk*), marvel at the feat of Victorian engineering and enjoy breathtaking views of the Thames from its now-covered walkway (a favoured hangout for prostitutes in the bridge's early days).

On the south bank of the Thames, east of Tower Bridge, stands the dismal bulk of the **Thistle Tower** hotel, **St Katherine's Way** (see **Hotels**, p10), which can be seen at the end of *Brannigan*. Barry Foster is held at the hotel before being deported in the film version of TV cop show *Sweeney!* but unfortunately, he's gunned down on the drawbridge at the entrance to **St Katharine's Dock (19)** before he can be put on the boat. It's on the Thames at the same dock that the boat where Bob Hoskins and Helen Mirren entertain the shady Yanks is moored in *The Long Good Friday*.

West London: Fitzrovia to Hatton Garden

A walk through some of London's more bohemian neighbourhoods, from the raffish literary enclave of Fitzrovia, through the eccentrically fey Bloomsbury to the diamond trading area of Hatton Garden. Film-makers though, seem more interested in the dark side of the district, so expect mummies, cannibals and a very nasty serial killer...

Starting Point: Euston Station

Euston Station (1) is the oldest of London's three great intercity termini, opened in 1838 as part of the West Coast Main Line (WCML) linking the capital to Birmingham. In the early sixties, the station was developed beyond recognition and, despite vigorous protests, its landmark smoke-blackened Doric arch-way was demolished, leaving the modern station lost within a characterless complex of shops and offices. Many discarded stone sections of the arch have been painstakingly tracked down, and persistent rumours suggest that it may one day be re-erected. There's a tantalisingly brief glimpse of the station as it used to be in Stanley Donen's 1958 lighter-than-lightweight romantic comedy *Indiscreet*, when Ingrid Bergman meets her sister Phyllis Calvert from the train. Euston

also appears in Michael Winner's 1962 look at rock-'n'roll, *Play It Cool*, with UK rocker and Elvis clone Billy Fury.

You may want to pick up a little, um, something at **Euston Books, Eversholt Street (2)** alongside the station, where sexually fraught bouncer Ray Burdis stocks up with rubber fetish gear to kick-start his love life in the wildly self-indulgent gangster movie *Love, Honour and Obey*.

South of the station lies Fitzrovia, which must be the only London neighbourhood to be named after a pub. The name, coined as recently as the thirties, is actually taken from literary watering hole the Fitzroy Tavern, and not from Robert Adams' Fitzroy Square.

Take a detour a little west, if you want, to the elegant Square, which lies between Great Portland Street and Warren Street tube stations, south of Euston Road. The name Fitzrovia inevitably conjures up the literary and bohemian life that flourished in the area in the thirties. At **29 Fitzroy Square** lived leading Bloomsburyite novelist Virginia Woolf, in a house previously inhabited by George Bernard Shaw. Woolf's rather internalised narratives have occasionally been adapted for the screen with variable results. *Mrs Dalloway*, with Vanessa Redgrave in the title role, was adapted by actress Eileen Atkins for director Marleen Gorris, but much more successful was Sally Potter's imaginative *Orlando*. A handful of Shaw's verbose plays were filmed, rather stagily,

Tom & Viv: the Faber and Faber office: John Foster House, Endsleigh Place

by Gabriel Pascal, but his biggest cinematic success came, of course, with the musicalisation of his play *Pygmalion* as *My Fair Lady* (which, incidentally, was filmed entirely in Burbank, California).

The walk proper begins at Gordon Street, running south from Euston Road opposite the railway station. Walk south and turn left into Endsleigh Place, where you'll find a fittingly literary film location. In 1994, Brian Gilbert directed the cinema version of *Tom & Viv*, Michael Hastings' play about the failure of emotionally constipated poet TS Eliot (Willem Dafoe) to cope with the increasingly erratic behaviour of his wife, Vivienne Haigh-Wood (Miranda Richardson). The office of the Association of Commonwealth Universities, **John Foster House, 36 Endsleigh Place** (**3**) on the corner of Gordon Square, became the offices of 'Faber and Faber', Eliot's publisher, where an enraged and slightly unhinged Viv pours melted chocolate through the letterbox. The real office where Eliot worked can be seen later, on Thornhaugh Street.

Just across Upper Woburn Place is the perfectly period, part-pedestrianised **Duke's Road** (**4**), one of the few streets in London to have been designed as a whole. **Grafton Mansions**, on the east side, is the flat where the war damaged Septimus Smith (Rupert Graves) impales himself on the railings in *Mrs Dalloway*. It is also home to Alex (David Ladd, son of Alan Ladd, and now a big-shot movie producer), in the grisly 1972 thriller *Death Line*.

French poets Paul Verlaine and Arthur Rimbaud (played by David Thewlis and Leonardo DiCaprio in Agnieszka Holland's film of Christopher Hampton's play *Total Eclipse*) lodged in **Howland Street**. Ruth Ellis, hanged for shooting her upper-class playboy boyfriend, and portrayed by Miranda Richardson in

Dance With a Stranger, lived in **Goodwood Court**.

Return to Euston Square Underground Station and turn left into Gower Street. Almost

Doctor in the House and The Mummy Returns: St Swithin's and the British Museum: University College, Gower Street

immediately on the left is the entrance to **University College, Gower Street** (**5**). If you're a fan of cosy fifties comedies, you'll doubtless recognise the domed, neo-Classical building, designed by William Wilkins, architect of the National Gallery, as 'St Swithin's', where oddly middle-aged medical students Dirk Bogarde, Kenneth More and Donald Sinden plunder every known enema and bedpan joke for Ralph Thomas's 1954 comedy *Doctor in the House*. The director's brother, Gerald Thomas (who helmed the *Carry On* series), tried to repeat the formula in 1961 with *Raising the Wind*, but a music academy proved no substitute for a teaching hospital, though the building remains suspiciously similar to St Swithin's. Although University College bears little resemblance to the British Museum – apart from having a dome – it stood in for the museum in not one but two mummy movies. In 1980 Mike Newell inflicted *The Awakening*, a turgid adaptation of Bram Stoker's novel *The Jewel of Seven Stars*, with a bewhiskered Charlton Heston unwittingly summoning up Queen Kara in the museum's Egyptian galleries, on the movie-going public. (Newell survived and went on to make *Four Weddings and a Funeral*.) Years later, Stephen Sommers' *The Mummy Returns*, a warmed-over rehash of his phenomenally successful *The Mummy*, also passed off UCL as the British Museum.

Continuing south on Gower Street brings you to the decorative entrance of the

Stage Fright: Richard Todd evades the police: Royal Academy of Dramatic Art, Gower Street

Royal Academy of Dramatic Art (RADA), 62-64 Gower Street (**6**), the training ground for countless of the UK's most revered stage

The Hunger, Richard III and Spy Game: the New York clinic, the King's bunker and CIA HQ: Senate House, Malet Street

95

Sliding Doors: Gwyneth Paltrow works or drinks: Bertorelli's, Charlotte Street

Naked: the empty office building: Ariel House, Charlotte Street

actors. Murder suspect Richard Todd evades the police by crashing Jane Wyman's acting class at the academy in Hitchcock's 1950 film *Stage Fright*.

Running parallel to, and east of, Gower Street, is Malet Street. At Montague Place stands the dazzling white Portland stone tower of the University of London. Legend has it that George Orwell based *1984*'s sinister Ministry of Truth on **Senate House, the University of London, Malet Street (7)**, and the severe, no-nonsense lines of its deco interior make it the ideal fascist bunker for the newly-crowned king (Ian McKellen) in Richard Loncraine's thirties-set *Richard III*. Director Tony Scott has twice passed off the cool marble foyer as a US location. Don't be fooled by the yellow cabs and the shots of Manhattan streets. The interior of Susan Sarandon's 'Park West Clinic', where David Bowie and Catherine Deneuve attempt to stave off the inevitable ravages of time in Scott's glossy exercise in vampire-chic *The Hunger*, is Senate House. As is the entrance lobby of the 'CIA HQ' in 'Langley, Virginia', where Robert Redford works, in Scott's hyperkinetic globetrotting thriller *Spy Game*. Senate House also provided the site of the bank robbery in Jonathan Glazer's quirky gangster movie *Sexy Beast*.

Go back to Gower Street, then head north and west into Tottenham Court Road. Facing the east end of Charlotte Street is trendy home accessories shop **Heal's, 196 Tottenham Court Road (8)**, where Francis Bacon (Derek Jacobi) glimpses visions in the window in *Love Is the Devil*, John Maybury's self-consciously arty biopic of the compulsive artist and brilliant drinker.

A crowd of unconventional artists of all sexualities gravitated to the liberal ambience of the Fitzroy Tavern in the thirties. It was also where waiters from the restaurant across the road, which had no alcohol licence, used to slip over to the Fitzroy to buy in drinks for the diners. Times change and now you certainly can get a drink in **Bertorelli's, 19-23 Charlotte Street (10**; see **Bars & Restaurants**, p16), which features in *Sliding Doors*.

Almost opposite Bertorelli's, on the southeast

Sapphire: Foscari's coffee bar: Thai Metro, Charlotte Street

corner of Windmill Street, stood 'Foscari's', the coffee bar where the student beatniks hang out in 1950s murder mystery *Sapphire*. It's currently the **Thai Metro, 14 Charlotte Street**.

Charlotte Street is overshadowed by the gawky pillar of the 1960s Telecom Tower, its revolving restaurant off-limits to the public since a bomb blast damaged the tower in the early seventies. It had come close to fictional destruction years earlier, by northerners Brenda and Yvonne (Lynn Redgrave and Rita Tushingham) during the wild party at the climax of slapstick comedy *Smashing Time*. At the end of the movie, the pair trudge glumly down **Charlotte Street** after their dreams of fame turn pear-shaped.

Ariel House, 74a Charlotte Street (9) is the "post-modernist gas chamber" where Johnny (David Thewlis) speculates on increasingly paranoid philosophical concepts with the obsessive security guard (Peter Wight) in Mike Leigh's *Naked*. Behind the block is the flat of lonely Deborah MacLaren, where Thewlis pops over for a bout of sex.

At **21 Tottenham Street**, on the south side, stands a block of luxury flats called Scala House, the only reminder that on this spot stood the Scala Theatre, where the Beatles perform their TV concert in *A Hard Day's Night*. Across the road you can still see **Charlotte Mews**, the alleyway from which the Fab Four emerge just in time for the final concert.

The newsagent on the cor-

A Hard Day's Night: running to the TV concert: Charlotte Mews

Peeping Tom: the newsagent: Percy Street

Peeping Tom: the first murder: Newman Arms, Newman's Court

Velvet Goldmine: Jack Fairy and the glitter kids: Hanway Place

ner of **Percy Street** at Rathbone Place is where apparently respectable gent Miles Malleson (who also played the Caliph in Powell's classic *The Thief of Baghdad*) furtively buys adult photographs in Michael Powell's *Peeping Tom*. **Newman's Court (11)**, off Rathbone Place, is where Carl Boehm picks up prostitute Brenda Bruce at the opening of *Peeping Tom*. Bruce takes him up to her room above the **Newman Arms** (see **Bars & Restaurants**, p16), where the unbalanced photographer films her murder.

Stephen Street, off Tottenham Court Road, houses the invaluable **British Film Institute National Library, 21 Stephen Street** (✆ 020.7255.1444; website: www.bfi.org.uk). You'll need to be a member to take advantage of the numerous facilities, though it is possible to get a day pass. There's a vast collection of books, magazines, microfiche records and special collections.

The small, angled backstreet of **Hanway Place (12)**, behind Hanway Street off Tottenham Court Road, is where the glitter kids first glimpse Jack Fairy at the opening of Todd Haynes' seventies fantasia *Velvet Goldmine*. At the eastern end of the street is the intimidatingly stark, slate frontage of **Hakkasan, 8 Hanway Place** (see **Bars & Restaurants**, p16). From the creator of the Wagamama chain of minimalist eateries, it can be seen in *About a Boy*.

Head east toward Bloomsbury, past the **Cinema Bookshop, 13-14 Great Russell Street** (see

About a Boy: Hugh Grant tries to come clean: Hakkasan, Hanway Place

Shopping, p23), leaving plenty of time to browse the jumble of new and used books on its packed shelves. The Bloomsbury connection continues with the beautifully preserved **Bedford Square (13)**, the backdrop to several scenes in the film of Virginia Woolf's *Mrs Dalloway*.

Shirley Valentine: Shirley meets her schoolfriend: Radisson Marlborough Hotel, Bloomsbury Street

Blackmail: the water fountain: British Museum, Bloomsbury

The **Radisson Marlborough Hotel, 9-14 Bloomsbury Street** (see **Hotels**, p10), can be glimpsed in *Shirley Valentine*.

The **British Museum, Bloomsbury (14**; see **Historic Sites**, p31), is not inevitably played by University College, but has occasionally appeared as itself. The blackmailer stops at the drinking fountain at the entrance in *Blackmail*. Its Assyrian statues can be seen in *Maurice*, while Vanessa Redgrave and Jane Horrocks are both entranced by the Elgin marbles here in *Isadora* and *Born Romantic* respectively. The sculpture court pops up in *Percy*, the museum's Great Court appears in *Kabhi Khushi Kabhie Gham...*, and the Round Reading Room features in *The Day of the Jackal*. Unusually, *Possession* filmed extensively in both the public and private areas of the museum.

Immediately south of the museum, hidden away behind New Oxford Street, is **AKA, 18a West Central Street (15**; see **Bars & Restaurants**, p16) off Museum Street, whic features in *Intimacy*. It also holds a weekly Monday Night at the Movies.

Russell Square tube station (16) is the haunt of cannibalistic zombies, descendants of the survivors of an underground accident, trapped in the tunnels and feasting on unwary late-night passengers, in Gary Sherman's seriously nasty 1972 horror *Death Line*. The real office where TS Eliot worked, by the way, can be seen on **Thornhaugh Street** at the northwest corner of Russell Square. A blue plaque marks the building. The **National**

Intimacy: the West End bar: AKA, West Central Street

The Passenger: Jack Nicholson arrives in London: Bloomsbury Centre

Hospital for Neurology, Queen Square, appears in *Sliding Doors*.

In Michelangelo Antonioni's 1975 film *The Passenger*, disaffected TV documentarist David Locke (Jack Nicholson) swaps identities with a dead man in North Africa, only to find that his new persona is that of a dodgy arms dealer. Arriving in London to put together the pieces of his new identity, Locke first claps eyes on Maria Schneider in the then-new **Bloomsbury Centre (17)**. Since he's heading for Notting Hill, Locke seems to be here for no other reason than that the intimidating, arena-like construction represents another of Antonioni's favoured austere, brutalist backdrops.

In its favour, the centre does contain the **Renoir Theatre** (*℗ 020.7837.8402*), an arthouse cinema outside which Catherine McCormack waits in *Born Romantic*.

Red Lion Square (18) can be seen in Robert Bierman's 1997 adaptation of George Orwell's novel *Keep the Aspidistra Flying*. The aspidistra, if you didn't know, is a huge, ugly, leafy plant, invariably planted in a huge, ugly pot, without which no suburban front window was complete during the thirties and forties. It's now practically extinct. This uniquely British institution is virtually unknown across the Atlantic, where the film was lumbered with the ghastly title *A Merry War*.

Conway Hall, 25 Red Lion Square (*website: www.conwayhall.org.uk*), was established in 1929 by the South Place Ethical Society, which still runs the hall. Although it has a tradition of hosting radical, and occasionally scandalous, meetings, it was quite innocuously used as the concert theatre in the 1961 music college comedy *Raising the Wind*. It's at the entrance to **Hol-**

The Avengers: the entrance to the Ministry: Kingsway Tram Tunnel

born Underground Station (19) that Brenda Blethyn first meets daughter Marianne Jean-Baptiste in Mike Leigh's *Secrets & Lies*. In keeping with the director's improvisational style, the two actors had never met before the scene was shot. The Aldwych entrance of the station had previously been used as the fictitious 'Camden Road' tube station, where IRA man Dirk Bogarde plants a bomb in Basil Dearden's 1952 film *The Gentle Gunman*.

A little to the north, in the middle of Kingsway, you can see the gaping, though now gated, northern entrance to the abandoned **Kingsway Tram Tunnel**, which apparently led into the Ministry in Jeremiah Chechik's disastrous film of *The Avengers*. In the film, computer trickery sent the tunnel to run beneath the Thames to Greenwich. In reality, it emerges under the arch of Waterloo Bridge, but has lain unused since the last tram ran in 1952.

There's nothing to see now, but 242-243 High Holborn, now Blackwell's bookshop, was the site of the famous Holborn Empire music hall. Built in 1906 as Weston's, the Empire was a premier palace of varieties, and it was here in 1914 that the first colour feature film, Kinemacolor production *The World, the Flesh and the Devil*, opened. The music hall was severely damaged by bombing in 1941, and was finally demolished in 1960. It's on the traffic island opposite the Holborn Empire (or rather an impressive studio mock-up) that Rex Harrison plucks Vivien Leigh from the obscurity of Charles Laughton's busking troupe in the 1938 melodrama *St Martin's Lane*.

Turn into the peaceful Lincoln's Inn Fields to feel you've travelled back in time. The **Sir John Soane's Museum, 13 Lincoln's Inn Fields** on the north side (*℗ 020.7405.2107; website: www.soane.org*), is certainly worth a visit. Incidentally, the set for the flat of John Steed (Ralph Fiennes) in *The Avengers* was based on the celebrated architect's striking home. It's open from Tuesday to Saturday and admission is free. Check ahead for special tours.

Walk down Serle Street. If it's open, on weekdays, stroll

Witness for the Prosecution: Charles Laughton is driven to his chambers: New Square, Lincoln's Inn Fields

Tom Jones: the London street: New Square, Lincoln's Inn Fields

A Fish Called Wanda: John Cleese's chambers: New Square, Lincoln's Inn Fields

through the gate on the left into **New Square (20)**, a quaintly civilised square of gentlemanly solicitors' chambers. Sir Wilfrid Robarts (Charles Laughton) and his fussing nurse Miss Plimsoll (Elsa Lanchester) are driven through the imposing gates to Robarts' chambers in Billy Wilder's immaculate 1957 film of Agatha Christie's play, *Witness for the Prosecution*. It's all second-unit stuff, of course (that can't be Laughton in the car), as the movie was shot in Hollywood and the chambers are unmistakably an LA soundstage. Cynical Partridge (Jack MacGowran) suggests that the penniless Tom (Albert Finney) get out of his entanglement with Lady Bellaston by proposing to her, as they walk along the square's west side, in Tony Richardson's 1963 movie *Tom Jones*. **2 New Square**, in the southeast corner, is the office of barrister Archie Leach (John Cleese), where Wanda (Jamie Lee Curtis) breaks all the rules by calling on him, in *A Fish Called Wanda*.

Lincoln's Inn was also used for the little-seen 1998 period drama *Basil*, with Christian Slater, and in the previous year, for *Mrs Brown*, with Judi Dench as Queen Victoria.

From the northeast corner, continue through to Old Square and **Lincoln's Inn Chapel**. Beneath the chapel is the elaborately vaulted undercroft. This is where Tom duels with Fitzpatrick and, for his pains, ends up arrested for armed robbery, in *Tom Jones*. Algy (Rupert Everett) accuses Jack (Colin Firth) of being a Bunburyist here in Oliver Parker's *The Importance of Being Earnest*, with **Stone Buildings** running to the east, transformed into an Edwardian street. The undercroft was also ingeniously glazed and furnished to provide the queen's lodgings in Richard Loncraine's *Richard III*.

Tom Jones: Tom is arrested after fighting the duel: the undercroft of Lincoln's Inn Chapel

The next street east is **Chancery Lane**, where King's College's **Maughan Library** (formerly the Public Records Office) became the exterior of the 'Tower of London' from which, despite the best efforts of Johnny English (Rowan Atkinson), Pascal Sauvage (John Malkovich) manages to lift the Crown Jewels.

The Saint: the Moscow hotel: Renaissance London Chancery Court Hotel, High Holborn

Head back to High Holborn. Almost alongside the site of the old Empire stands the **Renaissance London Chancery Court Hotel, 252 High Holborn (21**; ✆ *020.7829.9888*), housed in the magnificent old Pearl Assurance Building. Having stood empty for years, the grandiose marble interior has done frequent service as a film location. It became the 'Porphyrion Insurance Company', where Mr Bast (Sam West) works – until he ill-advisedly takes the advice of Anthony Hopkins, for *Howards End*. The interior of Hopkins' rubber company was filmed in the same building. The bowels of this Grade II listed building provided the 'hospital' and 'mortuary', where Richard (Ian McKellen) woos Lady Anne (Kristin Scott Thomas) over the body of her husband, in *Richard III*. It also became the hotel where Earl Rivers (Robert Downey Jr) is murdered in the same film. Its marble-pillared entrance stood in for the 'Russian' hotel lobby, where Elizabeth Shue catches up with Val Kilmer (not too hard a task, since all Kilmer's aliases are the names of Catholic saints), in Philip Noyce's *The Saint*.

Take a quick detour south of Holborn Circus to **New Street Square**, seen in Po Chih Leong's rather pretentious 1998 vampire flick *The Wisdom of Crocodiles*, with Jude Law and Kerry Fox.

Head back to Holborn, and walk north on Leather Lane. Turn left into **Hatton Wall (22)**, behind Clerkenwell Road and west of the junction with Farringdon Road, which became fifties 'Soho' in *Mojo*. The film of Jez Butterworth's stage play, about underworld corruption in the emergent pop music biz, remains inertly stagey despite an excellent cast, which includes playwright Harold Pinter. **24-28 Hatton Wall** (in reality the office of *The Idler* magazine) was transformed into the 'Atlantic Club' run by Ricky Tomlinson, supposedly on 'Dean

Mojo: the Atlantic Club, Soho: Hatton Wall

High Heels and Low Lifes: Goldmax Safe Deposit Centre: Hatton Garden

A Fish Called Wanda: the jewel robbery: Diamond House, Hatton Gardens

Snatch: Doug the Head's local: Ye Olde Mitre Tavern

Street'.

Continue on to **Hatton Gardens (23)**, centre of the diamond business, and therefore robberies in the movies. **63-66 Hatton Gardens** became the 'Goldmax Safe Deposit Centre' ripped off by Kevin McNally's crew in *High Heels and Low Lifes* and, across the street, **Diamond House, 37-38 Hatton Gardens,** is the site of the jewellery heist pulled off by Jamie Lee Curtis and Kevin Kline in *A Fish Called Wanda*. Hatton Gardens was transformed into 'Greenwich Village', where Tom Cruise is stalked by the sinister baldy man after leaving the apartment of hooker Domino, in *Eyes Wide Shut*: a couple of New York-style payphones were added between numbers 32 and 38 Hatton Gardens, a London fire hydrant sign was covered up and shop awnings were decked out with US '(212) 555' phone numbers. Although 212 is the genuine New York dialling code, 555 is a fictitious area code generally used in American movies to avoid the expensive litigation which can result from unintentionally using a real phone number on screen. The stalker, by the way, is on a different street altogether (see East London, p118). You might recognise **Premier House, 12-13 Hatton Gardens**, as 'Denovitz Diamonds', the store of Jewish-wannabe

Eyes Wide Shut: Tom Cruise is stalked in Greenwich Village: Hatton Gardens

Snatch: Denovitz Diamonds: Premier House, Hatton Gardens

Doug the Head (Mike Reid) in Guy Ritchie's far-too-laddish *Snatch*.

A little further on, between 8 and 9 Hatton Gardens, is a narrow alleyway leading to **Ye Olde Mitre Tavern** (see **Bars & Restaurants**, p16). Reid is first seen getting a phone call ('Hava Nagila'

plays on his mobile, of course) here in *Snatch*, and Ritchie puts in a micro-cameo as Man Reading Newspaper.

West London: Paddington to Notting Hill

A wander through London's bedsit-land, the faded gentry of Bayswater and the shabby little rooms of Notting Hill, where notorious property-owner Peter Rachman gave his name to exploitative landlords. Cinematically, all human life is here, tucked away behind anonymous front doors that hide dark secrets and copious amounts of drugs.

Starting Point: Paddington Station

We start from **Paddington Station (1)** itself, which serves Worcester and the West of England. This is one of the truly great railway buildings, consisting of three vast arched spaces as awe-inspiring as any cathedral. Take a moment to admire the swirling ironwork of the arches and the almost Moorish balconies. The station was built in 1853 from designs by the ubiquitous Isambard Kingdom Brunel. It's now the terminus for the Heathrow Express, which will whisk you off to London's main air terminal at top speed every fifteen minutes. The station can be seen in the 1947 suspenser *The October Man*, with John Mills.

Julie Christie and Dirk Bogarde lie to their respective spouses from a phone box in the station, before sneaking off to a hotel, in John Schlesinger's *Darling*. Mrs Benson collects the body of her husband, murdered in Northern Ireland while doing a spot of work for Geoff Hughes, from here at the beginning of *The Long Good Friday*. But, although the real Paddington Station is glimpsed in *Performance*, the buffet where Chas (James Fox) – on the lam after a spot of freelance violence – overhears the address of Turner's house, is actually at Olympia Station in West Kensington.

Mimet House, 5 Praed Street, opposite the Hilton London Metropole, stands on the site of the demolished People's Club, which was once the legendary Q Club, a soul-reggae dive presided over by Count Suckle. The club was transformed into the venue where a strangely glamorous Poly Styrene performs with seminal punk band X-Ray Specs in Alex Cox's 1986 film *Sid and Nancy*.

Paddington Station is surrounded by seemingly endless streets of anonymous hotels, some grand, some rather faded. Turn right into Craven Road. The Edinburgh boys from *Trainspotting* might be expected to fetch up in King's Cross when they find themselves with two kilos of skag to offload, but it's here,

Trainspotting: heading to the drug deal: Royal Eagle Hotel, Craven Road

The Italian Job: Charlie Croker's coming out: Royal Lancaster Hotel, Lancaster Terrace

amid the shabby anonymity of Bayswater, that they make a cool £16,000. Sick Boy leads the "small-time wasters with an accidental big deal" out of **Smallbrook Mews**, across **Craven Road** (**2**), to the **Royal Eagle Hotel, 26-30 Craven Road** (see **Hotels**, p10), in a parody of the Beatles' *Abbey Road* album cover.

Continue west to Craven Hill Gardens. More upmarket than the Royal Eagle is the **Royal Lancaster Hotel, Lancaster Terrace** (**3**; see **Hotels**, p11), which can be seen in *The Italian Job*.

Just to the east, off Westbourne Street, runs Bathurst Mews. No drugs here, but plenty of sex and sleaze. **42 Bathurst Mews** (**4**) stands in for the flat of society osteopath Stephen Ward in *Scandal*, Michael Caton-Jones' account of the John Profumo-Christine Keeler scandal which rocked the Tory government in the sixties. Redevelopment of the area around Ward's actual flat, 17 Wimpole Mews in Marylebone, meant that it had changed too much to recreate the period. Bathurst Mews also housed *Connecting Rooms'* 'Johnny's Car Mart', where smarmy conman Alexis Kanner hires flashy sports cars.

You'll need to head west to find *Connecting Rooms'* main location, on the way passing **16 Lancaster Gate** (**5**), traditionally the home of the FA (Football Association) until the organisation upped sticks and moved to Soho Square. Immediately after the building was vacated, with fixtures and fittings left 'as was', the production team for *Mike Bassett: England Manager* – a kind of *This Is Spinal Tap* of English football – took over and shot the boardroom scenes in this most accurate of locations.

Scandal: Stephen Ward's Marylebone flat: Bathurst Mews

Connecting Rooms started out as Marion Hart's downbeat and sentimental play *The Cellist*, which throws together a middle-aged musi-

Mike Bassett: England Manager: the old Football Association HQ: Lancaster Gate

cian and a retired schoolmaster in shabby Bayswater lodgings. Franklin Gollings' 1969 film (his only feature) is notable mainly for the pairing of Hollywood legend Bette Davis as the titular gut-scraper, with stage knight Sir Michael Redgrave as the secretive teacher. **37 Craven Hill Gardens** (**6**) is the boarding house where the two protect their respective guilty secrets.

And how our notions of temporary accommodation have changed. Next door but one is Anouska Hempel's drop-dead stylish white-on-white **Hempel Hotel, 31-35 Craven Hill Gardens** (see **Hotels**, p10). Its Zen Garden, just across the road, can be seen in *Notting Hill*.

On to **Porchester Hall, Porchester Centre, Queensway** (**7**). In the sixties, Porchester Hall became

Connecting Rooms: Bette Davis' Bayswater lodging: Craven Hill Gardens

Notting Hill: the wedding reception: the Hempel Hotel's Zen Garden, Craven Hill Gardens

Monty Python's The Meaning of Life: Porchester Hall, Porchester Centre: the disgusting Mr Creosote

synonymous with the lavish drag balls hosted by larger-than-life Canadian trombonist Jean Fredericks. The annual event was virtually the sole outlet for ostentatious trannie glam in an age when homosexuality was still a criminal offence in the UK (you can glimpse Fredericks and a bevy of her camp followers in *The Adventures of Barry McKenzie*). In 1983, Porchester Hall was transformed into the upper-class restaurant where the disgusting Mr Creosote explodes after that final, fatal "waffer-theen" mint, in *Monty Python's The Meaning of Life*. The complex also contained public baths, now gone, though the Turkish bath is still functioning. It's while using the public baths that old pals Jimmy (Phil Daniels) and Kevin (Ray Winstone) meet up in *Quadrophenia*, only to realise that they've fallen on opposite sides of the Mod-Rocker divide when they come to get dressed.

For such an elegant hotel, the **Inverness Court Hotel, 1 Inverness Terrace (8**; see **Hotels**, p10) at Fosbury Mews, a block east, has been the scene of some raucous cinematic goings-on, including hard drinking in *Valentino* and disruptive behaviour from Sid Vicious and Johnny Rotten in *Sid and Nancy*. The hotel can also be seen in *Sweeney!*

Head back to Bayswater Road. Alongside Queensway Underground Station is **Hilton Hyde Park, 129 Bayswater Road (9**; see **Hotels**, p10), overlooking Hyde Park. Not to be confused with London's famous first Hilton, at the foot of Park Lane. The hotel is probably better known by its former name, the Coburg Hotel, as it was when Hitchcock used it as a location in *Frenzy*.

Whiteley's, Queensway (10), London's first real department store, recently given a flashy makeover, is where agent Harry Palmer (Michael Caine) uses

Sid and Nancy: Rock Head's hotel: Inverness Court Hotel, Inverness Terrace

Frenzy: 'Mr and Mrs Oscar Wilde' check in: Hilton Hyde Park, Bayswater Road

the shoe store pedoscope (a primitive X-ray device used to check the fit of shoes) to check out the contents of a suspicious flask in flashy sixties spy thriller *Billion Dollar Brain*. Down-at-heel cellist Bette Davis does her shopping here in *Connecting Rooms*. Incidentally, the store's founder, Yorkshireman William Whiteley, was not averse to expecting his female staff to indulge in extracurricular activities, and was shot on the store's premises in 1907 by a young man claiming to be his unacknowledged son. The murder inspired the plotline of *Gosford Park*.

A bit of old Russia in Bayswater has proved to be a gift to London-based film-makers needing to conjure up that country's unique atmosphere. The elaborately gilded Russian Orthodox **St Sofia's Cathedral (11**), aptly enough on **Moscow Road**, is the scene of the inevitably doomed wedding between homosexual composer Tchaikovsky (Richard Chamberlain) and the naïvely romantic Nina (Glenda Jackson) in Ken Russell's *The Music Lovers*. Its glittering interior is also the 'St Petersburg' church, where Natalya (Izabella Scorupco) bumps into Boris (Alan Cumming) in *GoldenEye*, though the film doesn't use the Cathedral's exterior (for that, see **Southwest London**, p141).

Continue west to the fringes of Notting Hill, which seems to be the exclusive cinematic domain of sexually duplicitous men. **62 Princes Square (12**) is the flat Gwyneth Paltrow shares with philandering John Lynch in *Sliding Doors*, before her life forks into alter-

The Music Lovers and **GoldenEye**: Russia: St Sofia's Cathedral, Moscow Road

Sliding Doors: Gwyneth Paltrow finds out the truth: Princes Square

native realities. **1 St Stephen's Crescent** (**13**), opposite St Stephen's Church at Talbot Road, is home to single mother Rachel (Rachel Weisz), conned into believing Hugh Grant is also a doting parent, in *About a Boy*. **22 St Stephen's Gardens** (**14**), off Chepstow Road, is the seedy bedsit of archetypal womaniser Michael Caine in *Alfie*. It's not really changed at all since 1966 – apart from a little pedestrianisation of the area, which means that Jane Asher would no longer be able to leg it straight onto a convenient passing bus.

Cash Bar, 105-107 Talbot Road (**15**; see **Bars & Restaurants**, p17), used to be Coins Café, which can be seen in Rose Troche's *Bedrooms & Hallways*.

About a Boy: Rachel Weisz's house: St Stephen's Crescent

Alfie: Alfie's gaff: St Stephen's Gardens

We're now into Notting Hill proper. Even more seedy than Alfie's gaff is the hideaway of reclusive ex-rock star Turner Purple (Mick Jagger) in Nicolas Roeg and Donald Cammell's dazzlingly fractured *Performance*. Filmed in 1968, but left on the shelf by a gobsmacked Warner Bros for two years, it's now recognised as one of the most original and influential British films. However, you're no longer likely to find magic mushrooms left on the doorstep of the smart townhouse at **25 Powis Square** (**16**). The peeling paint has gone and the rubble-strewn site in front of the house is now a railed-off playground.

Alfred Lynch walked past the house during the opening credits of Michael Winner's *West 11*, to his shabby bedsit at **26 Colville Terrace** (**17**). A downbeat little melodrama, the film makes excellent use of its West London locations.

Notting Hill in the fifties and sixties was bedsitland – streets of crumbling, under-maintained hotels run by absentee landlords. In the fifties, the first wave of West Indian immigrants, invited by the government to help rebuild Britain after the war, settled here. Before long, the area became the site of race riots,

Bedrooms & Hallways: sexual exploration at the bakery: Cash Bar, Talbot Road

dramatised in Julien Temple's extended pop promo *Absolute Beginners*, which was filmed on a huge recreation of Notting Hill's streets (nicknamed 'Napoli' in the movie), built on the backlot at Shepperton Studios.

The L-Shaped Room: the Brockash Road bedsit; St Luke's Road

It was the real Notting Hill which often supplied the scruffy, flaking backdrop to the new wave of socially concerned dramas in the sixties, typical of which is Bryan Forbes' 1962 movie *The L-Shaped Room*. In the film, French actress Leslie Caron (the movie needed a big international star) shares a rundown house with cohabitees representing a daring compendium of sixties issues: Brock Peters (race), Patricia Phoenix (prostitution) and Cicely Courtneidge (lesbianism), while Caron herself is in town for an abortion. The bedsit on the fictitious 'Brockash Road' was **4 St Luke's Road** (**18**) at Westbourne Park Road.

Performance: Turner Purple's retreat: Powis Square

Immediately to the right of number 4 is the arch of the cobbled **St Luke's Mews**, where Sunny (Sienna Guillory) lives in Alex Jovy's *Sorted*. And, yes, it is true what the characters say, this is the mews where Paula Yates lived and died. It's here, too, that Bill

The Man Who Knew Too Little: Bill Murray gets involved: St Luke's Mews

Withnail & I: the Mother Black Cap, Camden: Babushka, Tavistock Crescent

Murray gets mugged, all the while assuming it's part of the Theatre of Life experience, in Jon Amiel's comedy thriller *The Man Who Knew Too Little*. **6 St Luke's Road** is '6 Bishop's Mews', where Murray first encounters Joanne Whalley in her fetching French maid outfit in the same movie.

Continue north on St Luke's Road. **Babushka, 41 Tavistock Crescent** (**19**; see **Bars & Restaurants**, p17), used to be the old Irish boozer the Mother Black Cap, which can be seen in *Withnail & I*. Babushka itself can be glimpsed briefly in *Virtual Sexuality*.

Notting Hill landmarks such as Trellick Tower and the **Westway Flyover**, roaring behind Babushka, are an indication that maybe we're not in Camden anymore. Beneath the flyover, behind Babushka, lay the vacant lot where the encampment stood in *Sammy and Rosie Get Laid*, Stephen Frears and Hanif Kureishi's failed attempt to repeat the success of *My Beautiful Laundrette*.

Continue on to Lancaster Road. In the Beatles 1964 film début *A Hard Day's Night*, when Ringo Starr escapes the pressure of the TV theatre and goes walkabout with his camera, it's in **Lancaster Road** that he's spotted by a brace of squealing teen fans while taking arty shots of a milk crate. **20 All Saints Road** (**20**), on the northeast corner of Lancaster Road, is the old junk shop he dives into for a disguise of peaked cap and old raincoat. The shop is now a ladies' lingerie boutique.

Turn left into All Saints Road itself. **Manor, 6-8 All Saints Road** (see **Bars & Restaurants**, p18), which used to be Mas Café, was transformed into

A Hard Day's Night: the junk shop: All Saints Road

Clive's restaurant, where Helen organises the grand opening in *Sliding Doors*.

Continue on to Bosworth Road. **The Earl**

Derby, 50 Bosworth Road (**21**; see **Bars & Restaurants**, p17) at Southern Row, appears in *Intimacy*.

One of Notting Hill's great attractions, of course, is the Portobello Road market. The famous street market runs from Notting Hill north to Ladbroke Grove.

Sliding Doors: Clive's new restaurant: Manor, All Saints Road

Intimacy: the pub theatre: The Earl Derby, Bosworth Road

The southern Notting Hill end is the famous antiques market. Time was, you could take a chance on picking up a bit of discarded junk that might just turn out to be a treasure, but now it caters largely to tourists and you'll need to be a bit more imaginative in your choice of street market to find that unspotted Rembrandt. The centre of the market is fruit and veg, while north of the Westway it remains a local flea market. But wherever there's picturesque squalor and cheap accommodation, the artsy bohos are bound to move in, and gentrification follows. Notting Hill is now the heart of West London medialand, with writers, actors and popstars hiking up the property values. The release of the film *Notting Hill* finally sent rents and house prices into the stratosphere and, ironically, forced out some of the smaller local businesses.

Portfolio, Golborne Road (**22**), at Bevington Road, has been through several incarnations, most usually as an art gallery, but it has twice featured in films as a restaurant. In 1991, it was the diner belonging to American Brad Dourif in Hanif Kureishi's low-key directorial début *London Kills Me*, but it is much more famous as the failed restaurant of Hugh Grant's friend Richard McCabe in *Notting Hill*. Also on **Golborne Road**, Simon Penry-Jones earns a crust cleaning windscreens in sex-swap comedy *Virtual Sexuality*.

The section of **Portobello Road** (**23**) just north of Westway is where Bill Murray gets the wrong phone call that plunges him into a murky world of intrigue in *The Man Who Knew Too Little*. You won't be invited to join in, as there is no phone

Notting Hill: the failed restaurant: Portfolio, Golborne Road

The Man Who Knew Too Little: the 'Theatre of Life': Portobello Road

box. **309 Portobello Road**, at Raddington Road, is the house where the 'Theatre of Life' scenario goes horribly wrong when a real hitman gets involved.

A little off the tour is a ghoulish sidetrack. **Ruston Mews (24)** has been developed beyond all recognition, and had a name change too. Not surprising, since it was originally known as Rillington Place. Number 10, the last house on the left of this small cul-de-sac, was the home of serial killer John Reginald Christie, who murdered a number of young women as well as his own wife and hid the bodies in the garden and within the house itself, as a subsequent tenant discovered. Among his victims was Beryl Evans, the wife of one of Christie's lodgers, Timothy Evans. Christie also killed the couple's young baby. He found a perfect fall-guy in the gullible and none-too-bright Evans, ensuring his silence with a story that Beryl and the child had died during a botched illegal abortion. Evans was subsequently hanged for the double murder in one of the most notorious miscarriages of British justice. *10 Rillington*

Place, Richard Fleischer's grim account of the case, with Richard Attenborough as the seedy sadist – undercutting his usual cosy image – paints a far more accurate picture of glum, grey post-war London than the usual pop-coloured confections. It was filmed in the real Rillington Place before the street was redeveloped.

Notting Hill: bumping into Julia: Coffee Shop, Westbourne Park Road

Notting Hill: Hugh Grant's famous front door: Westbourne Park Road

The Frog and Firkin, 96 Ladbroke Grove (25; see **Bars & Restaurants**, p17), can be seen in *Mike Bassett: England Manager*.

Coffee Shop, 303 Westbourne Park Road (26; see **Bars & Restaurants**, p17), appears right at the beginning of *Notting Hill*. Next door, on the corner of Westbourne Park and Portobello Road, was the empty property outside which Hugh Grant bumps into Julia Roberts. And it's now – Coffee Republic. A few yards away across Portobello Road, **280 Westbourne Park Road** is the exterior of Grant's flat in the film. The rundown bedsit interior was a studio set and bore no resemblance whatsoever to what actually lay behind the famous blue door, for this was actually home to the screenwriter Richard Curtis. Rather than the homely mess of a flat which confronted Roberts, the converted chapel boasts a courtyard garden, a 1,000 square-foot reception room and a galleried mezzanine. Shortly after filming it was put on the market for £1.3 million, which must make *Notting Hill* the most expensive house ad ever. The blue door, since removed and auctioned off for charity, has now been replaced by a rather anonymous black one.

I Hired a Contract Killer: Jean-Pierre Léaud's flat: Westbourne Park Road

The strangest thing about *Notting Hill* the movie is its total lack of ethnic diversity. Since the fifties, the area has been defined by its large and vibrant Afro-Caribbean community, and hosts the annual Notting Hill Carnival, one of Europe's most spectacular street festivals, held over the August Bank Holiday (*website: www.nottinghillcarnival.net.uk*). In fact, the size of the event has grown out of all proportion to the narrow streets of the area, and there's talk of diverting the festivities to the more manageable open space of Hyde Park.

The door immediately to the left of number 280, the corner flat at **227 Portobello Road**, was home to the terminally depressed Jean-Pierre Léaud in *I Hired a Contract Killer*, from Finnish director Aki Kaurismäki, the genius or fruitcake – according to taste – who gave us the bequiffed *Leningrad Cowboys Go America* and *Hamlet Goes Business*, with the titular character running a rubber duck factory. Léaud's flat overlooks what was the Warwick Castle pub, where he meets improbable flower seller Margi Clark. In line with the gentrification of the area, the bar

Notting Hill and Dirty Weekend: the tattoo parlour: Saints Tattoo Parlour, Portobello Road

Crimetime: after the crime re-enactment: Ground Floor Bar, Portobello Road

has been given a smart makeover and is now the **Castle**.

Saints Tattoo Parlour, 201 Portobello Road, is where the guy who got drunk and now can't remember why he chose a tattoo reading 'I love Ken' emerges from, under the opening credits of *Notting Hill*. It's also the 'Brighton' tattoo parlour that Bella (Lia Williams) peeks into in Michael Winner's film of Helen Zahavi's *Dirty Weekend*.

Look down **Blenheim Crescent**, the side street full of snow during the winter section of the 'four seasons' scene in *Notting Hill*. This is also where you'll find the real Travel Bookstore, the model for Hugh Grant's bookshop in the film.

Opposite the tattoo parlour, on the corner of Talbot Road, is **Ground Floor Bar, 186 Portobello Road (27**; see **Bars & Restaurants**, p17) at Talbot Road, where Sadie Frost and Stephen Baldwin grab a drink in *Crimetime*. They then head over the road for a raunchy sex session in the doorway alongside the **Electric Cinema, 191 Portobello Road** (see **Entertainment: Cinemas**, p25). Chas (Luke de Lacy) and Justine (Laura Fraser) walk past the cinema during their row in *Virtual Sexuality*. It can also be seen in *London Kills Me* and *Circus*, and during the bravura 'four seasons' sequence in *Notting Hill*. The scene ends, in spring, at the **Salvation Army Building, 205 Portobello Road**, which is also where Chas and Justine finish their spat.

Gong, 142 Portobello Road (28), a furniture and furnishings shop, was transformed into the 'Travel Book Company', where Anna Scott (Julia Roberts) browses through books on Turkey in *Notting Hill* (at the time of filming it was Nicholls Antique Arcade).

Continue north on Portobello. The antiquey section of the road, around

Circus: the Brighton cinema: Electric Cinema, Portobello Road

Notting Hill: Hugh Grant's travel bookshop: Gong, Portobello Road

Otley: Tom Courtenay's digs: Portobello Road

Westbourne Grove, was a favourite backdrop during the sixties. Tom Courtenay strolls past the stalls behind the opening credits of Dick Clement's sixties spy spoof *Otley*. Courtenay's digs are at **67 Portobello Road** – the shop was called Trad at the time. Almost directly opposite, alongside the red-painted junkshop Alice's, is Denbigh Close. **18 Denbigh Close (29**), is the bric-a-brac strewn pad of Charlie Croker (Michael Caine) in *The Italian Job*. Yul Brynner discovers that **Lipka Antique Gallery, 282 Westbourne Grove (30**), is the front for smooth villain Charles Gray (famous as The Criminologist in *The Rocky Horror Picture Show*) in Sam Wanamaker's 1969 spy thriller *The File of the Golden Goose* in the days when it was the Antiques Supermarket.

The Italian Job: Michael Caine's swinging pad: Denbigh Close

On the corner diagonally opposite is **The Earl of Lonsdale, 277-281 Westbourne Grove (31**; see **Bars & Restaurants**, p17), formerly Henekey's, which can be seen in *Otley*.

22 Portobello Road was, incidentally, the real home of George Orwell, author of *1984*, *Animal Farm* and *Keep the Aspidistra Flying*.

Turn right into Chepstow Villas. Facing you is a pair of houses. The right-hand one is **47 Kensington Park Road (32**), home of villainous Charles Gray, where Edward Woodward is given house room, in *The File of the Golden Goose*.

Notting Hill hangouts such as Damien Hirst's The Pharmacy and Café Rouge feature in the book of *Bridget Jones's Diary*,

The File of the Golden Goose: villain Charles Gray's house: Kensington Park Road

The File of the Golden Goose: the villain's gallery: Lipka Antique Gallery, Westbourne Grove

Madame Sousatzka: home of music teacher Shirley MacLaine: Stanley Crescent

but not in the film. The **Notting Hill Coronet, 103 Notting Hill Gate** (see **Entertainment: Cinemas**, p26), is where William Thacker watches fictitious Anna Scott movie *Helix* in *Notting Hill*. Notting Hill's other cinema is the **Gate Cinema, 87 Notting Hill Gate** (see **Entertainment: Cinemas**, p25).

On to **Stanley Gardens (33)**, a lot more upscale than it appears, littered with builders' skips, in John Schlesinger's 1988 film *Madame Sousatzka*. At the end of the road is **10 Stanley Crescent**, home to eccentric music teacher Shirley MacLaine in this drama, co-written by Ruth Prawer Jhabvala, the regular screenwriter of the Merchant-Ivory team. At the other end of Stanley Gardens is the 1875 Victorian Classical **St Peter's Church**, also seen in the movie, with a lavish interior designed by Charles Barry Jr, son of the architect of the Houses of Parliament. This is the church tower seen from the roof of Hugh Grant's flat in *Notting Hill*, and it also features in *Spiceworld the Movie*.

On **Ladbroke Grove (34)** at Lansdowne Road, Richard E Grant hangs onto the side of the wheel-clamping vehicle as it attempts to shake him off in *Jack & Sarah*. **91 Lansdowne Road** is the home of Gina McKee and Tim McInnerny, where Hugh Grant amazes everyone with his surprise date, megastar Julia Roberts, at the birthday party in *Notting Hill*. The entrance to the private communal garden Grant and Roberts climb into is **Rosmead Gardens, Rosmead Road (35)**, and it's not as cutesy as it looks in the movie. This is a private garden, by the way, so don't even think about trying the same trick (there is also quite a drop into the garden).

After the success of *Blowup*, Michelangelo Antonioni returned to West

Notting Hill: the birthday party: Lansdowne Road

Notting Hill: the communal gardens: Rosmead Gardens, Rosmead Road

The Passenger: home of doomed TV reporter Jack Nicholson: Lansdowne Crescent

London to film scenes for his equally inscrutable 1975 film *The Passenger*. TV reporter David Locke (Jack Nicholson) lurks by **St John's Church, Lansdowne Crescent (36)**, opposite his house at **4 Lansdowne Crescent**, before deciding to follow the itinerary of the dead man with whom he's swapped identities.

Turn down **Lansdowne Rise (37)**, the hill the baby carriage careers down as the Antichrist Damien Thorn (Sam Neill) attempts to rub out the opposition in *The Final Conflict*.

Go west on Notting Hill Gate and turn into Hillsleigh Road, then right into Campden Hill Square. **13 Campden Hill Square (38)** is the house that gorilla-fixated Trotskyite Morgan Delt (David Warner) shares with his upper-class wife Leonie (Vanessa Redgrave) in Karel Reisz's archetypal sixties movie *Morgan – A Suitable Case For Treatment*. Around the corner, opposite the gardens, you can see the bay-front where the workmen clamber over the scaffolding. Coincidentally, a blue plaque opposite, at **16 Campden Hill Square**, records that Charles Morgan, writer and critic, lived here, while **number 23** was home to war poet Siegfried Sassoon. **96 Campden Hill Square** is the birthplace of Daniel Day-Lewis.

Holland Park School, Airlie Road (39), off Campden Hill Road, is where gauche teacher Michael Crawford teaches in *The Knack*.

The Halcyon Hotel, 81 Holland Park (40; see **Hotels**, p10), features in *The Saint*. Meryl Streep's

The Final Conflict: the careering baby carriage: Lansdowne Rise

Morgan – A Suitable Case For Treatment: Morgan's house: Campden Hill Square

The Saint: hideout of Simon Templar: The Halcyon Hotel, Holland Park

It Happened Here: punch-up with the SS: The Prince of Wales, Pottery Lane

'Battersea' house in *Plenty* is actually in Holland Park. But though Bridget Jones lives in the area in the original book, she moved south of the river (to Borough) for the movie.

The Prince of Wales, Pottery Lane (41) at the junction of Portland Road, is the pub where the locals get into a violent fracas with the British SS in Kevin Brownlow's astonishing fake documentary of life under Nazi occupation, *It Happened Here*.

Penzance Place, on the right, leads into Portland Road. **Orsino Restaurant, Penzance Place (42)**, used to be a pub. Rita Tushingham and Michael Crawford wheel an iron bedstead around the outside of the pub in *The Knack*, while Donal Donnelly (who went on to play Archbishop Gilday in *The Godfather: Part III*) takes a short cut through it, picking up a stack of ashtrays and bottles in a sight gag that Richard Lester had left over from the Beatles' movie *A Hard Day's Night.*

Blowup: David Hemmings' studio exterior: Pottery Lane

Jack & Sarah: bringing up baby: St James's Gardens

Continue north on Pottery Lane. **77 Pottery Lane**, next to the currently closed Earl of Zetland pub, was the exterior of David Hemmings' photographic studio in Michelangelo Antonioni's seminal *Blowup*. The name of the road reflects the area's history. In the 19th century this was an area of potteries and brickfields, and these very desirable properties were among the poorest housing in London. Just to the north, on Walmer Road opposite Avondale Park, stands one of the few remaining bottle kilns (as in 'bottle shaped'), where the pottery was fired.

Head down Princedale Road. On the right, **49 Princes Place** was the studio of *Vogue* photographer John

Cowans, who acted as advisor on *Blowup*. This is the studio interior where Hemmings snaps away for the archetypal sixties fashion shoot.

Head west into the quiet square of St James's Gardens. The house, where Jack (Richard E Grant) brings up baby Sarah, with the help of gentleman-of-the-road William (Ian McKellen) and American kook Amy (Samantha Mathis), in *Jack & Sarah*, is **22 St James's Gardens (43)**.

On the south side of the square, opposite St James Norlands church, **2 St James's Gardens (44)** (which, at the time of filming, was the house of TV presenter Robin Day) is the London home of smitten Victorian gent Charles (Jeremy Irons) in *The French Lieutenant's Woman.*

Addison Avenue, at St James' Gardens, is where the Griswalds – Chevy Chase and family – knock Eric Idle off his bike in *National Lampoon's European Vacation.*

The Sikh temple, **Central Gurdwara, 62 Queensdale Road (45)** at the corner of Norland Road, with its gleaming gold domes, is the scene of the boisterous wedding in *Bend It Like Beckham.*

In the starry, but universally-panned, *Parting Shots*, Michael Winner takes the revenge-movie premise to its logical conclusion, with Chris Rea terminating just about everyone who ever crossed him. As always, the police look on helplessl, and **Latimer Road** is the tube station where Rea evades them.

The Bramley Arms, Freston Road (46; see **Bars & Restaurants**, p17), has a long history as a film location, appearing in *The Lavender Hill Mob, Betrayal, Leo the Last, Quadrophenia* and *Sid and Nancy.* Opposite the Bramley is the scrapyard where smoothy Pete works in *Quadrophenia.*

The French Lieutenant's Woman: the London house of Jeremy Irons: St James's Gardens

Bend It Like Beckham: the wedding at the Sikh temple: Central Gurdwara, Queensdale Road

The Lavender Hill Mob, Quadrophenia and Sid and Nancy: familiar pub: The Bramley Arms, Freston Road

Far North London: Muswell Hill to Brimsdown

There's an odd mix of Mike Leigh suburbia and gun-toting gangsterism in this section, which is less a walk than a scattered selection of north London locations. If you're not driving, you'll be relying on the rail networks.

Starting Point: Muswell Hill

Alexandra Palace, Muswell Hill, was a great Victorian project, the 'People's Palace', built in 1873 to rival South London's Crystal Palace, but seems to have proved extraordinarily flammable. Destroyed by fire two weeks after it opened, it was rebuilt, only to burn down again in 1980. In the intervening years, it acted as a WWII POW camp, and its commanding position overlooking North London made it ideal for the first BBC television transmissions. The eastern section of Alexandra Palace, affectionately known as 'Ally Pally', was the British Broadcasting Corporation's main transmission centre for the twenty years from 1936 to 1956, when it was downgraded to providing news broadcasts only. While still a gutted ruin, the Palace's central Concert Hall became 'Victory Square' for Michael Radford's 1984 film of George Orwell's satire *Nineteen Eighty-Four*. There are historic tours, where you can see the original 'Beeb' studios and the enormous Harry Willis organ, one Sunday every month (℃ *020.8365.2121; website: www.alexandrapalace.com*). Stuart Townsend and Dan Futterman rummage in a rubbish skip in front of the Palace in underrated comedy caper *Shooting Fish*. The Palace was rebuilt and reopened as a conference venue in 1988.

Fortismere School, Tetherdown, is the school where Arsenal fan Colin Firth teaches in the movie adaptation of Nick Hornby's novel *Fever Pitch*.

1999's *Love, Honour and Obey* isn't so much bad exactly as irritating. Did the world really need another London gangster movie, with cool boys showing off their shaky knowledge of incomprehensible hardman slang? But Kathy Burke is always watchable, and Ray Winstone also manages to rise above the self-indulgence, even while he indulges in a bit of karaoke at **The Queen's Hotel, 26 Broadway**

Nineteen Eighty-Four: Victory Square: Alexandra Palace, Muswell Hill

Love, Honour and Obey: the karaoke bar: Queen's Hotel, Hornsey

Parade (see **Bars & Restaurants**, p18), Hornsey.

Just to the east, in Harringay, is another Grade II listed boozer built for the same entrepreneur, John Cathles Hill, **The Salisbury, 1 Grand Parade, Green Lanes** (see **Bars & Restaurants**, p18), at the corner of St Ann's Road. The Salisbury's slightly faded ambience can be seen in *Chaplin*, as 'Fagan's' in *The Long Good Friday* and as itself in *Spider*.

Cross Green Lanes to Duckett Road. It's gangsters again and, guess what, Ray Winstone again. Antonia Bird's *Face*, though, with Robert Carlyle as the embittered post-Socialist trading agitation for aggravation, has a bit more substance than the average heist movie. **56 Duckett Road**, alongside Haringey Passage, is the house where Damon Albarn is found murdered. Robert Carlyle legs it from the crime scene down **Haringey Passage**, past **South Harringay Infants School, Pemberton Road**. Ray Winstone and Philip Davis get caught up in a major shoot out on **Allison Road**, where the cop car bursts into flames.

The **Castle Climbing Centre, Green Lanes** (*www.castle-climbing.co.uk*), is where Heather Graham meets Joseph Fiennes to learn how to climb in Chen Kaige's thriller *Killing Me Softly*.

The Long Good Friday, Chaplin and **Spider:** classic boozer: The Salisbury, Grand Parade, Green Lanes

During the late fifties, **83 Oakleigh Avenue, Whetstone**, was home to Peter Sellers, and dubbed 'St Fred's' in that chortlesome Goonish style.

Princess Park Manor, 52 Friern Barnett Road, New Southgate, is now a luxury apartment complex. This seems a fitting coda to Lindsay Anderson's scabrous state-of-the-nation satire *Britannia Hospital*, as this

Face: Damon Albarn is shot: Duckett Road

Face: burning cop car: Allison Road

was once that very hospital. Friern Barnett Hospital, built in the mid-19th century as the notorious Colney Hatch Asylum, but closed and crumbling for years,

Britannia Hospital: state-of-the-nation hospital: Princess Park Manor, Friern Barnett Road

provided the ideal backdrop to the third and least of Lindsay Anderson's Mick Travis trilogy, which began so spectacularly with the anarchic *if....* and meandered with the Brechtian *O Lucky Man!* before plummetting to earth with this bilious allegory. Friern Barnett is also the institution where psycho Keith Allen is incarcerated in Vadim Jean's 1994 horror movie *Beyond Bedlam*. This film also features the **Grove Inn, Friern Barnet Road**, in the days when it was The Turrets pub.

The North London suburbs of **Totteridge** and **Woodside** were used for much of Monty Python's first movie, an assembly of the most famous TV sketches, *And Now For Something Completely Different*. The film, made entirely on location, was based in a disused dairy in Totteridge.

Continue on to Mill Hill East (*tube: Northern line*). In Stefan Schwartz's comedy *Shooting Fish*, scam artists Stuart Townsend and Dan Futterman inventively turn a disused **gasometer** into a cosy home. You can see the entrance to this desirable residence between numbers 12 and 13 on **Lee Road, Mill Hill East**, off Devonshire Road.

The **Aegean Pools, 2 Hale Lane** (℡ *020 8959.6845*), Mill Hill, is where Paul Freeman is first seen doing high dives in *The Long Good Friday*, before he's offed by a young Pierce Brosnan – though the murder was filmed in another swimming baths.

If you go to Brighton to check out the dance hall in *Quadrophenia*, where Jimmy leaps from the balcony to impress the crowd, you'll find that the interior is an aquarium. **LA Fitness, Winchmore Hill Road** at Dennis Parade, used to be the old Royalty Ballroom, which provided the exterior.

The streamlined deco lines of **Southgate Underground Station** appear in Angela Pope's 1994 film *Captives*, with prison dentist Julia Ormond conducting an unlikely affair with convicted murderer Tim Roth. The station and **Grovelands Park**, can also be seen in *Stevie*, a rather stagey adaptation of Hugh Whitemore's play about the poet Stevie

Shooting Fish: the gasometer home: Lee Road, Mill Hill East

Quadrophenia: the Brighton dance hall: LA Fitness, Winchmore Hill Road

Stevie: Stevie's home – in the movie: Avondale Road, Palmer's Green

Smith ("not waving but drowning…"), with Glenda Jackson excellent as usual in the title role and Lindsay Anderson regular Mona Washbourne as her formidable Aunt. **17 Avondale Road, Palmer's Green**, is the home they share in the film, though the poet's real home, as a blue plaque indicates, was **1 Avondale Road**.

Grovelands House, The Bourne, Southgate, is the hospital where Michael Denison recovers in the 1949 wartime melodrama *Landfall*.

Southgate is also the neighbourhood of photographer Timothy Spall in Mike Leigh's award-winning film *Secrets & Lies*. **87 Whitehouse Way**, at Hampden Way, is Spall's house, while the **Studio on the Green, 34 The Green, Winchmore Hill**, became his photographic studio.

What, no cello? Mike Leigh's *Life Is Sweet* bounces onto the screen with a happy-happy-happy dance tune. The hall where Alison Steadman is taking a dance class for tots is **Celbic Hall, 77 Lancaster Road**, Enfield. The house she shares with incurable procrastinator Jim Broadbent and bulimic daughter Jane Horrocks, is **7 Wolsey Road**, off Brick Lane. I'm sure there's no culinary connection whatsoever between Timothy Spall's truly disturbing 'Regret Rien' restaurant ("Pork cyst… tongues in a rhubarb hollandaise… liver in lager and clams in ham.") and the establishment where it was filmed. After a spell as a Greek taverna, it's now **Chaseside Indian Restaurant, 135-137 Chase Side** (© 020 8367.9919), Enfield. Just don't ask for Tripe Soufflé.

David Niven takes an untypically unsympathetic role as Jasper O'Leary, the arro-

Secrets & Lies: Timothy Spall's home: Whitehouse Way

Secrets & Lies: Spall's studio: Studio-on-the-Green, The Green, Winchmore Hill

gant English squire descending on the jovially 'Oirish' village of 'Rathbarney' like a supercilious plague, in Mario Zampi's 1954 film *Happy Ever After*.

Life Is Sweet: the Regret Rien: Chaseside Indian Restaurant, Chase Side

Kicking off like *The Quiet Man*, it soon turns into a blackish, slightly sub-Ealing farce, with the locals unwittingly vying with each other to bump off their bumptious landlord. But it's not quite as Irish as it might seem. The home of Major McGlusky (Michael Shepley) and his daughter Serena (Yvonne De Carlo) is **Forty Hall Banqueting and Conference Centre, Forty Hill**.

Roy (Ward) Baker's 1957 movie *The One That Got Away* tells the true story of Franz von Werra, the WWII flying ace with the distinction, as the title suggests, of being the only German POW to have escaped and made it back to the Fatherland. The camp seen in the movie is **Trent Park Mansion, Bramley Road, Trent Park**, now part of the campus of Middlesex University, which was indeed once a POW camp. The mansion can be seen again in Michael Winner's 1967 satire on the advertising business *I'll Never Forget What's 'is Name*, with Orson Welles.

Trent Park, now the Middlesex University campus, has been used frequently in films, particularly horror movies: **West Lodge Park** and **Trent Park** appear in *The Devil Rides Out*, **Oak Wood** in *The Satanic Rites of Dracula*, and the eastern edge of **Rough Lot Wood** in Ken Russell's *The Lair of the White Worm*. **Cat Hill Campus** features in *Buster*.

The disused **Prince of Wales Hospital, Tottenham Green East**, is the building site where Robert Carlyle and Ricky Tomlinson work in Ken Loach's *Riff Raff*.

Mildred (the late and much missed Yootha Joyce) takes driving lessons around Hadley Green in UK TV sitcom spinoff *George and Mildred*. The stables of **Hadley House** are the prep school attended by the son of their long-suffering, sniffy neighbours, the Fourmiles.

Unfortunately now much modernised, **Brimsdown Station** is where a fraught Sidney Stratton (Alec Guinness) tries to catch a train in the Ealing classic *The Man in the White Suit*.

East London: Liverpool Street to Beckton

Hollywood's East End, perpetually fog-shrouded, and thronged with gin-soaked whores, has been a cinematic staple of cinema from DW Griffith's *Broken Blossoms* to the Hughes brothers' *From Hell*. The real East End was indeed for a long time an area of dismal poverty, where waves of immigrants – Huguenots, Jews, Bengalis – huddled together in the narrow streets around the bustling old port. The fierce sense of neighbourhood and distrust of outsiders and authority allowed such notorious gangs as the Krays to flourish. So it's no surprise that this tour is heavy on gangsterism and atmosphere.

Starting Point: Liverpool Street Station

Liverpool Street Station is mainly a commuter station, servicing Essex (with the Great Eastern Line), East Anglia and Stansted Airport. The station was given a radical makeover, including some rebuilding, as part of the massive Broadgate development in the eighties. The bright, airy concourse is hardly recognisable as the smoke-blackened, 19th-century edifice of David Lynch's *The Elephant Man*, but this is indeed where John Merrick (John Hurt), arriving back in London from the continent, is chased by a roaring mob down into the toilets: "I am not an animal. I am a human being." The decayed Victorian splendour of the station would have been reason enough to film here, but Liverpool Street really is where Merrick arrived from Brussels. Look up at the delicate wrought iron spider webs to imagine what the station once looked like, and at the sparkly clean brickwork and gothicky windows above Platform 1 to see the shell of the building as it was in the movie. The bright new station with its modern facilities is a boon for the traveller, but it's hard not to feel the loss of the original wooden

The Elephant Man: "I am not an animal": Liverpool Street Station

Mission: Impossible: meeting up with Voight: Liverpool Street Station

Spiceworld the Movie: the Turin TV special: Broadgate Arena

The Golden Bowl: buying the bowl in Bloomsbury: Brushfield Street

walkways. A carefully framed shot transforms Liverpool Street Station into 'Liverpool Station' for Sam Wanamaker's 1969 film *The File of the Golden Goose*, when Yul Brynner and Edward Woodward head 'up North' to track down a gang of international counterfeiters. And the revamped station is changing already. A row of cash-machines at the foot of the stairs from the Liverpool Street entrance has replaced the telephones where Tom Cruise meets up with Jon Voight in *Mission: Impossible*.

Walk through Octagon Arcade, the row of shops at the west end of the station concourse, turn right at the huge rust-iron sculpture, and find yourself in sunny Italy. Remember *Spiceworld the Movie*, and the girls' trip to Turin for the TV special? You didn't really believe the budget stretched to overseas filming did you? The 'Turin' arena where the Spices perform 'I'm the Leader of the Gang (I Am)' – without Gary Glitter, whose role was judiciously excised after filming when the nasty details of his private life became public – is the **Broadgate Arena**.

Attached to Liverpool Street Station is **The Great Eastern Hotel, Liverpool Street** (see **Hotels**, p11), which was used for scenes in Lindsay Anderson's *O Lucky Man!* It's also where Bill Murray ends up perched on a ledge in *The Man Who Knew Too Little*.

Across Liverpool Street from the rail terminus is **Liverpool Street Underground Station**, above which is the safe house where Tom Cruise

The Man Who Knew Too Little: teetering on the ledge: The Great Eastern Hotel

Mission: Impossible: the safe house: Liverpool Street Underground Station

holes up, with Jean Reno, in *Mission: Impossible*. It's in front of the tube station that the firm picks up another member of the team for the big job in Antonia Bird's *Face*.

A casualty of the area's redevelopment is the site of one of the most enduring images in recent London cinema. Whenever the social problems of the King's Cross area are discussed, there's an inevitable reference to Neil Jordan's *Mona Lisa* and the hellish bridge where prostitutes ply their trade. In fact, the scene was filmed on Pindar Street, a road bridge which once spanned the railway lines at the rear of Liverpool Street Station.

The basement HQ of the monks out to destroy Antichrist Damien in *The Final Conflict* is now part of the **One Gun Street** development, opposite the eastern end of Artillery Passage.

Head north up Crispin Street and turn left onto Brushfield Street. On the north side of the street is the old **Spitalfields Market**. It can be seen in the 2003 version of *Nicholas Nickleby*, with Charlie Hunnam in the title role and Jamie Bell as Smike. The old eastern section is listed, but the 1920 west section is up for redevelopment.

Opposite the market is a row of perfect period shops. **52 Brushfield Street** became 'Harris's', the jeweller shop where Uma Thurman and Jeremy Northam discover the titular gift in the Merchant-Ivory adaptation of Henry James' novel *The Golden Bowl*. Notice how carefully positioned greenery hides the more modern London Wool and Fruit Exchange buildings further down the street. In the background of the scene you can see Nicholas Hawksmoor's magisterial **Christ Church Spitalfields**, on Commercial Street at the eastern end of Brushfield Street. Inside the church, the newly-awakened Jim (Cillian Murphy) discovers the sea of dead (and not-so-dead) bodies, before being attacked by the infected priest, in *28 Days Later*. The church, or rather a recreation of it, looms over the Victorian East End seen in the Hughes brothers' *From Hell*, with Johnny Depp on the trail of Jack the Ripper. In fact a great swathe of Spitalfields was immaculately recreated in Prague for the film,

28 Days Later: the corpse-strewn church: Christ Church Spitalfields

The Crying Game: Dil's hairdressing salon: Fournier Street

The Crying Game: spying on the leak: City Spice, Brick Lane

Lock, Stock and Two Smoking Barrels: 'Hatchet' Harry's porn empire: Blackman's Shoes, Cheshire Street

Born Romantic: Jimi Mistry's house: Sclater Street

including a facsimile of the Ten Bells pub, where the prostitutes congregate.

On the northern corner of Fournier Street, opposite Christ Church, is the real **Ten Bells** (see **Bars & Restaurants**, p19), for many years renamed the Jack the Ripper, and containing memorabilia from the case. It has now reverted to its original name.

The dilapidated look of Fournier Street belies its position as the current centre of Britart, being longtime home to Gilbert & George and, more recently, to Tracey Emin. **3 Fournier Street**, almost alongside the Ten Bells, was transformed into the hairdressing salon where Dil (Jaye Davidson) works in Neil Jordan's *The Crying Game*. The Georgian terraced houses of the area are a national treasure. Fortuitously saved from redevelopment by the poverty of the area, they're now up for grabs and renovation as the area is relentlessly gentrified.

Follow your nose on to Brick Lane, home to the famous market. This narrow thoroughfare, guaranteed to set your stomach rumbling with the spicy smells emanating from its many restaurants, was once the East End's Jewish ghetto, and is now, cleaned up and prettified, the heart of the Bengali community.

The corner of **Osborn Road** and **Old Montague Street**, at the south end of Brick Lane, can be seen in the 1950 movie *Night and the City*.

City Spice, 138 Brick Lane (see **Bars & Restaurants**, p18), was once

the famed Clifton Restaurant, where Irish terrorist Miranda Richardson spies on Jaye Davidson and Stephen Rea in *The Crying Game*.

Turn right into **Pedley Street** and continue along the narrow road to the dark turning under the railway line. Just ahead of you is Vallance Road, home to Ronnie and Reggie, the notorious Kray twins who ruled this manor in the sixties, though 'Fortress Vallance', their house at 178 Vallance Road, has been demolished. This is real bruiser territory in the movies too. The stretch of cobbled street in front of the arch is where the Young Gangster (Paul Bettany) drops a taxi onto the recalcitrant debtor to impress boss Freddie Mays (David Thewlis) in *Gangster No. 1*. Eddie (Nick Moran) and Bacon (Jason Statham) leg it down the rather intimidating steps to the railway bridge at the end of the tunnel after the law descends on their street stall scam at the opening of *Lock, Stock and Two Smoking Barrels*.

Cross over the bridge onto Cheshire Street and turn right towards Ramsey Street. On the left is **Repton Boys Club**, where the boxing-mad Krays once worked out. This is the site of the catastrophic three-card-brag game in *Lock, Stock and Two Smoking Barrels*, as well as Terence Rigby's boxing club, where he's quizzed by US cop Harvey Keitel in *The Young Americans*.

Turn back toward Brick Lane. On the left, **Blackman's Shoes, 42-44 Cheshire Street**, is the exterior of 'Hatchet' Harry's office – "Harry Lonsdale: Porn King" – in *Lock, Stock and Two Smoking Barrels*.

There is a bit of a respite from the relentless machismo at **97-99 Sclater Street**, just off Brick Lane, where bumbling mugger Eddie (Jimi Mistry) lives in casual squalor with his vague dad Barney (Kenneth Cranham) in *Born Romantic*.

Just to the south is Elder Street, a tiny cobbled street off Folgate Street. The audacious

Gangster No. 1: dropping the taxi: Pedley Street

Lock, Stock and Two Smoking Barrels: the catastrophic card game: Repton Boys Club

Velvet Goldmine: the Dublin doorway: Elder Street

Snatch: Sol's pawn shop: Teesdale Street

Gangster No. 1: burning down Freddie's club: Corbridge Crescent

Shiner: Andy Serkis' flat: Apollo House, St Jude's Road

Spider: sex under the bridge: Regent's Canal

opening of Todd Haynes' *Velvet Goldmine* has the infant Oscar Wilde deposited on a Dublin doorstep by aliens. Just north of Spitalfields Market, you can find the doorway of **15 Elder Street**. Across the street, at **number 32**, lived painter Mark Gertler, played by Rufus Sewell in *Carrington*.

Mansford Street, which has been completely redeveloped, and **Hackney Road** are the backdrops to Carol Reed's 1955 film *A Kid for Two Farthings*, a colourful and sentimental fable set in the old Jewish East End, with young Jonathan Ashmore convinced his one-horned goat is a unicorn.

Enough of this softie stuff. **88 Teesdale Street** became the pawn shop of Sol (Lennie James) in *Snatch*.

Apollo House, St Jude's Road, is the home of Mel (Andy Serkis) in a misjudged scene of extreme nastiness in *Shiner*.

In **Bethnal Green Town Hall, Cambridge Heath Road** at Patriot Square, is the wood-panelled office interior of 'Hatchet' Harry (PH Moriarty) in *Lock, Stock and Two Smoking Barrels* (supposedly above his Cheshire Street porn shop). The same office became Benicio Del Toro's tailor's in another Guy Richie film, *Snatch*. With a bit of dressing, it was also transformed into the glamorous deco office of 'Bijou' record company supremo Jerry Devine (Eddie Izzard) in *Velvet Goldmine*. You can see the wood panels again, in the police station, in Julian Simpson's 1999 conspiracy thriller *The Criminal* – which also features the Town Hall's austerely deco entrance hall and exterior – and in *I Capture the Castle*. Oh, and conveniently, this frequently-seen location happens to house the London Film Office.

The **Genesis Cinema, 95 Mile End**

Lock, Stock and Two Smoking Barrels and Velvet Goldmine: 'Hatchet' Harry's office and Jerry Devine's office: Bethnal Green Town Hall, Cambridge Heath Road

Road (see **Entertainment: Cinemas**, p26), is a very comfortable and sizeable five screen auditoria, concealed by a deceptively small frontage.

Corbridge Crescent, on the Regent's Canal north of Cambridge Heath Station, is the site of Freddie Mays' club, torched by the goons of arch enemy Lennie Taylor, in *Gangster No. 1*. In the shadow of the omnipresent gasometers, Gabriel Byrne and Miranda Richardson enjoy a brief sexual liaison under the **canal bridge** in David Cronenberg's *Spider*.

At this point, you can take a detour north to explore Hackney. From Cambridge Heath Station you can travel a couple of stops to Hackney Downs. There are several locations dotted about you might want to check out. In Hackney itself, the famous **Hackney Empire, 291 Mare Lane** (© 020.8510.4500; website: www.hackneyempire.co.uk), is where Chaplin performs his drunk act before moving to Hollywood in the Richard Attenborough biopic *Chaplin*. The stage-side box was built for the movie. Glitter star-to-be Jonathan Rhys-Meyers learns a bit about life, and theatre, watching panto dame Lindsay Kemp perform here in Todd Haynes' *Velvet Goldmine*. The theatre also became the 'Hippodrome' where Harry Houdini (Harvey Keitel) performs in *Fairy Tale: A True Story*.

To the east runs **Belsham Street**, home to Minnie Driver in comedy thriller *High Heels and Low Lifes*.

A little further east is the brand new Homerton Hospital. There's nothing to see now, but the old hospital, demolished in the eighties, stood in for Whitechapel's Royal London Hospital in *The Elephant Man*.

To the north is Downs Road, on the north side of Hackney Downs, and another vanished location. Clive Donner's 1964 film of Harold Pinter's play *The Caretaker* was shot entirely on location (with cinematography by director-to-be Nicolas Roeg),

Chaplin and Velvet Goldmine: the music hall: Hackney Empire, Mare Lane

Die Another Day: the Cuban cigar factory: Simpson House, Stoke Newington Road

Naked: Johnny's London base: St Mark's Rise

in a rundown house at 31 Downs Road, which has since been demolished. When the financing fell through, friends of the cast and crew, including Peter Hall, Peter Sellers, Elizabeth Taylor and Richard Burton, stumped up the cash to bring the project to the screen.

To the west runs Stoke Newington Road. The interior of **Simpson House, 92 Stoke Newington Road**, became the 'Cuban' cigar factory, where Bond drops the magic name Universal Exports in his search for Zao in the twentieth Bond movie *Die Another Day*.

Mike Leigh's *Naked* is one of his most problematic films. For all his self-lacerating rage and self-loathing, there's no getting away from the fact that the central character, Johnny, is essentially a rapist, though David Thewlis' towering performance transcends the paint-by-numbers yuppie role. **33 St Mark's Rise**, off Downs Park Road, Dalston, is the house where sardonic Mancunian misanthrope Johnny holes up.

Stephen Frears' *Dirty Pretty Things* was shot in the area, on **Kingsland High Street**, **Birkbeck Mews** and in the **Ridley Road market**.

76 Quilter Road is Brenda Blethyn's terraced house, darlin', in Mike Leigh's *Secrets & Lies*.

The disused **Queen Elizabeth Hospital, Hackney Road** at Goldsmith's Row, is frequently drafted in to serve as a film location. Recently it's been used in *High Heels and Low Lifes*, *Born Romantic*, *Shiner* and *Sorted* (as the customs office where Jason Donovan works).

Before taking on Julia Roberts and Hugh Grant in *Notting Hill*, and Samuel L Jackson and Ben Affleck in *Changing Lanes*, Roger Michell directed *Titanic Town*, the story of housewife Bernie McPhelimy (Julie Walters) and her attempts to establish a peace movement in Belfast. The junction of **Hackney Road** and **Cremer Street** is the site of the 'Falls Road' riot, and the disused Flying Scud pub,

Secrets & Lies: Brenda Blethyn's house: Quilter Road

137 Hackney Road, is where Annie McPhelimy (Nuala O'Neill) and Dino/Owen (Ciarán McMenamin) take shelter.

Titanic Town: the Falls Road riot: Hackney Road

The Royal Oak, 73 Columbia Road (see **Bars & Restaurants**, p18), at the heart of the famous flower market, appears as 'Samoan Jo's' in *Lock, Stock and Two Smoking Barrels*, as well as a typical East End boozer in *Honest* and *The Krays*.

On **Boundary Passage** at Boundary Street, behind Shoreditch High Street, is the less than salubrious drinking club where Lennie met Freddie

Lock, Stock and Two Smoking Barrels and **The Krays:** East End boozer: The Royal Oak, Columbia Road

in *Gangster No. 1*. While Freddie Mays is all sharp Italian suits and glitzy establishments in Mayfair, his arch-rival Lennie Taylor (Jamie Foreman) operates out of this bare bricks drinkery. For the film, Boundary Passage was blocked off with a fake dead-end to disguise the High Street.

Head back to Old Street for a detour to Yorkshire, with maybe just a whiff of Minnesota... San Francisco-born, but Minnesota-raised, Josh Hartnett has little more than a subsidiary role in *Blow Dry* – a kind of northern 'Strictly Hairdressing' with a screenplay by Simon Beaufoy, the writer of *The Full Monty* – but by the time the video was released, he was the star of *Pearl Harbor* and had ousted Alan Rickman and Natasha Richardson from the cover. Set in Keighley, Yorkshire, the grand hairdressing tournament was filmed inside **Shoreditch Town Hall, 380 Old Street**. It is closed for major renovations until 2004.

Blow Dry: the Yorkshire hall: Shoreditch Town Hall, Old Street

An empty building on the cobbled **Coronet Street**, at the corner of Boot Street, is the exterior of the fictitious 'Metro Bar'

Gangster No. 1: Lennie Taylor's club: Boundary Passage

The Crying Game: exterior of the Metro Bar: Coronet Street

in *The Crying Game*. The interior was provided by famous gay bar The London Apprentice at **333 Old Street**. It has since been revamped and reopened as the (straight) **Mother** (see **Bars & Restaurants**, p18), which can be seen in *High Heels and Low Lifes*. Around the corner is Hoxton Square, which we were constantly being informed a couple of years ago was the coolest place on the planet. Ahead of the trends, **9 Hoxton Square** is the flat of Dil, where the goldfish meet a sad end on the pavement.

Turn into Hoxton Street and walk north, leaving behind the wine bars and jazz clubs to enter the real old Hoxton and its busy street market. At Bacchus Walk, on the left, is **Bacchus, 177 Hoxton Street** (see **Bars & Restaurants**, p18), which stands in for Whitechapel's Blind Beggar in *The Krays*. Philip Ridley's film script, arch poetics aside, depicts a very different East End from that usually seen on screen – a fiercely matriarchal society where women shoulder the burdens while overgrown boys play gangsters.

Rose Troche, who wittily dissected lesbian relationships in the successful indie *Go Fish* in 1994, explores the sexual complications of a group of Londoners of all sexualities in *Bedrooms & Hallways*, with Kevin McKidd, James Purefoy and Hugo Weaving (playing a sexually rampant estate agent). **15 Westland Place** at Ebenezer Street, off City Road, is the

The Crying Game: Dil's apartment: Hoxton Square

spacious loft apartment of Leo (McKidd) and flatmate Darren (Tom Hollander). It's famous now, of course, as Jamie Oliver's **Fifteen** restaurant (see **Bars & Restaurants**, p18).

Across Nile Street, **Underwood Street** was transformed into the 'Soho' backstreet where Jasper is ushered into the peepshow office of the sinister Noble (Barry Stearn) in *The Criminal*.

Bunhill Fields Burial Ground, 38 City Road, is the cemetery where Chiwetel Ejiofor reveals to Audrey Tautou that he's married, in Stephen

The Krays: shooting George Cornell at Whitechapels' Blind Beggar: Bacchus, Hoxton Street

Frears' *Dirty Pretty Things*. The burial ground, originally much larger than the remnant left today, was restored as a peaceful park after being severely bombdamaged during W W I I . Established in 1315, it was, unusually, not consecrated, which meant that it became the last

Bedrooms and Hallways: Kevin McKidd's spacious loft: Fifteen, Westland Place

Dirty Pretty Things: Chiwetel Ejiofor reveals his secret: Bunhill Fields Burial Ground, City Road

resting place for nonconformists and liberal humanists. In 1853, with 120,000 occupants, overcrowding meant that it was closed. Famous graves include those of John Bunyan (author of *Pilgrim's Progress*), Daniel Defoe (author of *Robinson Crusoe* and *Moll Flanders*) and mystic poet and painter William Blake. The most unusual monument, though, must be the huge sarcophagus of one Dame Mary Page, with an enthusiastically detailed inscription which gives just a little too much information: 'In 67 months she was tapd [tapped] 66 times. Had taken away 240 gallons of water without ever repining at her case or ever fearing the operation.'

When Tom Cruise walks along Hatton Garden, masquerading as Greenwich Village, in *Eyes Wide Shut* (see **West London: Fitzrovia**, p100), his sinister stalker Phil Davies is actually on **Worship Street** – look out for **Nicon House, 21 Worship Street**, in the background.

Continue to Whitechapel. Directly opposite the tube station is the **London Hospital, Whitechapel Road**, where the real John Merrick, the Elephant Man, stayed, under the protection of Dr Treves, after being rescued from life as a sideshow attraction. Its modern annexes rendered it unsuitable for filming, and the movie was shot elsewhere.

South from Whitechapel Road, the huge, redbrick **Tower House, Fieldgate Street**, was one of six Methodist missions built around London for the destitute (the only other still remaining is the

Eyes Wide Shut: the sinster stalker in Greenwich Village: Worship Street

I Hired a Contract Killer: the Hotel Splendide: Tower House, Fieldgate Street

famous Arlington House in Camden). In 1990 it was the 'Hotel Splendide', where Jean-Pierre Léaud and Margi Clarke hole up to escape the relentless hitman in Aki Kaurismäki's strangely somnambulistic *I Hired a Contract Killer*. Author Jack London dismissed Tower House as a "monster doss house" in his 1902 *The People of the Abyss*, though George Orwell was kinder in his 1933 *Down and Out in Paris and London*, saying it was the best of all common lodging houses. It was certainly good enough for the young Joseph Stalin, who stayed there, at sixpence a night, in 1907, while attending the Fifth Congress of the Russian Social Democratic Labour Party. It is currently empty, weed-ridden and boarded-up, the statuary gone from over the grand ornamental entrance.

The **Blind Beggar, 337 Whitechapel Road**, is where Ronnie Kray shot George Cornell after he'd, rather recklessly, referred to the psychopathically violent gangster in public as a "fat poof".

Go one stop east, to Stepney Green (*tube: District and Hammersmith & City lines*). **Bancroft Road, Mile End**, can be seen in Antonia Bird's 1997 film *Face*, with Robert Carlyle.

'Fabian Court', the apartment block of Jasper (Steven Mackintosh) in *The Criminal*, has a pleasantly deco appearance, but if you were thinking of eyeing the local estate agents, you're out of luck. The fictitious court is actually a side entrance (through gates to the right) to the **Queen Mary and Westfields College, Mile End Road**, east of Stepney Green Underground Station. The name 'Fabian Court' is an homage to Harry Fabian, the Richard Widmark character in Jules Dassin's stunning 1950 London noir *Night and the City*. The striking 1936 college building, decorated with stylish art deco bas reliefs, was built as the People's Palace, replacing a Victorian philanthropic venture of the same name, intended to bring culture, enertainment and education to the people of the East End.

Return to Whitechapel and take the East London line to Shadwell. **Wilton's Music Hall, 1 Grace's Alley, Wellclose Square**, off Cable Street, was the first, and one of the most successful of London's music halls. Built in 1858, it has had a chequered history and, until recently, lay dilapidated. During the fallow years it found regular employment as a film backdrop. It became the 'Aldershot' music hall where the precocious young entertainer takes over from his troubled mother in *Chaplin*, the interior of the twins' nightclub in *The Krays* (for the exterior,

see **Southwest London**, p145) and the 'US' theatre where Isadora Duncan (Vanessa Redgrave) performs high kicks as 'Peppy Dora'

The World Is Not Enough: the boat chase: Tobacco Dock, Wapping Lane

to earn enough to take her to Europe in Karel Reisz's *Isadora*. Scenes for *Interview With the Vampire* were also supposedly shot at Wilton's but don't seem to have survived the final cut. The music hall is now home to the Broomhill Opera Company.

Tobacco Dock though, on the tiny **Ornamental Canal** at Wapping Lane, still exists. It's on the right-angle bend of the Ornamental Canal that the traffic wardens (dated cameos by long-forgotten, minor celebs from reality-TV) get drenched during the 'Thames' boat chase in *The World Is Not Enough*. Bond's Q boat leaps up the canal's steps and tears through the 'London Canoe Club' clubhouse (specially built for the movie) alongside the pirate ships of Tobacco Dock, before coming aground at Chatham in Kent.

Running south from the dock is **Reardon Street**, where Sidney Poitier alights a bus on his way to the funeral in *To Sir, With Love*. In the movie, you can glimpse the spire of Nicholas Hawksmoor's church of St George-in-the-East at the end of the street, and it was at the school of St George-in-the-East that ER Braithwaite, author of *To Sir With Love*, taught. The story goes that the headmaster of the school remembered events somewhat differently from the book and refused to allow filming on the premises.

Turning right onto Watts Street leads to the the forbidding brick bulk of the **John Orwell Sports Centre, Tench Street** (© 020.7488.9421), the health club where Bridget Jones sheds the pounds on an exercise bike in *Bridget Jones's Diary*.

Turning left into Green Bank takes you to Dundee Street, running south to Wapping High

Bridget Jones's Diary: Bridget burns off the pounds: John Orwell Sports Centre, Tench Street

The Long Good Friday: Harold's mum at the Good Friday service: St Patrick's Church, Green Bank

Gandhi: Gandhi stays in the East End: Kingsley Hall, Powis Road

28 Days Later: the deserted station: Canary Wharf Underground Station

Street. **St Patrick's Church, Green Bank**, is the site of the Good Friday service, where Harold Shand's mum narrowly escapes being blown up, triggering the chain of events in *The Long Good Friday*. The street runs down to the Thames near Wapping New Stairs at a stretch known as the **Pool of London** which, not surprisingly, was the backdrop to Basil Dearden's semi-documentary drama *Pool of London*, shot around the then bomb-damaged and now largely rebuilt area. It was on the riverfront here that Harold Shand's 'Lion and Unicorn' pub was built – and blown up – for *The Long Good Friday*. **Wapping** tube station remains pretty much as it's seen during the opening credits of *To Sir With Love*, except that the crumbling warehouses are now smart loft conversions.

Head to Mile End. **Mile End Road** can be seen in Antonia Bird's *Face*. Cross the road to Tredegar Square. The large house at **3 Tredegar Square** supplied period interiors for *Wilde* and also appears in Brit gangster flick *Love, Honour and Obey*. There are two more locations north of the area: **Zealand Road** pops up in quirky sex comedy *Virtual Sexuality*, and **Wendon Street** in *Face*.

Next, to Bromley by Bow. By an odd coincidence, **Kingsley Hall, Powis Road**, is where Gandhi (Ben Kingsley) stays during his visit to London in Richard Attenborough's biopic. And, yes, as a blue plaque attests, it's also where the real Gandhi stayed in 1931. To the south, the Grade II listed **Balfron Tower, St Leonard's Road**, is the sister of North Kensington's more famous Trellick Tower, by the same architect, Erno Goldfinger (Ian Fleming nicked the name for his villain). It's the deserted highrise

28 Days Later: the deserted tower block exterior: Balfron Tower, St Leonard's Road

28 Days Later: "The end is extremely fucking nigh": St Anne's Church, Commercial Road

where Jim and Selena hide out with Frank and Hannah in Danny Boyle's *28 Days Later*, which also filmed on nearby **Spey Street**.

Further southwest is **St Anne's Church, Commercial Road** at Newell Street. Another Nicholas Hawksmoor church, it supplied the entrance and the stairwell in which Jim sees the writing on the wall: "The end is extremely fucking nigh".

To Stratford, home of the famous **Stratford East Theatre, Gerry Raffles Square**, where the legendary Joan Littlewood produced groundbreaking theatrical productions in the sixties and launched countless careers from her Rep company, including Barbara Windsor. *Oh! What a Lovely War* started life here as an ironic Pierrot show. In 1962, Littlewood directed the film version of one of her stage shows, *Sparrows Can't Sing*, with regulars including Windsor, James Booth and Murray Melvin. The film was shot around **Angel Lane**.

North of Stratford is Leytonstone. You might want to pay homage at the birthplace of one of the real giants of cinema here. **517 Leytonstone High Road** is the birthplace of Alfred Hitchcock.

Continue to the Isle of Dogs. At the **New Billingsgate Market**, Jason (Sean Bean) inflicts some serious damage on a supposed grass (an informer) in front of the horrified workers at the beginning of the violent *Essex Boys*. The market also features in the post-apocalyptic horror-sci-fi film *28 Days Later*. In the same film, Jim and his fellow survivors run down the vast, deserted escalators of **Canary Wharf tube station**

A couple of stops south on the DLR is Crossharbour. **1 Canada Square** (otherwise known as the Canary Wharf tower) became the headquarters of wannabe ruler Pascal Sauvage (John Malkovich) in *Johnny English*. West of the station, in the shadow of the London Arena, is **Glengall Bridge** across **Millwall Inner Dock**, the bridge which Bond dives under as it closes during the boat chase which kicks off *The World Is Not Enough*. East of the station is the unlovely complex of the **Samuda Estate, Manchester Road**, which can be seen in

Johnny English: Pascal Sauvage's HQ: Canada Square

The Long Good Friday: Harold Shand searches for a lead: The Waterman's Arms, Glenaffric Avenue

Dirty Pretty Things.

Further south still, legendary waterfront boozer **The Waterman's Arms, 1 Glenaffric Avenue** (see **Bars & Restaurants**, p19), is 'The Governor General' in *The Long Good Friday*.

It must have seemed a great idea at the time to end the Thames boat chase at the **Millennium Dome** for *The World Is Not Enough*, but the sight of the uncompleted Dome dates the movie forever.

The **Royal Victoria Dock, Canning Town**, was used for the 'rollover' during the boat chase in *The World Is Not Enough*. The **CWS Flour Mill** provided the grim passageways and stairwells of 'Shangri La Towers', the home of the unfortunate Buttles in Terry Gilliam's *Brazil*. The interior of the mill also provided the vast clerks pool in the Department of Records, where Jonathan Pryce works, as well as the deserted corridors of the Expediting Department. South of the dock stood the old Tate and Lyle Sugar Factory, Plaistow Wharf. Recently demolished, the factory was turned into a makeshift studio for the filming of *The Criminal*.

King George V Dock, south of London City Airport, is the quayside where Harold Shand (Bob Hoskins) gets the name of the grass from his bent cop friend (Dave King) in *The Long Good Friday*.

Beckton Gasworks was famously transformed into 'Vietnam' by Stanley Kubrick for *Full Metal Jacket*. The dreadful opening of the otherwise quite good Bond movie, *For Your Eyes Only*, sees a wacky, wheelchair-bound 'Blofeld' character being dumped into an industrial chimney on the site. Beckton also supplied the WWI battlefields for the 1986 spoof *Biggles*, and the house for the creepy adaptation of Ian McEwan's novel *The Cement Garden* was built here, with the tower of Canary Wharf needing to be digitally removed from the background. The 'Japanese detention centre' in Steven Spielberg's film of JG Ballard's autobiographical novel *Empire of the Sun* was also filmed inside the old gaswork buildings. Part of *Brannigan* was filmed here too. The gasworks is currently being redeveloped.

Southeast London: Peckham to Eltham

The locations in southeast London are too scattered for a walking tour, so I've arranged the tour by district. Time for a rail pass. If you're travelling on a Sunday, check ahead, as routine maintenance means that lines are often out of service.

PECKHAM

Alongside pleasant streets and some lively bars, there's also urban deprivation. Don't get paranoid, but – as in any inner city area – exercise the usual awareness.

It seems like a dream cast – Bob Hoskins, Michael Caine, David Hemmings, Tom Courtenay, Helen Mirren and Ray Winstone – and it is, but the film of Graham Swift's Booker Prize-winning novel *Last Orders* never really catches light. The exterior of the

Last Orders: the Coach and Horses: The Wishing Well, Choumert Road

fictitious 'Coach and Horses' in the film is actually **The Wishing Well, 79 Choumert Road** (see **Bars & Restaurants**, p19) at the corner of Bel-

lenden Road. Walk up Bellenden Road to Danby Street. The smart new premises at **192 Bellenden Road** was 'Dodds & Son', Michael Caine's butcher shop in *Last Orders*, before renovation. Just across the road you might recognise the distinctive little archway of Tom Courtenay's undertakers, **157 Bellenden Road**.

Blowup: David Hemmings beneath the railway arch: Consort Road

Head along Copeland Road to **Consort Road**. The railway arch over Consort Road, just east of Peckham Rye Station, is where David Hemmings mingles with the factory workers at the opening of Michelangelo Antonioni's *Blowup*.

NEW CROSS TO DEPTFORD

Gary Oldman's intense *Nil by Mouth* was filmed around New Cross, though the high-rise estate used for the film has since been demolished. The local boozers seen in the movie are **The Five Bells Public House, New Cross Road** (see **Bars & Restaurants**, p19), **The Royal Archer, Camplin Street** at Egmont Street, and **The Hatcham Liberal Club, 369 Queens Road**.

241 New Cross Road was home to Sir Barnes

Nil by Mouth: South London boozer 1: The Five Bells Public House, New Cross Road

Nil by Mouth: South London boozer 2: The Royal Archer, Camplin Street

Wallace, designer of the Wellington bomber and inventor of the bouncing bomb, and played by Michael Redgrave in *The Dam Busters*.

You might experience a slight culture shock moving from the stiff upper lips of *The Dam Busters* to the altogether different stiffness on display in Patrice Chéreau's *Intimacy*. A kind of 'Last Tango in New Cross', Mark Rylance and Kerry Fox go way beyond the call of duty as the couple locked in a near-wordless physical relationship. Rylance's house, where they make the beast with two backs on a regular weekly basis, is **2 Alpha Road**, just south of New Cross Road as it becomes Deptford Broadway.

John Osborne's bilious rant *Look Back in Anger* was probably equally shocking when it was premièred at the Royal Court Theatre. The play broke new ground but the film hasn't worn particularly well. It was shot at a time when classically trained actors were still faking working-class accents, and when British movies were tentatively venturing outside the confines of the studio. *Look Back in Anger* features the old Deptford Market.

Local papers got quite excited when it was rumoured that Tom Cruise would be filming in Deptford. It never happened. It was Brad Pitt who shot scenes for *Interview With the Vampire: The Vampire Chronicles* in South London. **St Paul's Church, Deptford High Street**, became the interior of a 'New Orleans' church where Pitt attacks a priest, in Neil Jordan's film of the Anne Rice novel. Sadly the scene never made it to the final cut of the movie. Not to worry, South London's fans of the undead can catch the church in another vampire movie, Shimako Sato's little-seen 1992 film *Tale of a Vampire*, with Julian Sands.

At the north end of Deptford High Street, across Creek Road, is **St**

Intimacy: Mark Rylance's flat: Alpha Road

Spider: the Dog and Beggar: Crown and Sceptre, Friendly Street

Nicholas's Church, Stowage, where playwright Christopher Marlowe is buried. Marlowe was stabbed in the eye in a pub brawl in Deptford, possibly over a bar bill, though since Marlowe was also gay, a professed atheist and a spy, there are plenty of more colourful theories about his death. The incident was fancifully incorporated into *Shakespeare in Love*, with an uncredited Rupert Everett as Marlowe.

Just around the corner is the **Crown and Sceptre, 92 Friendly Street**, an old-fashioned little local corner pub which became the 'Dog and Beggar' for David Cronenberg's *Spider*.

Deptford grew to enormous fame as the home of Henry VIII's Royal Naval Dockyard (Russia's Peter the Great stayed here to learn about building a navy), but as ships grew ever larger, the dockyards moved elsewhere. To the east, on Creek Road, is **Deptford Creek**, the riverside setting for the *Frankenstein*-like scene between the mutating astronaut (Richard Wordsworth) and the little girl (a very early, uncredited appearance by Jane Asher) in Hammer's 1955 sci-fi flick *The Quatermass Xperiment*.

Ladywell Leisure Centre, Lewisham High Street (*© 020.8690.2123; rail: Ladywell*), is the swimming bath where Harold Shand's right hand man is slain by the IRA man (Pierce Brosnan in an early role, credited as First Irishman) in *The Long Good Friday*.

BROCKLEY

South of New Cross. The famous **Rivoli Ballroom, 350 Brockley Road**, opposite Crofton Park Railway Station, is where Kathy Burke sings backing vocals for her band in the 'Camden'-set *This Year's Love*. It's also the ballroom where Natalie Appleton and Melanie Blatt waltz while Nicole Appleton gets smashed at the rock festival in David A Stewart's *Honest*. Less recognisably, its bar became the interior of 'East Berlin's Eck Bar', where Tom Bishop (Brad Pitt) stops off to contact Nathan Muir (Robert Redford) – "Vodka did me in, I'm coming home" – as he attempts to get Schmidt (Jörg Stadler) across the East-West border in Tony Scott's *Spy Game*.

Spy Game: the East Berlin bar: Rivoli Ballroom, Brockley Road

Entertaining Mr Sloane: Kath's house: Camberwell Old Cemetery, Forest Hill Road

HONOR OAK PARK

Further south still, turn right from the station on Honor Oak Park into Forest Hill Road. The lodge of **Camberwell Old Cemetery, Forest Hill Road**, is the home of Kath (Beryl Reid) in the 1969 film of Joe Orton's play *Entertaining Mr Sloane*. The performances are priceless, but it's more black sitcom than Orton, changing the drab semi in the middle of a rubbish tip for this Victorian Gothic folly. In 1993, the Grade II listed building was in a sad state of disrepair, and was put on the market by owners Southwark Council. It's now a private home, fenced off from the cemetery.

GREENWICH

East of Deptford is the nautical town of Greenwich, with its **Old Royal Naval College** (see **Historic Sites**, p31) regularly cropping up on the big screen in a variety of guises. The **Royal Naval College Chapel, King William Walk**, can be seen as the site of 'Wedding II' in *Four Weddings and a Funeral* and in the 2002 remake of *The Four Feathers*. The *trompe-l'œil* **Painted Hall** appears in all its glory in the 1983 remake of *The Wicked Lady*, *The Avengers* and *Quills*. It is also the suitably beautiful setting for the bellringing concert in *The Madness of King George*, and the interior of a 'Venice' church in *Lara Croft: Tomb Raider*. The college exterior, meanwhile, has proved to be extremely adaptable, standing in for Buckingham Palace, the Pentagon and even wartime London, as well as occasionally playing

Shanghai Knights: Charing Cross: Old Royal Naval College

The Madness of King George and **Lara Croft: Tomb Raider**: the Painted Hall, Old Royal Naval College

itself, in *Shining Through*, *The Bounty*, *King Ralph*, *Patriot Games* and *Charlotte Gray*. It also appears in the fifth, 2002 version of *The Four Feathers*, as the site of the bus chase in *The Mummy Returns*, and as 'Charing Cross' in *Shanghai Knights*.

In the 2002

The Four Feathers: the Cutty Sark, Greenwich

adaptation of AEW Mason's novel *The Four Feathers*, the parade, with over 500 soldiers, bands and horses, marches from **King Charles** along **College Way** to the **Cutty Sark**. For the first time since 1938 (when she sailed from Falmouth to her current berth next to HMS Worcester), the yards of the famous tea clipper were decked out with sails, specially made by sailmakers M Putt.

Stop off at the Cutty Sark Tavern on Ballast Quay, looking across the river to the Millennium Dome. Scenes for *The Four Feathers* were to have been filmed at this historic pub (although the interior already has the appearance of a movie set), but it proved too expensive to restore the period look.

Around the corner, on Lassell Street stood the British Sailor, an empty pub taken over as the local boozer in Mike Leigh's *All or Nothing*. Sadly, the pub has now been bulldozed as part of the quayside redevelopment, but further along the road, **73 Lassel Street** became the cab office out of which Timothy Spall works.

Greenwich is the setting for Andrew Birkin's melodrama *The Cement Garden* (though the isolated house was built in the grounds of Beckton gasworks). Christopher Hampton's 1996 film of Joseph Conrad's novel *The Secret Agent* and George Sluizer's ambitious *Crimetime* both also filmed

All or Nothing: Timothy Spall's cab office: Lassel Street

some scenes in Greenwich.

Part of the National Maritime Museum is **Queen's House** (*© 020.8312.6565*), built by James I for Anne of Denmark who, inconsiderately, died before it was completed. It was nevertheless finished and given by Charles I to Queen Henrietta Maria. In the 1980s it was substantially restored and decorated in the style of the period. Its pillared walkway was used to represent a London street in Ang Lee's *Sense and Sensibility*, and also appears in Oliver Parker's film of *An Ideal Husband*.

The Krays: the twins' Vallance Road home: Caradoc Street

To the east, toward Greenwich Park, is **The Gloucester, 1 King William Walk** (see **Bars & Restaurants**, p19), a real gay bar which appears in *Beautiful Thing*. Another landmark in the cinema depiction of gays was filmed in part around Greenwich. Glenda Jackson and Murray Head take the precocious kids for a scamper around Greenwich Park in John Schlesinger's *Sunday, Bloody Sunday* (though the family home is about twelve miles away, in Wandsworth). And look out for Daniel Day-Lewis' first screen appearance as one of the kids vandalising cars by the gravestone-lined passageway alongside Nicholas Hawksmore's **St Alphege**.

Opposite Greenwich Theatre, **6 Crooms Hill** was the home of poet Cecil Day-Lewis, father of actor Daniel. A few doors along, the Georgian house at **14 Crooms Hill** is the home of Lady Drake (Phyllida Law), where Maddy (Anna Friel) appeals for help, in *Mad Cows*. On the other side of the park, **Vanbrugh Castle, 121 Maze Hill**, the house of architect and dramatist Sir John Vanbrugh, became the grand 'Highgate' house, where Cathy Tyson sends out a tray of refreshments to Bob Hoskins while she services a rich client in Neil Jordan's *Mona Lisa*.

Mike Leigh's grubbily downbeat film *All or Nothing* is set around a determinedly non-touristy Greenwich. No picturesque views of the Cutty Sark here. The shabby flat, where Timothy Spall and his family live their fast food and TV lifestyle, is on the **Haddo Estate**, just north of Greenwich Railway Station, now deserted and due for demolition. The hospital where

Mad Cows: the home of Lady Drake: Crooms Hill

Mona Lisa: the grand Highgate house: Vanbrugh Castle, Maze Hill

Spall's son James Corden suffers the inevitable consequences of his junk-food existence, is **Greenwich District Hospital, Woolwich Road**. It can also be seen in Danny Boyle's post-apocalyptic *28 Days Later*.

Head west on Trafalgar Road. **32 Caradoc Street** stands in for 'Fortress Vallance', the demolished home of the Kray twins, in *The Krays*. This period street is frequently used as a backdrop for TV shows and ads. It's used for the Coronation street party (that's a street party to celebrate HM's Coronation in 1953, not a soap opera convention) in Fred Schepisi's *Plenty*, with Meryl Streep and Charles Dance.

The **Millennium Dome**, of course, features as the climax of the river boat chase in *The World Is Not Enough* – and it's unfinished state forever dates the movie. A little south, scenes for the tough soccer violence movie *I.D.* were shot on **Boord Street** and **River Way**.

South of Greenwich Park, **11 The Paragon** (*rail: Blackheath*), one of a semi-circle of fourteen houses around a green, is home to Nicole Kidman's cousin, Martin Donovan, in Jane Campion's *Portrait of a Lady*. Between Tranquil Passage and Royal Parade runs the tiny, crooked, cobbled passageway of Brigade Street. **17 Brigade Street**, behind bar Mar Terra, became the entrance to the 'Sombrero Club' in Todd Haynes' *Velvet Goldmine*. Haynes films the scene as a romantic homage to the party scene in Orson Welles' *The Magnificent Ambersons*.

Portrait of a Lady: Martin Donovan's house: The Paragon

WOOLWICH

From Maze Hill Station head east to Woolwich Dockyard

Velvet Goldmine: entrance to the Sombrero Club: Brigade Street

Blowup: the eerie park: Maryon Park

High Heels and Low Lifes: villain Michael Gambon's house: Eltham Palace, Court Yard

Station, then west on Woolwich Road to **Maryon Park**, south of Woolwich Road. The east side of the park is the eerie park where photographer David Hemmings might or might not have seen something nasty, in Michelangelo Antonioni's much copied sixties classic *Blowup*. Antonioni notoriously manipulated reality to achieve the visual effects he wanted, painting paths black and grass, well, green. The bushes where the 'body' is hidden were put there for the film, and the large houses overlooking the park were simply false flats. The 'antique shop' (it was a grocery store) was in Cleveley Close, running from Woolwich Road to the park's northeast corner. It's since been demolished and the corner redeveloped.

Carry on to Woolwich itself, and head south to the old munitions factory, **Old Royal Military Academy, Academy Road**, which was dressed up to provide wartime London streets for *Charlotte Gray*, before being renovated to provide more classy loft apartments.

The entrance to **Woolwich Town Hall, Market Street**, is the 'Victoria Hotel, Keighley', where the competing hairdressers arrive in style in *Blow Dry*.

Woolwich Cemetery is the site of the funeral of Violet Kray (Billie Whitelaw) at the end of *The Krays*.

THAMESMEAD

Continue on to Abbey Wood Station. Go north on Manor Way to that ghastly sixties planning disaster, the **Thamesmead Estate**. A grim, windswept collection of tower blocks connected by intimidating walkways, it is the natural home for Alex (Malcolm MacDowell) and the 'droogs' in *A Clockwork Orange*. The 'Flat Block B Marina' is Thamesmead's artificially created **Southmere Lake**. Alex reasserted his dominance over his fellow droogs here by dumping Dim (Warren Clarke) in the water and slicing his outstretched hand at **Binsey Walk** on the lake's western shore, overlooked by the blocks of Yarnton Way. And now it's makeover time. Armed with little more than a bit of trellis, lovely geraniums and some Mama Cass records, Hettie Macdonald turns

A Clockwork Orange: Flat Block B Marina: Binsey Walk, Thamesmead Estate

a dystopian nightmare into a plebeian paradise for gayboys Glen Berry and Scott Neal in her 1996 feelgood romance *Beautiful Thing*, adapted from Jonathan Harvey's play.

South of Thamesmead is **Abbey Wood**, the neighbourhood where much of Terry Jones' *Personal Services* was filmed, with Julie Walters as Christine Painter, the fictional alter-ego of Luncheon Voucher madame Cynthia Payne.

DULWICH

Head west to Dulwich Station. *Legally Blonde* sees Reese Witherspoon as a not-so-dumb blonde leaving Beverley Hills Barbieland to cut it with the Ivy Leaguers in Harvard Law School. It's not surprising that there's not a lot of filming in the real Harvard University (a Pasadena high school stood in), but what is surprising is that the production ended up in SE21. After test screenings left audiences a tad disappointed, a new ending was commissioned. By now, though, Witherspoon was in the UK filming *The Importance of Being Earnest*, so the 'Harvard' graduation ceremony was filmed in **Dulwich College, College Road**, Dulwich Village. The college also features in *Lara Croft: Tomb Raider*.

Crystal Palace Road, East Dulwich, is home to the wife and daughter of George (Bob Hoskins) in *Mona Lisa*.

ELTHAM

To the north of Eltham Station, **Greenwich Cemetery** on **Well Hall Road**, off Shooters Hill, is where oddball Catherine McCormack looks after graves in *Born Romantic*.

And to the south, **Eltham Palace and Courtauld House, Court Yard** (see **Historic Sites**, p32), is an art deco treasure. It becomes a private cinema in *Richard III*, and appears in *High Heels and Low Lifes* and *I Capture the Castle*.

Avery Hill Tropical Plant House is the conservatory of General Sternwood (James Stewart), where he explains his problems to Philip Marlowe (Robert Mitchum) in Michael Winner's 1978 remake of *The Big Sleep*.

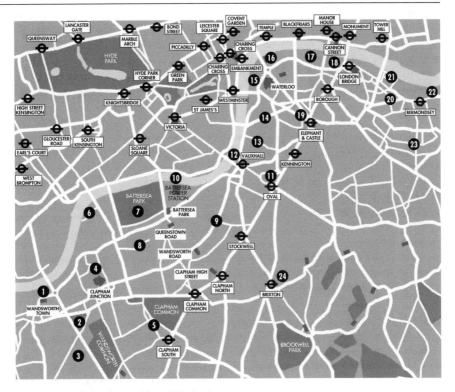

South-Central London: Wandsworth to Tooting

Like taxis, film-makers seem reticent to stray south of the river. Locations are, therefore, spread more widely. There are fewer tube lines, too, so you'll be relying more on the rail system. South London takes in the South Bank arts complex, unspoiled histori-cal locations and some of the capital's livelier neigh-bourhoods. Among the celebs who ventured south, you'll find Brad Pitt scrapping in a bareknuckle fight, Albert Finney achieving stardom and Tom Cruise chilling out...

Starting Point: Wandsworth

Three controversial British classics of the early sev-enties to start with: one kept on the shelf for a couple of years by a jittery production company, one with-drawn for two decades by its director, and one which took its production crew by surprise...

Just north of **Wandsworth Town Station** on **Old York Road (1)**, Chas (James Fox) phones his one-time boss Harry Flowers (Johnny Shannon) for help

after the killing of bookie Joey Maddocks (Anthony Valentine) in *Performance*. The northern subway beneath the huge circular advertising installation on **Trinity Road**, deserted, unswept and extremely unnerv-ing, is where the Alex and the 'droogs' attack the Irish tramp at the beginning of *A Clockwork Orange*.

Head south to the northwestern section of Wandsworth Common. **5 Spencer Park (2)** is the home of the dreadfully earnest Hodson family in John Schlesinger's *Sunday, Bloody Sunday*, so quin-tessentially 'Hampstead' that many people believe that's where it was filmed. The first mainstream film to take its char-acters' homosex-uality complete-ly for granted, it's

Performance: Chas calls for help: Wandsworth Town Station, Old York Road

A Clockwork Orange: Droogs in the subway: Trinity Road

127

Sunday, Bloody Sunday: the ghastly Hodson family: Spencer Park

The Amsterdam Kill: Robert Mitchum stays in Wandsworth: The Brewery Tap, Wandsworth High Street

hard to remember what a step this was. The film crew, hitherto assuming that the relationship between Peter Finch and Murray Head was uncle and nephew, were supposedly a bit taken aback by the full-on, tongues-and-all, smacker.

To the south on Earlsfield Road is the famous **Wandsworth Prison (3)**, where Anna Friel is banged up for shoplifting a bag of frozen peas (and they say British courts are soft) in the disastrous Britcom *Mad Cows*.

A flat above **The Brewery Tap, 68 Wandsworth High Street** (see **Bars & Restaurants**, p19), is home to Robert Mitchum in *The Amsterdam Kill*.

Wandsworth Town Hall, High Street, provides the lavish lobby of the 'Baltic Hotel', where Okwe (Chiwetel Ojiofor) finds a human heart clogging up the loo in Stephen Frears' *Dirty Pretty Things* (the rest of the hotel's interiors were studio sets, but for the exterior, see **Central London: Leicester Square**, p38).

Clapham Junction (4), the major rail hub, gives its name to *Up the Junction*. The 1967 film started life as a TV play directed by Ken Loach, and gets somewhat softened, with a sixties pop score from Manfred Mann, by director Peter Collinson (much happier with the lightweight *The Italian Job*). The movie was mostly shot to the east, around Battersea, but Suzy Kendall gets digs on **Ingrave Street**, off Falcon Road, though it has now been thoroughly redeveloped.

The old Clapham, before the area's fashionable rebirth as 'Cla'am', is the neighbourhood portrayed in David Lean's film of the play *This Happy Breed*, Noël Coward's rather patronising portrait of working class life between the wars. The local landmark department store, **Arding and Hobbs, St John's Road**, is apparently blown up by terrorists in

Dirty Pretty Things: lobby of the Baltic Hotel: Wandsworth Town Hall, High Street

the 1981 Sylvester Stallone actioner *Nighthawks* (which was predominantly set in New York).

Lavender Hill, which gave its name to the

The Winslow Boy: the Winslow house in South Kensington: Clapham Common West Side

Ealing classic *The Lavender Hill Mob*, runs east from the station.

To the southeast is Clapham Common, if you want a bit of a diversion. At first glance, tough-talking macho Yank David Mamet hardly seemed the obvious person to film Terence Rattigan's 1946 play *The Winslow Boy*. But it's clearly Rattigan's precision of language and immaculate stagecraft that appealed. The performances are faultless, but the reverence for the play's structure makes an oddly disjointed film. The Winslow family home is supposed to be in fashionably upper-crust South Kensington, but you'll find the mansion used for the movie tucked away off the green expanse of Clapham Common: it's **21 Clapham Common West Side (5)** at Thurleigh Road, now renovated and slightly remodelled.

If you follow the Thames east, you come to Battersea Church Road. **St Mary's, Battersea Parish Church, Battersea Church Road (6)**, looking across the river to Sands End and Chelsea Harbour, is where Julia Foster spends her lunchbreaks with nerdy, but dependable, bus conductor Graham Stark in *Alfie*. At the end of the movie, a suitably chastened Michael Caine balefully watches her baby's christening in the church. The road continues to the southern end of **Battersea Bridge**, which is where Tom (Jason Flemyng) is left floundering, with his ringing mobile and two very expensive shooters, at the end of *Lock, Stock and Two Smoking Barrels*.

A little to the east, at the foot of Albert Bridge, is **Waterside Point, Anhalt Road**, home to stressed-out young marrieds Hugh Laurie and Joely Richardson as they try every trick in the book to conceive a child in Ben Elton's *Maybe Baby*.

Across Albert Bridge Road is the entrance to **Battersea Park (7)**. Before cheap airline travel put the Balearics within reach for those little breaks, Battersea Funfair was where the working classes took their entertainment. The park remains, but the fair is long gone. However, you can see its blowsy charms in Val

Alfie: Alfie watches the christening: St Mary's, Battersea Church Road

Maybe Baby: Joely Richardson's flat: Primrose Mansions, Prince of Wales Drive

Brannigan: John Wayne's flat: York Mansions, Prince of Wales Drive

Guest's sci-fi film *The Day the Earth Caught Fire*. In Eugene Lourié's 1960 lovable dino-flick *Gorgo*, the captured saurian is exhibited in the funfair. (Had nobody seen *King Kong*? Will they never learn?) The twist here is that the cute dinosaur is only a toddler and soon Mummy Gorgo is making her way up the Thames to rescue baby. Battersea Park is famously film-friendly and often stands in for other London parks, including St James's Park in *101 Dalmatians*, when Jeff Daniels and Joely Richardson get dunked in the pond, Clapham Common for Neil Jordan's *The End of the Affair* and Hyde Park in *Wilde*. Irritatingly self-pitying Frank (Rufus Sewell) meets American tourist Martha (Monica Potter) in the park in *Martha Meet Frank, Daniel & Laurence*.

Defining the southern boundary of Battersea Park is Prince of Wales Drive. **Primrose Mansions, Prince of Wales Drive**, is the block Joely Richardson moves to after fertility problems lead to a marital bust-up in *Maybe Baby*. **61-80 York Mansions, Prince of Wales Drive**, was the temporary home of visiting Chicago cop John Wayne in *Brannigan* (though when the villains booby-trap his toilet with a bomb, the resulting hole in the wall reveals a view of the Albert Memorial in Hyde Park). York Mansions is also home to Wolfe Lissner (Ian McShane), boyfriend of the psychopathic Vic Dakin (Richard Burton), in *Villain*.

Head back toward the river. In 1960, Albert Finney shot to stardom as the disaffected factory worker Arthur Seaton in Karel Reisz's *Saturday Night and Sunday Morning*. One of the key movies of the British New Wave, the film made much of its Nottingham locations, but it's not entirely authentic Midlands. It's outside **The British Flag, 103 Culvert Road**

Saturday Night and Sunday Morning: Arthur Seaton gets beaten up in Nottingham: The British Flag, Culvert Road

(**8**), on the corner of Rowditch Lane, where Seaton and his pal witness a drunken old man smash a shop window, and later, where Arthur gets beaten up by squaddies.

By Battersea Park's southeast entrance, on **Queen's Circle**, stood the little tea-stall where Meryl Streep meets wide-boy Sting in Fred Schepisi's underrated film of David Hare's play *Plenty*, and it's in the park, beneath Chelsea Bridge, that she asks him to be the no-strings father of her child. Chelsea girl Suzy Kendall walks over **Chelsea Bridge** to experience life on the other side of the tracks in *Up the Junction*.

To the south on Queenstown Road, by Queenstown Road Station once stood Gladstone Terrace, home to sisters Adrienne Posta and Maureen Lipman in *Up the Junction*, another location lost as substandard housing is bulldozed. And further south still, near Wandsworth Road Station, is Larkhall Lane. The **Larkhall Tavern, Larkhall Lane** (**9**), was used for the interiors of the fictitious 'Coach and Horses', supposedly in Bermondsey, in the film of Graham Swift's novel *Last Orders* (for the exterior, see **Southeast London**, p122, and **Bars & Restaurants**, p19). The pub served up its last pint in 1999 and is due to be turned into luxury flats.

Return to Queen's Circle, and one of the most recognisable London landmarks, the old **Battersea Power Station** (**10**), a brick cube with four tall chimneys. Closed since 1983 and gutted, the many plans to turn it into a theme park or leisure centre have fallen through. In the meantime, though, it's found a use as a film location. Its dilapidated railway station is one of the shabby backdrops to Michael Radford's grim 1984 film*Nineteen Eighty-Four*, and hosts the climactic Battle of Bosworth in Richard Loncraine's *Richard III*. The rubble-strewn interior is one of the murder sites in George Sluizer's *Crimetime*. It's also where Hugh Laurie and Tom Hollander confront the BBC man in 2000's *Maybe Baby*.

The modernistic **Marco Polo House, Queenstown Road**, south of Chelsea Bridge, is HQ to the QVC shopping channel. It is the 'Presm Building', the fertility clinic where a somewhat embarrassed Annette Crosbie has to explain to Mark Frankel that he was the result of a misconception involving mixed-up test tubes, in *Leon the Pig Farmer*.

Following the Thames east, you pass through **Nine Elms**, home to the fruit and veg trade since it moved from Covent Garden in the seventies.

Spider: the halfway house neighbourhood: Oval Mansions, Kennington Oval

The World Is Not Enough: the attack on MI6: Vauxhall Cross, Albert Embankment

Anthony Simmons' 1973 comedy-drama *The Optimists of Nine Elms*, starring Peter Sellers, recalls the area's past.

Southeast of Vauxhall is Kennington. The halfway house in the shadow of the giant gasometer where Spider (Ralph Fiennes) stays in the David Cronenberg movie is **Oval Mansions, Kennington Oval (11)** at Vauxhall Street, behind the famous Oval Cricket Ground.

The stepped, post-modern bulk of the MI6 HQ building, **Vauxhall Cross, 85 Albert Embankment** (**12**), by Vauxhall Bridge is the start of the river chase in *The World Is Not Enough*. Special effects blow a hole in the building in the film, but the IRA did a more convincing job in real life. Pierce Brosnan returns to the building, as a shabbier, seedier agent, in John Boorman's film of John le Carré's novel *The Tailor of Panama*. The real exterior is, of course, matched to a studio set, this time in Bray Studios, Dublin. The block is overshadowed by **Camelford House, 87-89 Albert Embankment**, next door, atop which Matthew Rhys teeters, contemplating the death of his brother, in *Sorted*.

And one block upriver, **Peninsula Heights**, formerly Alembic House and home of disgraced peer Lord Archer, is the luxurious flat of Ian Hendry in cult favourite *Theatre of Blood*. In a surprisingly moving scene, Vincent Price recites the soliloquy from *Hamlet* on the balcony as the critics assemble, before plummeting into the Thames. The tower's unparalleled views over the Thames and the Houses of Parliament make it irresistible to film-makers. Michael Caine organises The Italian Job here. George Segal works in the building – although the entrance is clearly in the City of London – in the 1973 romantic comedy *A Touch of Class*. Three years later the Heights became the HQ of 'Media Incorporated', where an American-accented Barry Foster operates as a sinister PR man in *Sweeney!*

If you have the time, you can head down Salamanca Street to **Salamanca Place**, where Bricktop's heavies catch up with Tyrone (Ade) in *Snatch*, though it has since been completely redeveloped.

Never mind, walk along Black Prince Road. **The Jolly**

Theatre of Blood: Edward Lionheart takes a dive: Peninsula Heights

Gardeners, 49 Black Prince Road (**13**; see **Bars and Restaurants**, p20), became 'The Drowning Trout' in *Snatch*.

Now head back to the Embankment and turn right down Lambeth Road. In Henry Cornelius' 1949 farce *Passport to Pimlico*, WWII bomb damage uncovers documents revealing that the titular neighbourhood belongs to the Duchy of Burgundy and is therefore exempt from Britain's strict post-war regulations. The locals naturally declare independence. Yes, it's the classic little-folk-against-beaurocracy theme of the best Ealing comedies. Across Vauxhall Bridge is the real-life area of Pimlico, but if you stand between Hercules Road and Kennington Road, and look north toward the **railway bridge** (**14**), you'll recognise the film's 'Pimlico'. At the time of filming it was nothing more than a flattened bomb site, and a huge set was built to incorporate the arches of the real railway bridge.

Snatch: shootout at The Drowning Trout: The Jolly Gardeners, Black Prince Road

Passport to Pimlico: independence for Pimlico: the railway bridge, Kennington Road

Off Kennington Road is **Walcot Square**, at Sullivan Road, where Reggie Kray's violent reaction to two guys admiring his car sends his wife Frances into hysterics in *The Krays*.

Return to the Embankment. Outside **Lambeth Palace**, at the foot of **Lambeth Bridge**, Midnight Franklin (Jayne Mansfield) waits for the protection money pick-up – "Don't tell me they've got the Archbishop working for them, please!" – in strip-joint melodrama *Too Hot to Handle*.

Nearby, on **Lambeth Palace Road**, on the Thames Embankment by Lambeth Bridge, nerdish Ian Carmichael bumps into Janette Scott, prompting him to take Alastair Sim's course in lifemanship in Robert Hamer's 1960 comedy *School for Scoundrels*. The road was also used for the double-decker bus chase (supposedly from the British Museum to Tower Bridge) in *The Mummy Returns*.

Although *Brannigan* used the exterior of New Scotland Yard in Victoria, the interior of top cop Richard Attenborough's office has spectacular views over the Houses of Parliament, Westminster Bridge and County Hall, from south of the river. It's clearly an upper floor of **St Thomas Hospital**. In the hospi-

Johnny English: the sushi bar: Yo!
Sushi, Belvedere Road

tal grounds alongside the Thames, Bob Hoskins and Helen Mirren reminisce in *Last Orders*. Scenes for Michael Winner's *Death Wish 3* (supposedly set in New York) were also filmed in the grounds of St Thomas.

County Hall (**15**) was the seat of the old London County Council, which became the Greater London Council before being dissolved by Margaret Thatcher. It now houses a hotel and aquarium. The interior has been regularly used as a film location. It became the CIA HQ in 'Langley, Virginia' in *Mission: Impossible* and the Old Bailey in *Scandal*. County Hall's basement became the interior of the 'Tower of London' (the exterior was the Tate Modern) in Richard Loncraine's *Richard III*, while its entrance was the Lord Protector's HQ in the same film. A few computer-generated embellishments turn County Hall into the exterior of Austin Powers' groovy pad in *Goldmember*.

Opposite the south side of the hall is the branch of Japanese chain **Yo! Sushi, Belvedere Road** (*©* *020.7928.8871*), where Rowan Atkinson meets Natalie Imbruglia, and naturally gets his tie caught in the conveyor belt, in *Johnny English*.

The terrace in front of County Hall is the setting for the politician's lecture at the opening of Alfred Hitchcock's *Frenzy* – he claims that the Thames is free from foreign bodies, just as the body of the 'Necktie Killer' victim is washed up, while Hitch puts in his cameo as a bowler-hatted, unsmiling rubbernecker in the crowd. Harry Fabian (Richard Widmark) pretends to get a drinks licence at the southern entrance on **Westminster Bridge Road** in Jules Dassin's *Night and the City*. Scenes for *Die Another Day* were shot at the rear of County Hall, on **Belvedere Road**, and Bond finds the entrance to the abandoned 'Vauxhall Cross Underground Station' at the southern end of the bridge.

The **Royal Festival Hall** was built for the Festival of Britain in 1951, which you can see recreated on the actual site in *Prick Up Your Ears*, when playwright Joe Orton (Gary Oldman) and his partner Kenneth

Die Another Day: the entrance to
Vauxhall Cross Underground Station:
Westminster Bridge

Halliwell (Alfred Molina) visit the Festival. Anthony Hopkins and Judi Dench enjoy a civilised evening at the Festival in *84 Charing Cross Road*. On the Thamesside terrace, a miffed Hywel Bennett reveals to Hayley Mills that he's only just discovered she is the sixth richest girl in the country, in *Endless Night*. Since this is an Agatha Christie story, it seems unlikely she'll make it to the end of the last reel.

Further east, the terrace in front of the **National Film Theatre, South Bank** (**16**), is where a tongue-tied Hugh Grant eventually gets to the point about his feelings for Andie MacDowell in *Four Weddings and a Funeral*. While you're here, you might want to catch a film (see **Entertainment: Cinemas**, p26).

MOMI, the **Museum of the Moving Image, South Bank Centre, Belvedere Road**, with interactive exhibits exploring all aspects of cinema and TV, closed for renovation and was scheduled to re-open in 2003, but there is currently no sign of this happening.

On the terrace of the **National Theatre**, Jill Townsend and Patrick Drury decide to skip the second act of a particularly boring play in the particularly boring mummy adventure *The Awakening*.

Down Waterloo Road is **Waterloo Station**. Gary Cooper arrives at the station to attend the naval hearing in the 1959 courtroom drama *The Wreck of the Mary Deare*, and catches a black cab at the station's grand entrance. Two years later, John Schlesinger's career was launched with the half-hour documentary *Terminus*, which charts a day in the life of the station. Gregory Peck arrives at Waterloo only to discover that he was wanted for murder, in Stanley Donen's 1966 comedy-thriller *Arabesque*. The station was mocked up in Hollywood for Hitchcock's 1940 film *Foreign Correspondent*, when reporter Joel McCrea is met on his arrival in London, and for the 1944 melodrama *Waterloo Road*, though the latter was filmed in the area. **Waterloo Underground Station** can be seen in arty horror flick *The Wisdom of Crocodiles*. The **Waterloo & City line platform** is where Gwyneth Paltrow misses/catches the train in the alternative realities of *Sliding Doors*.

If size is important to you, you must catch a movie at the **BFI London IMAX Cinema, 1 Charlie Chaplin Walk** (see **Entertainment: Cinemas**, p26), the enormous cylinder planted in the old 'bullring' site in front of Waterloo Station. The choice of films is limited, but it is the largest screen in the country. Hugh Grant waits for his late date in front of the twinkling blue lights of the underpass in *About a Boy*.

The **Old Vic, The Cut** – home to the National Theatre for many years until the company moved to its purpose-built complex on the South Bank in the seventies – can be seen in Oliver Parker's film of Oscar Wilde's play *An Ideal Husband*. Just along The Cut

Richard III: the Tower of London: Tate Modern.

is excellent seafood restaurant **Livebait, 43 The Cut**, which appears in *Martha Meet Frank, Daniel & Laurence*. Continue east towards Southwark. On the left is the **Tate Modern** (**17**; © 020.7887.8000; website: www.tate.org.uk), which, as you can probably tell, was originally Bankside Power Station. Closed in 1980, like Paris' Gare d'Orsay the building has been given a new lease of life as a hugely successful modern art gallery. It has another new identity imaginatively bestowed on it in Richard Loncraine's thirties-set *Richard III*, where it becomes the 'Tower of London', a massively threatening Eastern European-style prison. Of course, it's really all sweetness and light inside, with a stunning exhibition space and a not bad café (© 020.7401.5020). Stop for a little refreshment, like Bridget (Renée Zellweger) and chums, who hang out here in *Bridget Jones's Diary*.

Alongside the Tate Modern, on Bankside, stands the re-creation of Shakespeare's **Globe theatre**, the culmination of years of campaigning by the late actor and director Sam Wanamaker. In Shakespeare's day, Southwark, then outside the bounds of the city, was the red-light and entertainment district. Brothels, taverns, bear-baiting and cockfighting flourished, along with the new-fangled entertainment form that marked the end of civilised values, the theatre. Apart from the rebuilt Globe, you can view the remains of **The Rose**, a genuine Elizabethan playhouse, where Shakespeare's earliest plays were performed.

A surviving pub from the same period on Bankside, at the foot of Southwark Bridge, is the **Anchor Tavern, 1 Bankside**. In 1666, an exhausted Samuel Pepys watched resignedly from the Anchor as the Great Fire of London consumed the city across the river. In 1996, Ethan (Tom Cruise) finally gets to chill out on the tavern's terrace after the pyrotechnics of Brian De Palma's *Mission: Impossible*.

To the east of Southwark Bridge Road is the old Borough Market, set within a knot of beautifully preserved period streets dear to the hearts of filmmakers, and so naturally a perfect area for redevelopment. See it now before it goes the

Mission: Impossible: chilling out after the chase: Anchor Tavern, Bankside

way of Battle Bridge in King's Cross.

Park Street (**18**) is a frequently used movie location, and can be seen in *Keep the Aspidistra Flying*, *Howards End* (Leonard Bast lives here) and, of course, *Lock, Stock and Two Smoking Barrels*. The gang's hideout is **15 Park Street**, while Dog's place is **13 Park Street**, next door – also the bike messenger HQ that Rupert Graves works out of in *Different for Girls*. Sean Connery brings Catherine Zeta-Jones here to buy the vase in *Entrapment*. For a brief moment, Park Street becomes the entrance to 'Kitchener Street', the site of Spider's childhood home in David Cronenberg's film.

Winchester Walk is the scruffy little sidestreet, apparently only minutes from Piccadilly Circus, where David Naughton is finally cornered and despatched in *An American Werewolf in London*. Also apparently in the West End is the tiny **Jubilee Café, 14a Winchester Walk** (easily missed, it's in a car park on the south side of the street), where David Thewlis meets waitress Gina McKee, in Mike Leigh's *Naked*. It's on **Stoney Street**, at, the western end of Winchester Walk, that US cop Harvey Keitel watches his British counterparts being incinerated in their car in Danny Cannon's *The Young Americans*. The triple-decker Knight Bus trundles down Stoney Street in *Harry Potter and the Prisoner of Azkaban*, and **Octopus House, 8 Stoney Street**, alongside the Market Porter pub, was transformed into the 'Third Hand Book Emporium'. **Number 7**, beneath the railway bridge, is the entrance to 'The Leaky Cauldron' in the

Lock, Stock and Two Smoking Barrels: Dog's place: Park Street

An American Werewolf in London: the climax in the West End alleyway: Winchester Walk

Naked: the West End cafe: Jubilee Café, Winchester Walk

Bridget Jones's Diary: Bridget's flat: The Globe, Bedale Street

The French Lieutenant's Woman: searching for Streep: Green Dragon Court

same movie (though *Harry Potter and the Sorcerer's Stone* used another door in Leadenhall Market: see **The City of London**, p91).

On the other side of Borough Market is **The Globe pub, 8 Bedale Street** (see **Bars & Restaurants**, p20), which appears in *Blue Ice*. Bridget's flat is above the pub in *Bridget Jones's Diary*. Across the street you can see the shops which were transformed into the cab office, the newsagent and, at **5 Bedale Street** (now Bedale's wine shop), the fictitious Greek restaurant where Daniel Cleaver (Hugh Grant) and Mark Darcy (Colin Firth) slug it out during a birthday party. Bridget plods glumly through the market in her Bunny Girl outfit after discovering Daniel with "Lara, from the New York Office". Cleaver's flat is behind an anonymous door on **Clink Street**, opposite the Clink Prison Museum. In *The French Lieutenant's Woman*, Jeremy Irons searches for Meryl Streep among the whores in **Green Dragon Court**, the dark, pillared space used as a carpark behind the Globe. The railway lines above the pub are where Natasha Little's sinister past is revealed in the flashback of *The Criminal*.

Take time out for a pint in **The George Inn, 77 Borough High Street** (see **Bars & Restaurants**, p20), which can be seen in *Tom Brown's Schooldays*.

Just around the corner stands the elaborate Victorian **Hop Exchange, 24 Southwark Street** (not generally open to the public, though you can peer through the glass doors at the iron-pillared and galleried central hall), which can be seen in *Spiceworld the Movie*.

Tom Brown's Schooldays: the coaching inn: The George Inn, Borough High Street

Spiceworld the Movie: the girls perform: Hop Exchange, Southwark Street

Looming over the area is the tower of **Southwark Cathedral**, the scene of Cinderella's wedding to Prince Edward at the end of Bryan Forbes' enjoyable but strangely underpopulated version of the traditional fairy tale, *The Slipper and the Rose*.

One stop

south from Borough on the Northern Line is Elephant and Castle, the neighbourhood which formed the backdrop to Kenneth Loach's slice of neo-realism *Poor Cow*, with Carol White and Terence Stamp, though since the film was made in 1967, much of the area has been bulldozed to make way for the shopping centre with its love-it-or-hate-it pink elephant. Off Newington Causeway, running north from the tube station, is Gaunt Street. **Ministry of Sound, 103 Gaunt Street** (**19**), is the disco which northerner Carl (Matthew Rhys) has to stump up £30 to get into in *Sorted*.

The Slipper and the Rose: the fairytale wedding: Southwark Cathedral

Return to Borough, and go south to Abbey Street. Currently closed and up for sale, **The Fleece, 160 Abbey Street** (**20**) at Neckinger, is the pub where the pathetic Jack 'The Hat' (Tom Bell) gets steaming drunk, before being dragged off by Ronnie's boyfriend Steve (Gary Love), past the **Marquis of Wellington, Druid Street**, under the railway bridge at **Gedling Place**, to the party to end all parties, in *The Krays*.

Head back to Tooley Street, past the London Dungeon (Madame Tussauds without the boring celebs) and Tower Bridge. The high, narrow passageways of **Shad Thames** (**21**), now so squeaky clean, were once time-blackened warehouses, the air heavy with the smell of spices impregnated in the very brickwork – you can still detect the faintest trace of cumin or pepper. The old Shad Thames can be seen in *The Elephant Man*, when Dr Treves (Anthony Hopkins) goes to look for John Merrick (John Hurt), and in *The French Lieutenant's Woman*, for which a beautifully elaborate dock office set was built on the Thames waterfront.

Now, of course, it's Starbucks and art galleries. On the Thames waterfront, **Cantina del Ponte, Butlers Wharf Building, 36c Shad Thames** (see **Bars & Restaurants**, p19), is where Renée Zellweger and Hugh Grant have a date in

Sorted: the nightclub: Ministry of Sound, Gaunt Street

The Krays: Jack 'The Hat' downs his last drink: The Fleece, Abbey Street

Bridget Jones's Diary: the date with Daniel Cleaver: Cantina del Ponte, Shad Thames

The French Lieutenant's Woman and Bridget Jones's Diary: the old warehouses: Shad Thames

Bridget Jones's Diary, before enjoying a clinch beneath the walkways of Shad Thames itself. Rohan and Pooja sit on the riverside terrace in *Kabhi Khushi Kabhie Gham....*

New Concordia Wharf,
Bermondsey Wall West, one of the renovated Thameside warehouses with a terrific view of Tower Bridge, became 'St Trevor's Wharf', the luxury pad John Cleese borrows for his tryst with Jamie Lee Curtis in *A Fish Called Wanda*. The window-hanging stunt was filmed a couple of blocks down at the, then undeveloped, **Reed's Wharf**.

There are a number of locations in South London you can visit at your leisure. A tube map and/or A-Z may be useful at this point.

A little further on, in **Bermondsey**, is the jolly red-and-green pop-arty apartment block **37-77 West Lane (22)**, where Sid Vicious (Gary Oldman) and Nancy Spungen (Chloe Webb) live in less-than-perfect harmony in Alex Cox's *Sid and Nancy*. 35 West Lane, now a smart office building, used to be the Two Brewers pub, outside which the fun couple have a blazing row.

Continue south to Lynton Road, and the huge crumbling bulk of the disused St Augustine's church. Alongside it, the gaunt and darkly Gothic **St Augustine's Vicarage, Lynton Road (23)** at Stevensons Crescent, looks like the last place on earth you'd want to rent a room. But if you did, would you really want to start messing with the occult? It comes as no surprise that very bad things hap-

Long Time Dead: consulting the ouija board: St Augustine's Vicarage, Lynton Road

Sid and Nancy: Sid and Nancy's love-nest: West Lane

pen here to the kids who play with a ouija board in the Brit shocker *Long Time Dead*.

Brixton (24;
tube: *Victoria line*) is pretty

South West 9: the Dog Bar: the Dogstar Bar, Coldharbour Lane

much defined in the public consciousness by the Afro-Caribbean community, who settled here, as in Notting Hill, during the fifties. As a riposte to the unforgiveably whitebread *Notting Hill* ("Notting Hill this ain't…"), Brixton's cultural buzz is portrayed, if not exactly celebrated, in Richard Parry's *South West 9*. Disturbingly reactionary – a drugs 'r' bad school project dressed up in the hipper-than-hip style of a Social Studies teacher – the movie does record the mix of railway arches, crumbling Victoriana and eye-popping street art that characterises the district. The **Dogstar Bar, 389 Coldharbour Lane** (see **Bars & Restaurants**, p19), formerly known as the Atlantic, appears pretty much as itself in the movie.

Not far from the tube station is the famed **Ritzy Cinema** (see **Entertainment: Cinemas**, p26), and beyond that, the empty, mural-covered building at **1-3 Effra Road** which became *South West 9*'s 'smoke house'.

In the other direction, **Brixton Academy, 211 Stockwell Road** (© *020.7771.3000; website: www.brixton-academy.co.uk*), is the theatre where Brian Slade (Jonathan Rhys Meyers) melodramatically fakes his onstage assassination in Todd Haynes' glam-rock epic *Velvet Goldmine*.

Turn down Villa Road, alongside Max Roach Park (named for the black American jazz drummer). **33 Villa Road** is the house of Erroll the grass (Paul Barber, now more famous as 'Horse' in *The Full Monty*), who gets cut up by Razors (PH Moriarty), in *The Long Good Friday*.

Back to *South West 9*. At the end of the road, you'll come to the church, which Essex boy Jake (Stuart

South West 9: the smoke house: Effra Road

Velvet Goldmine: goodbye to Brian Slade: Brixton Academy, Stockwell Road

The Long Good Friday: Erroll the grass: Villa Road

South West 9: Faith: St John the Evangelist, Wiltshire Road

Laing) transforms into "Faith – a celestial night of wholesome die-hard acid trance", **St John the Evangelist, Wiltshire Road** at Villa Road. Closed in 1998, the church has just reopened. No doubt the movie's location fee helped. Turn right onto Wiltshire Road. **70 Wiltshire Road** became the chaotic squat in the film.

Born Romantic, David Kane's follow-up to *This Year's Love*, is a multi-focus romantic comedy linked by a character, Adrian Lester's withdrawn but observant cab driver Jimmy, and a location, a salsa club seemingly yards from St Paul's Cathedral. In fact, it's in Brixton. And the good news is, it's for real. The **Loughborough Hotel, 39 Loughborough Road** at Evandale Road, is the place if you want to learn salsa, or even flamenco. There are four rooms on three levels, so whether you're a beginner wanting to impress your potential soulmate or a hip-swinger wanting to move up to a new level…

South of Brixton is Streatham. The thirty-six-lane **Streatham Megabowl, 142 Streatham Hill** (*© 020.8678.6007*), was used for – what else? – the bowl-

Born Romantic: the salsa club: Loughborough Hotel, Loughborough Road

South West 9: the chaotic squat: Wiltshire Road

ing scene in *Leon the Pig Farmer*.

A few doors away, **Caesars Nightclub, 156-160 Streatham Hill** (see **Bars & Restaurants**, p19), is the site of the 'boxing match' in *Snatch*.

Head to Balham (*tube: Northern line*). The Shakespearian Globe theatre within **The Bedford, 77 Bedford Hill** (*© 020.8673.1756; website: www.thebedford. co.uk*) at Fernlea Road, was transformed into the 'Sombrero Club', where the Bowiesque Brian

Slade (Jonathan Rhys Meyers) is discovered playing guitar in a frock, in *Velvet Goldmine*.

Finally, go west to Tooting. **Tooting Bec Lido, Tooting Bec Road** (*© 020.8871.7198*), at the eastern end of Tooting Common, is the swimming pool where Daniel Craig and Kelly Macdonald enjoy a brief idyll in *Some Voices*.

Snatch: the unlicensed fight: Caesar's Nightclub, Streatham Hill

Velvet Goldmine: the Sombrero Club: The Bedford, Bedford Hill

Southwest London: Hyde Park Corner to Wimbledon

A long and rambling tour from Hyde Park Corner to the outer reaches of Richmond and Wimbledon, which will require a bit of tube, train or bus travel. It takes in elegant Knightsbridge, the secret little mews of South Kensington, swinging Chelsea and the cosmopolitan bedsit-land of Earl's Court. Among the characters you'll meet are Colonel Blimp, Abe Lincoln, Count Dracula and Eva Peron...

Starting Point: Hyde Park Corner

The huge complex opposite Hyde Park Corner is the exclusive **Lanesborough Hotel, 1 Lanesborough Place** (**1**; see **Hotels**, p11). It's Royal Suite appears in *Eyes Wide Shut*.

The vintage cars assemble at **Hyde Park Corner** for the opening of *Genevieve*, while villainous John Vernon walks here with his lawyer, Mel Ferrer, in *Brannigan*. One of London's lost locations stood at

Hyde Park Corner: Londonderry House was used as the house of Lady Bellaston (Joan Greenwood) for Tony Richardson's 1963 film of *Tom Jones*.

Head west on Knightsbridge. The **Edinburgh Gate** entrance to Hyde Park, beneath the blandly modern **Bowater House**, is where Dirk Bogarde drives with car salesman Nigel Stock in *Victim*.

Continue along Knightsbridge. The side entrance to the grand **Wellington Court** (**2**) apartment block, in the tiny passageway off **Park Close**, is the entrance to the nightclub ("These places are glorified brothels...")

Eyes Wide Shut: Tom Cruise and Sydney Pollack: Lanesborough Hotel, Lanesborough Place

Dance With a Stranger: the nightclub: Wellington Court, Park Close

The Life and Death of Colonel Blimp: Candy's home: Ovington Square

where Desmond Cussen (Ian Holm) introduces David Blakeley (Rupert Everett) to "the glorified brothel keeper" Ruth Ellis (Miranda Richardson) in *Dance With a Stranger*.

Robert Fielding Salon, Knightsbridge, now gone, is the hairdresser's where Coral Browne gets fried (as Joan of Arc in *Henry VI*) in *Theatre of Blood*.

Head back towards Hyde Park Corner and turn down Brompton Road. In **Harrods (3)**, on Brompton Road between the two branches of Hans Crescent, Anne Bancroft breaks down as her marriage crumbles ("Harrods of all places!" splutters caring husband Peter Finch), in Jack Clayton's brilliant, all-but-forgotten *The Pumpkin Eater*. Peter Sellers takes Sinead Cusack shopping in the Food Hall in the glumly creepy *Hoffman*. The shop also appears in Robert Young's comedy *Splitting Heirs*. Rupert Penry-Jones and Laura Fraser glide past its illuminated exterior during the 'magic carpet ride' in *Virtual Sexuality*. The shop's owner, Mohamed Al Fayed, appears as a doorman giving directions to Anna Friel in the disastrous *Mad Cows*.

15 Ovington Square (4), off Brompton Road via Ovington Gardens, is the London home of Clive Candy (Roger Livesey) in Powell and Pressburger's masterly movie *The Life and Death of Colonel Blimp*.

In the 1998 remake of Disney's *The Parent Trap*, Lindsay Lohan takes over the Hayley Mills role of identical twins who scheme to get their separated parents back together. The rather nice Kensington home of mum Natasha Richardson is **23 Egerton Terrace (5)**, at Egerton Place. The owners of the house were not wildly keen to allow their house to be used, until they were persuaded by their young daughter, who was a big fan of the Hayley Mills original.

Go back across Brompton Road and follow Ennismore Street until it becomes Rutland Mews West. **Clock House, Rutland Mews West (6)**, is the home of bank chairman James Fox, where he gets suddenly offed by Ian McShane, in Jonathan Glazer's offbeat gangster movie *Sexy Beast*.

Opposite Clock House runs Rutland Mews South. From another era of British film

The Parent Trap: Natasha Richardson's house: Egerton Terrace

Sexy Beast: James Fox gets shot: Clock House, Rutland Mews West

altogether, **17 Rutland Mews South** is home to John Gregson and Dinah Sheridan in the 1953 comedy classic *Genevieve*. Don't recognise it? Walk to the south of the mews and look north. The ground floor of number 17 has been revamped, but the rest of the mews is recognisable. Halfway down on the right is the turnoff where the 1904 Darracq is garaged. The mews were once stables, and the name derives from the falcons that were kept there.

31 Ennismore Gardens Mews, in the same maze of streets, is the home of Brenda Blaney (Barbara Leigh-Hunt) in Alfred Hitchcock's *Frenzy*.

Heading back down **Brompton Road** to the intersection with Thurloe Place leads to the impressive **Brompton Oratory (7)**, the site of Alfred Hitchcock's marriage to Alma Reville in 1926.

South Kensington is famously featured in Roman Polanski's 1965 study of murderous psychopathy *Repulsion*. Standing alongside South Ken tube station, **Dino's (8)** has remained unchanged since Catherine Deneuve was filmed being taken by John Fraser for a fish and chip lunch. Opposite the station is the traffic island where she is disturbed by leering workman Mike Pratt. A few doors from Dino's, and also unchanged, is the **Hoop and Toy** pub, where Fraser drinks with his obnoxiously laddish mates, and further along, at **31 Thurloe Place**, is the beauty salon which became 'Madame Denise's', where Deneuve works.

To the north

Genevieve: the home of Gregson and Sheridan: Rutland Mews South

Frenzy: the home of Brenda Blaney: Ennismore Gardens Mews

stand two of London's great museums (and they're free). On **Cromwell Gardens** is the **Victoria and Albert Museum** (**9**; see **Historic Sites**, p32), which appears in *The Jokers* and *To Sir, With Love*.

Institute of Technology in Pasadena, California).

The **Royal Albert Hall, Kensington Gore** (**12**; © *020.7589.8212*; website: *www.royalalberthall.com*), is the site of sponger Alexis

Repulsion: Catherine Deneuve tucks into fish'n'chips: Dino's

Repulsion: John Fraser drinks with his mates: Hoop and Toy

The **X-Files**: the meeting of elders: Queen Alexandra's House, Kensington Gore

The **Natural History Museum, Cromwell Road** (**10**; see **Historic Sites**, p32), is where Professor Willingdon (Barry Jones) hears the Prime Minister's radio broadcast in *Seven Days to Noon*. Outside, he sees his face everywhere on posters. Tarzan is, understandably, spooked here in *Greystoke: The Legend of Tarzan, Lord of the Apes* and, along with the V&A, the museum is an inevitable destination of the school outing in *To Sir, With Love*. It also appears in *Loch Ness*.

Take a slight detour if you want. Down Old Brompton Road is Onslow Gardens. **69 Onslow Gardens** (**11**) is the home of Patricia Hayes, the old lady with the doomed little dogs, in *A Fish Called Wanda*.

Head back, towards Hyde Park. In *Greystoke: The Legend of Tarzan, Lord of the Apes*, Tarzan flees the opening of the 'Greystoke Wing' of the Natural History Museum to the glorious kitsch of Gilbert Scott's beautifully restored **Albert Memorial, Hyde Park**. Oliver Reed and Michael Crawford stage the first of their bomb hoaxes at the memorial in *The Jokers*.

Nearby is **Queen Alexandra's House, Kensington Gore**, where The Well-Manicured Man (John Neville) attends the meeting of elders in *The X-Files* (though the interior was the Athenaeum, the dining club of the California

Kanner's comeuppance at the end of the 1969 movie *Connecting Rooms*, the fantasy sequence from *The Knack*, Ann Todd's concert performance in the 1945 melodrama *The Seventh Veil* and the brass band competition finals in *Brassed Off*. However, it was, most famously, the site of the climax to both versions (1934 and 1956) of Alfred Hitchcock's *The Man Who Knew Too Much*. It can also be seen in *Follow Me, The Fourth Protocol* and *Spiceworld the Movie*. The hall was the brainchild of Queen Victoria's consort Prince Albert, following on the success of his Great Exhibition of 1851. Sadly, the prince died before the hall was built. It opened in 1871.

On the south side of the Royal Albert Hall, Sidney J Furie filmed a fight through the glass panes of a phone booth in *The Ipcress File* (there is no phone booth there).

Directly on the hall's west side is the **Kensington Road** section of the **Royal College of Art**, where Jennie Linden works in the film of Iris Murdoch's novel *A Severed Head*.

On the opposite side of the Royal Albert Hall is the **Royal Geographical Society** (open only by appointment; © *020.7591.3040; website: www.rgs.org*), is the king's sitting room in the 1995 film of *Richard III*.

Albert Court, the grand mansion block just off Kensington Gore, next to Imperial College, is home to Richard Hannay (Robert Powell) in the third film version of *The Thirty-Nine Steps*. Rita Tushingham is carried down the steps on a bedstead in *The Knack*, Peter Cushing scuttles over them to the home of Freddie Jones in *The Satanic Rites of Dracula* – the last, and possibly least, of Hammer's series – while George Segal sprints down the steps to catch a cab to Glenda Jackson's flat, while his wife enjoys a Beethoven concert in the Royal Albert Hall, in *A Touch of Class*.

Ann Todd hurries down the steps to study at the **Royal College of Music, Prince Consort Road**, in *The Seventh Veil* (in

Repulsion: Madame Denise's salon: Thurloe Place

A Fish Called Wanda: killing the old lady's dogs: Onslow Gardens

The Thirty-Nine Steps: Richard Hannay's home: Albert Court

Shine: David Helfgott studies in London: Royal College of Music, Prince Consort Road

The Ipcress File: contacting 'Bluejay': Science Museum Library, Prince Consort Road

which James Mason famously smashes down his walking cane on Todd's fingers: "If you won't play for me, you shan't play for anyone ever again!"). Another troubled youngster with a possessive guardian, the Adolescent David Helfgott (Noah Taylor), fumbles with his sheet music on the Albert Court steps in *Shine*, while Cecil Parkes (John Gielgud) watches from the college window.

Also on **Prince Consort Road** is the **Science Museum Library**, where Harry Palmer (Michael Caine) makes contact with 'Bluejay' in *The Ipcress File*. The library is open to the public for personal research – you can get a day pass on production of ID.

There's nothing to see now at 121 Queen's Gate, but this was the site of legendary sixties club Blaises. Named after cartoon character Modesty Blaise (incarnated by Monica Vitti in Joseph Losey's leaden fantasy), the basement venue hosted legendary performances from the likes of Jimi Hendrix. It's the club where Mike Roscoe (Ian Ogilvy) hangs out in Michael Reeves' 1967 movie *The Sorcerers*.

Queen's Gate Mews (13), running between Queen's Gate and Gloucester Road, is where the unfortunate chauffeur gets his head shaved in *Performance*.

To the south, **Queen's Gate Lodge, 23a Elvaston Place** at Elvaston Mews, became 'The Keeley Foundation for Science', where Peter Cushing confronts scientist Freddie Jones, who's incubating plague viruses for some obscure reason, in *The Satanic Rites of Dracula*.

Head up Gloucester Road and Palace Gate towards Kensington High Street. The old Biba store on Kensington Church Street can be seen in Michael Winner movies *The Jokers* and *I'll Never Forget What's 'is Name*. **40 Brunswick Gardens (14)**, off Kensington Church Street,

Performance: torturing the chauffeur: Queen's Gate Mews

was used for *102 Dalmatians*.

On the top floor of the old Biba store, **99 Kensington High Street** – previously Derry and Tom's, and now housing **Marks and Spencer** and **British Home Stores** – are the **Rainbow Room** and the **Roof Garden (15**; see **Bars & Restaurants**, p20). The Rainbow Room was once the legendary Regine's, which was transformed into a restaurant for *The Long Good Friday*. It appears in it's current incarnation in *Brazil*. You might also recognise it from the David Bowie video for 'Boys Keep Swinging'.

Barkers, Kensington High Street, is the department store to which Cecil Parker follows the mysterious woman in the glossy 1956 thriller *23 Paces to Baker Street*.

The anonymous doorway of 142-144 Kensington High Street was once the entrance to the real Sombrero Club (aka Yours or Mine), the gay club wildly romanticised by Todd Haynes in *Velvet Goldmine* (see **Southeast London**, p125, for the location used in the movie).

Just off Kensington High Street is **Durward House, 31 Kensington Court (16)**, the quite posh apartment block of ill-assorted robbers Terry-Thomas, Hattie Jacques and Athene Seyler in the 1960 comedy *Make Mine Mink*. Nearby **Esmond Court**, on Thackeray Street was the home of Joan Sims, stalwart of the *Carry On* movies, and **1-14 Kensington Court Gardens** was home to poet and dramatist TS Elliot.

Tucked away in this quiet enclave, the starkly modernist house at **51-52 Kelso Place (17)** is home to therapist couple Harriet Walter and Simon Callow, where Kevin McKidd and James Purefoy work out their psychosexual problems in Rose Troche's spot-on satire of sexual mores *Bedrooms & Hallways*.

10 Kynance

The Satanic Rites of Dracula: The Keeley Foundation: Queen's Gate Lodge, Elvaston Place

Make Mine Mink: the robbers' apartment block: Durward House, Kensington Court

Bedrooms & Hallways: the men's group: Kelso Place

Mews (**18**), to the east, is Juliette Binoche's classy 'bachelor girl' pad, where Jeremy Irons suffers a bout of *amour phooey*, in Louis Malle's laughably pretentious melodrama *Damage*.

On the other side of Kensington High Street is **Linley Sambourne House, 18 Stafford Terrace** (**19**; see **Historic Sites**, p32), which

Damage: Juliette Binoche's 'bachelor girl' pad: Kynance Mews

was used in two Merchant-Ivory films, *A Room with a View* and *Maurice*.

5 Melbury Road, now gone – replaced by an anonymous block of flats – is the home of Carl Boehm in Michael Powell's *Peeping Tom*. But over the road, **8 Melbury Road** is the house's twin. An impressive Norman Shaw artist's home with huge windows, it was home to director Powell, and the home movie scenes of *Peeping Tom* were shot in the garden with Powell himself as Boehm's sadistic father. A Directors Guild of Great Britain plaque records that Powell lived here from 1951 to 1971. The house was also home to artist Marcus Stone from 1840 to his death in 1921. **31 Melbury Road**, the real house of director Michael Winner, is the home of scallywag brothers Michael Crawford and Oliver Reed, who plan to steal the Crown Jewels for a lark, in *The Jokers*.

The famous blue-tiled **Arab Hall** of **Leighton House, 12 Holland Park Road** (**20**; see **Historic Sites**, p32), can be seen in *Brazil*, albeit camped up with copies of Michelangelo's David in its alcoves. The hall is part of the Leighton House Museum.

Head towards Holland Park. **Oakwood Court, Abbottsbury Road** (**21**), is the luxury 'Victoria' pad of the hooker where Sid Vicious (Gary Oldman) and Johnny Rotten (Andrew Schofield) terrorise the poor doggy in the car and feast on baked beans and fag-ends at the beginning of *Sid and Nancy*.

Brazil: Katherine Helmond's facial surgery: Leighton House, Holland Park Road

A Room with a View: Daniel Day-Lewis' London home: Linley Sambourne House, Stafford Terrace

Michael Winner brought Raymond Chandler to the mean streets of Kensington with his unfortunate

1978 remake of *The Big Sleep*, which features **The Orangerie, Holland Park** (**22**). John Thaw meets informer Joe Melia by the fountain (now the Iris Fountain) alongside the Arcade behind what is now Marco Pierre White's Belvedere, in *Sweeney!*

Sid and Nancy: the luxury pad: Oakwood Court, Abbottsbury Road

The Big Sleep: The Orangerie, Holland Park

The striking, peacock blue-tiled mansion of **Debenham House, 8 Addison Road** (**23**), back towards Kensington High Street, cries out to be a movie location, and that's what US ex-pat Joseph Losey thought as he drove his son to school. It became the setting for the impenetrable psychodrama *Secret Ceremony*, with Elizabeth Taylor and a black-wigged Mia Farrow playing disturbing mindgames. The house also supplied the bathroom of Queen Elizabeth (Annette Bening) in Richard Loncraine's *Richard III*, and was seen in period dramas *Trottie True* and *The Wings of the Dove*. The Grade I listed house – built in 1906 for the founder of the Debenham's department store chain, Sir Ernest Debenham, but lately used as offices of the Richmond Fellowship, a care and rehabilitation charity – was designed by Halsey Ricardo at the fag-end of the Arts and Crafts movement. It's rumoured that the tiles, by the William de Morgan company, who also supplied the tiles for Leighton House, were overstocks originally made for the Tsar's yacht and P&O liners.

In 1986, long before the Tom Hanks movie, there was a Nicolas Roeg film called *Castaway*, with Amanda Donohoe replying to Oliver Reed's ad for a partner to retire with him to a South Seas island. The tax office in **Charles House, Kensington High Street**, is where Donohoe works before taking off for a dubious paradise with Reed.

The buffet of **Kensington Olympia Station** (**24**) stands in for 'Paddington', where on-the-lam gangster Chas (James Fox) overhears that there's a basement flat vacant in Powis

Secret Ceremony: the creepy house: Debenham House, Addison Road

Blowup: David Hemmings meets his agent: El Blason, Blacklands Terrace

A Clockwork Orange: the record store: McDonald's, King's Road

Square, in *Performance*.

The basement of the old Post Office building on **Blythe Road**, behind Olympia, becomes the downstairs of the radical meeting addressed by Paul Sorvino (itself filmed in the Zion Institute, Manchester) in *Reds*.

Now jump on a bus or catch the tube (*tube: Circle line*) from High Street Kensington to Sloane Square. **Albrissi, 1 Sloane Square (25)** – actually at the start of Cliveden Place off Sloane Square – is an interior design service which became the bridal gown shop where Andie MacDowell tries on dresses in *Four Weddings and a Funeral*.

The English Stage Company at the **Royal Court Theatre, Sloane Square**, launched the original productions of many plays which have gone on to become equally famous films. Jimmy Porter first railed against the world here in John Osborne's *Look Back in Anger*, and Laurence Olivier caught up with the new wave as Archie Rice in *The Entertainer*.

El Blason, 8-9 Blacklands Terrace (26; see **Bars & Restaurants**, p20), just off King's Road, is still much the same as it was when scenes for *Blowup* were shot here in 1966.

The **McDonald's, King's Road**, at the northwest corner of Royal Avenue, used to be the trendy polished metal and glass Chelsea Drugstore, the record shop where Alex picks up two girls in *A Clockwork Orange*.

The Vestry, 120 King's Road, opposite Royal Avenue, was Thomas Crapper, Sanitary Engineer, seen in the opening credits of 1963's *The Servant*, where creepily camp gentleman's gentleman Dirk Bogarde is first seen. He's heading for the house where he ostensibly serves but actually destroys effete aristo James Fox, **30 Royal Avenue (27)**. It's opposite the one-time home of W Somerset Maugham, uncle of Robin Maugham, author of *The Servant*. Director Joseph Losey was

The Servant: James Fox's house: Royal Avenue

I Don't Want to Be Born: the monstrous baby: Wellington Square

clearly impressed with the area, living directly opposite, at **29 Royal Avenue**, from 1966 until his death in 1984.

At the southern end of Royal Avenue you can see the home of *Dracula* author Bram Stoker at **18 Leonard's Terrace**.

It's not looking good for stripper Joan Collins in 1975's *I Don't Want to Be Born*, what with Donald Pleasence as her obstetrician and Eileen Atkins as her sister-in-law nun. True to form, her bouncing bundle of joy is no sooner out of the womb than it's trying to rip her face off. Joan's home in this trashy horror flick is **32 Wellington Square**, off King's Road.

Continue west on King's Road then turn right onto Sydney Street. The huge **Chelsea Parish Church of St Luke, Sydney Street (28)** at Britten Street, is where Joely Richardson marries Jeff Daniels while a crowd of doggies wait outside in *101 Dalmatians*.

Go back to King's Road. Not an arthouse cinema as such, but tending to specialise in non-blockbuster fare, is the **Chelsea Cinema, 206 King's Road** (℡ *020.7351.3742*). Across the road, **213 King's Road** was the home of Sir Carol Reed, director of *The Third Man* and *Oliver!*

Heading back up King's Road brings you to **La Bersagliera, 372 King's Road (29**; see **Bars & Restaurants**, p20), an Italian restaurant which is the 'Cavern' coffee shop in *Dracula A.D. 1972*.

Turn into Glebe Place. On the right, about halfway down

101 Dalmatians: the doggy wedding: Chelsea Parish Church of St Luke, Sydney Street

Dracula A.D. 1972: the coffee shop: La Bersagliera, King's Road

The Killing of Sister George: the lesbian club: Bramerton Street

There's a Girl in My Soup: Goldie Hawn's basement flat: Glebe Place

the street, the basement at **15a Glebe Place (30)** is the chaotic pad of hippie chick Goldie Hawn, where oleaginous TV cook Peter Sellers vies for her affections with rock musician Nicky Henson, in Roy Boulting's 1970 sex farce *There's a Girl in My Soup*.

The unremarkable door in the middle of the featureless wall on the east side of Bramerton Street was the site of legendary lesbian club The Gateways, long since closed, where Beryl Reid and Susannah York, in Laurel and Hardy drag, meet Coral Browne, the lady from the BBC, in *The Killing of Sister George*.

Go back down Glebe Place and turn right at the end. **West House, 35 Glebe Place**, tucked away in a crook of the street off Bramerton Street, is the grand home of Uncle Monty (Richard Griffiths) in *Withnail & I*.

Upper Cheyne Row is where Passepartout (Cantinflas) is seen riding his penny-farthing on the way to the employment office where he gets the job as butler to Phileas Fogg (David Niven) that takes him *Around the World in Eighty Days*.

8 Cheyne Walk at Royal Hospital Road, is the home of theatre critic Jack Hawkins, duped into strangling his wife, Diana Dors, in the *Othello* segment of *Theatre of Blood*. **Cheyne Walk** is also the site of the police station in Joseph Losey's 1959 film *Blind Date*. On Cheyne Walk, east of Battersea Bridge, houseboats are traditionally moored. On one of the boats lives caddish blackmailer Dennis Price in Mario Zampi's 1957 black comedy

Withnail & I: Uncle Monty's: West House, Glebe Place

Around the World in Eighty Days: Passepartout rides his penny-farthing: Upper Cheyne Row

Theatre of Blood: the 'Othello' murder: Cheyne Walk

The Naked Truth. Advertising tycoon Orson Welles visits his ex-employee Oliver Reed on Carol White's boat in Michael Winner's 1967 *I'll Never Forget What's 'is Name*.

On the **Chelsea Embankment** at Oakley Street, the newly-defenceless Alex meets a former victim at the end of *A Clockwork Orange*, and it's under the **Albert Bridge** that the tramps take their revenge. Albert Bridge is also where Gwyneth Paltrow and John Hannah hang out and eventually reconcile in *Sliding Doors*, and where Eddie O'Connell sings 'Have You Ever Had It Blue' in Julien Temple's *Absolute Beginners*. If you want to take your characters south of the river, this beautifully delicate – and enormously photogenic – bridge is the one you want them to cross. See it illuminated at night from the Chelsea Embankment.

Go west along Cheyne Walk and turn right up Beaufort Street towards Fulham Road. Tony Richardson's 1961 film of Shelagh Delaney's play *A Taste of Honey* is famous for being the first major British production to be shot entirely on location. And although that's true, it's not entirely the canals and terraced streets of Salford. It's partly Chelsea. It might be difficult to envisage, but SW10 was not always quite as expensively 'chichi' as it is today. The production base, which was used for the rickety flat Rita Tushingham shares with Murray Melvin, was the scenic workshop of the English Stage Company (based at the opposite end of the King's Road, in Sloane Square's Royal Court Theatre). The workshop and yard (where the film ends with a firework display) have since been demolished, but **74 Elm Park Road (31)**, just around the corner, is the house – then in a state of disrepair – used for the interior of Dora Bryan's 'Salford' home.

The huge revolving doors of the new **Chelsea and Westminster Hospital** complex, **Fulham Road (32)**, lead into the spacious atrium where Dr William Harford (Tom Cruise) goes to look for the unfortunate Amanda Curram (Julienne Davis) in Stanley Kubrick's *Eyes Wide Shut*. The hospital is also where Imogen Stubbs dies in childbirth, leaving Richard E Grant bringing up baby in *Jack & Sarah*.

A Clockwork Orange: the tramps' revenge: Albert Bridge, Chelsea Embankment

The **Finborough Theatre**, above the **Finborough Arms, Finborough Road** (**33**) at Ifield Road, was part of screenwriter Hanif Kureishi's perfect day in London in *Sammy and Rosie Get Laid*. The pub is currently closed for major renovations.

Head north towards Old Brompton Road. The current-

A Taste of Honey: the northern interiors: Elm Park Road

ly empty **Knave's Kitchen, Finborough Road**, the basement of which was once the Catacomb, a gay coffee club, became the nightclub run by Borgia Ginz (Jack Birkett, credited as Orlando) inside Westminster Cathedral for Derek Jarman's punk museum piece *Jubilee*.

The building opposite, on the southwest corner of **Finborough Road** and **Old Brompton Road**, now a hostel, used to be the Princess Beatrice Maternity Hospital. After closure, while it stood empty, it was used as the hospital where David Naughton recuperates from a wolf bite in John Landis' *An American Werewolf in London*.

To the east is **Redcliffe Court, Redcliffe Square**, the house of the prostitute staked out by the press, after a tip-off that both a government minister and a KGB agent are using her services, in the dark conspiracy thriller *Defence of the Realm*.

64 Coleherne Road is home to nurse Jenny Agutter, where David Naughton undergoes some changes in *An American Werewolf in London*.

Around the corner, on Old Brompton Road, is the recently expanded **Troubadour, 265 Old Brompton Road** (**34**; *website: www.troubadour.co.uk*). This legendary coffee house (now blessed with a drinks licence), has a fascinating history dating from the coffee boom of the fifties. In the sixties, the Black Panthers met here, and the first issues of satirical magazine *Private Eye* were produced. The Troubadour hosted performances by such musical legends as Paul Simon, Joni Mitchell, Jimi Hendrix and Sammy Davis Jr, and it

Eyes Wide Shut: Tom Cruise looks for the woman: Chelsea and Westminster Hospital, Fulham Road

Defence of the Realm: the brothel: Redcliffe Court, Redcliffe Square

was the first London venue for Bob Dylan. It's where Richard Harris met his wife-to-be, and where Ken Russell, who recruited for his short films here, met Oliver Reed. The Troubadour features in two early Michael Winner films: Alfred Lynch hangs out in the coffee bar with girlfriend Kathleen Breck in the 1963 lowlife melodrama *West 11*, and Oliver Reed and Carol

An American Werewolf in London: Jenny Agutter's flat: Coleherne Road

White meet up amid the odd clutter of period ads and farm implements in *I'll Never Forget What's 'is Name*.

The extravagantly Victorian and unkempt **Brompton Cemetery, Old Brompton Road** (**35**), is where Helena Bonham Carter tends her mother's grave in *The Wings of the Dove*, and Eileen Atkins her daughter's (beneath the vast, noisy stand of Stamford Bridge) in the bittersweet romance *Jack & Sarah*. It also appears in Mark Peploe's strange arthouse chiller *Afraid of the Dark*. Among its celebrity plantings are suffragette Emmeline Pankhurst and operatic tenor Richard Tauber, who played Franz Schubert in the 1934 musical *Blossom Time*. Both graves are on the left of the main path near to the Old Brompton Road entrance. Toward the south of the cemetery, the rear of the 1839 chapel (the Fulham Road side) was used as the exterior of the 'St Petersburg' church where Natalya (Izabella Scorupco) hides out in *GoldenEye*. Appropriately, the cemetery is also the graveyard where Rowan Atkinson disrupts the funeral service in Bond spoof *Johnny English*.

South of the cemetery, and looming over its southern reaches, is the home of Chelsea FC, **Stamford Bridge**, the old Fulham Road entrance of which pretends to be 'Wembley Stadium' in *Nuns on the Run*. The entrance has now gone, replaced by the massive Chelsea Village development.

GoldenEye: the Russian church: Brompton Cemetery, Old Brompton Road

Directly opposite Chelsea Village is salon **Hair Brazil, 469 Fulham Road** (**36**), which is the betting office of Joey Maddocks (Anthony

Performance: smashing up the betting shop: Hair Brazil, Fulham Road

Deep End: the swimming bath: Fulham Public Baths and Wash-Houses, North End Road

Richard III: the royal palace interior: St Cuthbert's Church, Philbeach Gardens

The Stud: the toyboy's flat: Earl's Court Road

Sunday, Bloody Sunday: Peter Finch's surgery: Pembroke Square

Valentine), smashed up by Chas (James Fox) and his pals in *Performance*. At **368 North End Road** stand the old **Fulham Public Baths and Wash-Houses (37**), the setting for Jerzy Skolimowski's skewed 1970 romance *Deep End*, with John Moulder-Brown as the teenage bath-house attendant developing an unhealthy obsession with Jane Asher.

Hop on a bus or the Underground at Fulham Broadway to Earl's Court (*tube: District Line*). The **Earl's Court Exhibition Centre, Warwick Road (38**), is the site of the 'Virtual Reality 2000' expo, where a computer malfunction results in Justine (Laura Fraser) not *making* the man of her dreams, but getting *transformed into* him, in *Virtual Sexuality*. The bowels of the vast centre also provided the backstage preparation for the fascist rally (which was finally held in the Horticultural Hall, Westminster) in Richard Loncraine's imaginative Shakespeare adaptation, *Richard III*.

St Cuthbert's Church, Philbeach Gardens (a short crescent on the opposite side of Warwick Road), was dressed up to become the interior of the royal palace (the exterior is St Pancras Station) for the opening party scene – "Come live with me and be my love…"– of *Richard III*.

Go south on Warwick Road to **Trebovir Road**. **Kensington Mansions**, on the north side of Trebovir Road, is the gloomy apartment block where Catherine Deneuve goes scarily bonkers in Roman Polanski's *Repulsion*.

It's hard to believe, but the shabby door at **250 Earl's Court Road**, alongside Burger King, leads to the flat of ambitious toyboy Tony Blake (Oliver Tobias), aka the titular 'Stud', in seventies trash classic *The Stud*.

It could be argued that the whole gross-out comedy genre was born in Earl's Court in 1972, not with John Landis

Repulsion: Catherine Deneuve's gloomy apartment block: Kensington Mansions, Trebovir Road

or John Waters, but with Bruce Beresford. Yes, that's the Bruce Beresford who scored a brace of Best Picture nominations for *Tender Mercies* and *Driving Miss Daisy*. Then working as Film Officer at the British Film Institute Production Board, Beresford brought to the screen Barry Humphries' outrageous *Private Eye* comic strip about a naïve, sex-starved, Fosters-swilling Aussie adrift in the strange world of pervy Poms. *The Adventures of Barry Mackenzie* has, as they say, something to offend everyone. Across Earl's Court Road you'll find **The King's Head, Kenway Road** (see **Bars & Restaurants**, p20) at Hogarth Road, where Bazza (Barry Crocker) is asked to advertise 'High Camp Cigarettes'.

Head north to Pembroke Square, off Earl's Court Road. Behind the garden centre, **37 Pembroke Square** is the surgery of doctor Peter Finch in John Schlesinger's superb character study *Sunday, Bloody Sunday*.

Unlike Bruce Beresford, Mike Hodges doesn't have the 'first film' excuse. He'd already made the hard-as-nails classic *Get Carter* in 1971 (and survived to direct the critically lauded *Croupier*), but in 1985 he found time to helm the lame Britcom *Morons From Outer Space*. And, yes, that's about the length and breadth of the plot. **28 Mornington Avenue (39**), the last house on the left in the small cul-de-sac off North End Road, is where Griff Rhys Jones holes up with the alien idiots.

78A Talgarth Road, at North End Road, opposite West Kensington tube station, is Renton's

Morons From Outer Space: the aliens hole up: Mornington Avenue

Trainspotting: the Victorian townhouse: Talgarth Road

The Omen: the spiked priest: All Saints Church

"beautifully converted Victorian townhouse" – well, he is working as an estate agent – where Begbie and Sick Boy come to squat in *Trainspotting*.

At **Baron's Court Underground Station** (**40**), Regan (John Thaw) and Carter (Dennis Waterman) run for the tube after oversleeping in the film version of cop series *Sweeney!*

You can take the tube from Baron's Court straight to Putney Bridge (*tube: District line*), or take another small diversion if you feel like it. **Craven Cottage, Stevenage Road** (**41**), home of Fulham Football Club, stands in for Arsenal's Highbury ground in David Evans' 1996 film of Nick Hornby's novel *Fever Pitch*. The team have temporarily relocated while Craven Cottage is being radically redeveloped. It is promised that the ground's historic frontage will be preserved.

Gregory Peck meets up with manic priest Patrick Troughton on **Thames Path**, west of Putney Bridge, in *The Omen*. The nearby **All Saints Church** (**42**), on the north side of Putney Bridge, is where the priest gets spiked by a lightning conductor.

Cross **Putney Bridge**, which stands in for the now-modernised Waterloo Bridge in Richard Attenborough's biopic *Chaplin*. The snack bar on the Thames Embankment at the southern end of the bridge, where Dennis Waterman meets up with the lads at the beginning of *Sweeney 2*, has been replaced by a stylish new restaurant.

It's on **Putney Embankment** that Sir Guy Grand (Peter Sellers) bribes the Oxford crew (led by straight-as-a-die Graham Chapman) and their cox, Richard Attenborough, to ram the opposing team during the Oxford-Cambridge boat race in *The Magic Christian*, while slipping traffic warden Spike Milligan £500 to eat his parking ticket.

The rear of the boathouse on **Putney Embankment, Ashlone Road** (**43**), (now the Wandsworth Youth River Club) was transformed into the 'Second Chance animal shelter' run by Ioan Gruffudd, with a little help from Cruella De Vil, in *102 Dalmatians*.

The Magic Christian: bribing the Oxford crew: Putney Embankment

It's private property, but you should recognise the view from the public footpath to the west.

On Putney High Street at Felsham Road

102 Dalmatians: Ioan Gruffudd's animal shelter: Putney Embankment, Ashlone Road

once stood the old Putney Hippodrome, which was used as Edward Lionheart's decrepit lair, the 'Burbage Theatre', in the wildly camp *Theatre of Blood*. Built in 1906 as a vaudeville variety house, the theatre was converted into a cinema in the thirties, but had been closed for fourteen years when it was chosen as Lionheart's hideout. The proscenium was specially built and the grand chandelier added for the movie. Five hundred seats were bought (at a cost of 50p each) from Croydon Odeon, to fill the long-empty stalls. The theatre was demolished shortly after filming.

Take the train from Putney Station to Kew Bridge. **Kew Bridge Steam Museum** can be seen in the strange horror film *The Wisdom of Crocodiles*, and Nick Nolte visits the engine here in *The Golden Bowl*.

Abingdon House, 61 Kew Green, is Ralph Fiennes' house, supposedly on Clapham Common, in Neil Jordan's film of Graham Greene's novel *The End of the Affair*. The corrugated iron alongside the house masks, not a bombed site, but Kew Gardens' Herbarium, but you can catch a glimpse of the entrance to the gardens in the background as Fiennes runs across the green to stop Julianne Moore's cab. The church, where the V1s (flying bombs) fall, is the **Parish Church of St Anne** on the green.

The Georgian **Templeton House, 118 Priory Lane**, Roehampton, appears in *Ali G Indahouse*.

Another quick tube or train journey, this time from Kew Gardens to Richmond (*tube: District line*). The **Richmond Theatre, The Green** (*©020.8940.0088;*

The End of the Affair: Ralph Fiennes' house: Abingdon House, Kew Green

The End of the Affair: the V1s falling: Kew Green

The Krays: the exterior of the twins' club: Richmond Theatre, The Green

The Phantom of the Opera: Hammer's opera house: Wimbledon Theatre

website: www.theambassadors.com/richmond), has a long history as a film location. Back in 1957, it became the 'Palace Theatre', from where TV celeb Sonny MacGregor (Peter Sellers) broadcasts his ghastly faux-Scots *Here's Tae Ye* game show in *The Naked Truth*. Outside the theatre, decked out with a fake canopy, he's confronted by blackmailer Nigel Dennis (Dennis Price). The exterior of the theatre has since been used as the brothers' nightclub in *The Krays* (the interior was Wilton's Music Hall). Stephen Baldwin and Sadie Frost watch a production of *Macbeth* here in George Sluizer's *Crimetime*. Richard E Grant bumps into his parents outside the theatre in *Jack & Sarah*. The theatre is the setting for the audition scene in Alan Parker's first feature *Bugsy Malone* but, more exotically, became the 'Buenos Aires' theatre where Eva Duarte (Madonna) first meets Juan Perón (Jonathan Pryce) in Parker's visually lush filming of Andrew Lloyd Webber and Tim Rice's overblown school play *Evita*. In 2000 it was transformed into 'Ford's Theatre, Washington DC', where Brendan Fraser, unfortunately transformed into Abe Lincoln by Devil Elizabeth Hurley, loses his pager in Harold Ramis' remake of *Bedazzled*. The Richmond also stood in for the Savoy Theatre for Mike Leigh's film about Gilbert and Sullivan, *Topsy-Turvy* (the real thing, on the Strand, has been updated to twenties deco style), and the St James Theatre for *Wilde*. More recently, it was transformed into the Duke of York's for *Neverland*, the story of the genesis of Peter Pan, with Johnny Depp as JM Barrie.

West of Richmond Green is the tiny row of houses between King Street and Old Palace Lane. **Oak House, Old Palace Place**, is the 'Oxford' house where Young Iris Murdoch (Kate Winslett) and Young John Bayley (Hugh Bonneville) lunch with a nonplussed Young Maurice (Sam West) in *Iris*.

Iris: lunch at the Oxford house: Oak House, Old Palace Place

You can jump on a bus or take the train (via Clapham Junction) to Wimbledon. **Wimbledon Theatre** (© *020.8540.0362*), with its original Edwardian rope flytowers and fly gallery, became the 'Duke of York's Theatre' for the performance of *Peter Pan* in *Fairy Tale: A True Story*. The theatre developed delusions of grandeur in 1962 when it became the opera house (though transferred from Paris to London) for Hammer's remake of *The Phantom of the Opera*, with Herbert Lom as the masked composer. The theatre is also where Franz Liszt (Roger Daltrey) plays for an audience of fluttery groupies – and a sinister Richard Wagner (Paul Nicholas) – in Ken Russell's 1975 comic strip fantasia *Lisztomania*.

In 1964 Bryan Forbes achieved more quietly disturbing creepiness in *Séance on a Wet Afternoon*, with little more than two class actors and a rather gothic suburban house, than Hollywood can conjure up with a seven-figure budget and a credit roll that runs for ten minutes. Kim Stanley nabbed an Oscar nomination as the dubious medium who hopes to make her name by revealing the whereabouts of a missing child, conveniently kidnapped by her submissively doting husband Richard Attenborough (whose false nose remains one of cinema's great unexplained mysteries). **41 Marryat Road** at Burghley Road, overlooking Wimbledon Park, is the house where Stanley and Attenborough are locked together in their doomed *folie a deux*.

Wimbledon Lawn Tennis Club, between Church Road and Somerset Road, appears in Ralph Thomas' 1968 thriller *Nobody Runs Forever*, with Rod Taylor and Christopher Plummer.

Séance on a Wet Afternoon: the medium's house: Marryat Road

Far West London: Shepherd's Bush to Osterley Park

This trip takes in the old Hammersmith Palais and the old Hammersmith Odeon (now the London Apollo), so there's a strong musical theme, ranging from the Beatles and the Who, through to glam rock and punk, with Hollywood cartoons and a spot of northern dancing thrown in along the way. The tour covers quite a bit of ground, so you may need to use public transport.

Starting Point: Shepherd's Bush

Shepherd's Bush Underground Station is where Michael Caine attempts to shake off the MI6 tail in Don Siegel's seventies thriller *The Black Windmill*. Caine eventually eludes his pursuer after a chase across the footbridge, quirkily designed to look like an Intercity train flying over the bustling traffic of Uxbridge Road, which used to join the station to Shepherd's Bush Centre. The bridge has gone and after a recent makeover of the West 12 Shopping and Leisure Centre, it now includes a 12-screen Warner Village cinema complex (*© 0870.240.6020).

Walk west along Uxbridge Road, on the northern boundary of **Shepherd's Bush Green**. The area has a long history in the performance media. It was home to Lime Grove film studios, which became the BBC's television studio until BBC Television Centre was built on Wood Lane. The western fringe of Shepherd's Bush Green was home to two cinemas (both of which have

closed down) and two theatres. The Bush, as Shepherd's Bush Green is affectionately known, was the locale for the 1974 film of British TV sitcom *Man About the House*. It was more notably home to founder members of the Who, and so naturally featured as the local neighbourhood in Franc Roddam's 1979 film *Quadrophenia*. Alex Cox's *Sid and Nancy*, which also evokes a past phase of Brit Pop, uses some of the same territory.

Turning south on Shepherd's Bush Green takes you past the two defunct cinemas: the **Odeon**, now closed and boarded, and the Walkabout Inn, a raucous Australasian bar which was clearly once a picture house. South of the Walkabout stands the old **Shepherd's Bush Empire**, for many years the BBC TV Theatre from which much classic television was broadcast. It's now a music venue. Take a look at the still-legible legend on the side of the Walkabout on Rockwood Place alongside the Empire: 'Cinematograph Theatre, 1s, 6d & 3d' (pre-decimal prices, roughly 5p, 2 $^1/_2$p and 1p).

Alongside, on the corner of Goldhawk Road, above O'Neill's pub, is the **Bush Theatre**. Once the dance studio of hoofer Lionel Blair, since 1972 it has been an invaluable showcase for new writing, staging works by playwrights such as Snoo Wilson, Stephen Poliakoff and Jonathan Harvey. Three cinematic Mikes – Figgis, Leigh and Newell – have directed plays here.

Continue through Rockwood Place into Pennard Road. Directly opposite is **17**

Sid and Nancy: the gaff of Wally the punk: Pennard Road

Quadrophenia: chasing the Rocker: Shepherd's Bush Market

Pennard Road, the gaff of Wally, the crimson-haired punk (a character loosely based on Billy Idol) in *Sid and Nancy*.

Walk south to Goldhawk Road and turn west toward **Shepherd's Bush Market**. This narrow, bustling alley of stalls, running alongside the railway between Goldhawk Road Station and Shepherd's Bush Station, is the benighted passage where Jimmy's greaser pal Kevin (Ray Winstone) is chased from Goldhawk Road tube station and beaten up by Mods in *Quadrophenia*. During the day, however, it's a great place to pick up cheap household goods or exotic fabrics. Ray (Daniel Craig) is overwhelmed by the market's noise and colour in Simon Cellan Jones' *Some Voices*.

Schizophrenia in the movies usually means an evil twin wearing his mother's nightie plunging a steak knife into co-eds – a rare form of the condition. In Cellan Jones' unsensational 2000 film, Ray attempts to live without medication. The flat he moves into with Laura (Kelly Macdonald) is above the textile store at **51 Goldhawk Road**, and somehow contrives to make the rooftop terrace look quite enticing. Jimmy the Mod rides his scooter along **Goldhawk Road** in *Quadrophenia*, and both the super- market where Steph (Leslie Ash) works, and the pie and mash shop where Jimmy and the greaser eat, were also on the Goldhawk Road.

Alongside Goldhawk Road tube station, on the south side of the road, is the tiny **Metro Café**. You can grab a filling fry-up here, or just a cup of tea. This is the café where Nancy Spungen is told she's not wanted on the

Some Voices: Kelly Macdonald's flat: Goldhawk Road

Sid and Nancy: the 'caff': Metro Café Goldhawk Road

tour by the rest of the shade-wearing entourage in *Sid and Nancy*.

Across the road, just past the market, is **Lime Grove**, once the site of one of

The old Gaumont-British Lime Grove Studios in the early 1990s

London's great film studios, the Gaumont-British Lime Grove Studios. Hitchcock movies such as the 1934 versions of *The Man Who Knew Too Much* and *The 39 Steps* were shot here, as well as the classic Jessie Matthews musical *Evergreen*, and many of the Gainsborough costume melodramas (including *The Man in Grey* and *The Wicked Lady*). 'Folkestone Promenade' was built here for the 1941 film of HG Wells' *Kipps*. In 1949, the studio, failing after being taken over by the Rank Organisation, was sold to the BBC to become TV studios. The huge white complex, built in 1932, which stood on the west side of the road, was finally demolished in the nineties and the site is now a housing estate. Only street names, such as Gaumont Terrace and Gainsborough Court, recall that, for many years, this was the home of classic British cinema.

Continue north to Uxbridge Road. **The Harp Café, 304 Uxbridge Road** at Arminger Road, became 'Pete's', David Morrissey's restaurant, where he gives a job to his schizophrenic brother Ray in *Some Voices*.

Turn right, back towards the green, and then left onto Wood Lane, the main A40 road north. A few minutes walk and you'll find yourself in Hollywood. Robert Zemeckis' 1988 film *Who Framed Roger Rabbit* is set in Los Angeles, but as the groundbreaking animation was entrusted to the British studio of Richard Williams, the production was based at Elstree. Many of the sun-drenched locations are unmistakably California, but some are a little closer to the film's UK base. On **Wood Lane**, opposite the junction with Macfarlane Road, stands the **Dimco Building**, a huge, red brick building which, with the addition of a neon sign and a couple of palm trees, became Tinseltown's 'Acme warehouse', where Marvin Acme is killed by the falling safe. Somewhat disappointingly, you can't peek over the wall into Toontown, but on Saturdays and Sundays there's a car-boot sale in front of the buildings if you want to see them up close.

Past the railway bridge and across the road is the entrance to

Some Voices: Pete's restaurant: The Harp Café, Uxbridge Road

Who Framed Roger Rabbit: the Acme warehouse: the Dimco Building, Wood Lane

Who Framed Roger Rabbit: the wall of Toontown: the Dimco Building, Wood Lane

the famous 'concrete doughnut', the circular complex of the **BBC Television Centre**, where Beryl Reid causes ructions in *The Killing of Sister George*, and where Hugh Laurie works in Ben Elton's *Maybe Baby* (although for this movie, the BBC interior is actually the Epsom Race-course building).

Further north is the **White City** neighbourhood, where the police chase ends in *The Blue Lamp*. The area is now dominated by the BBC's brand new White City office, but used to be the site of White City Stadium, the famed dog racing track where Dirk Bogarde is cornered at the end of the 1949 classic. The stadium, built originally to house the 1908 Olympic Games and the Anglo-French Exhibition, was finally torn down in the 1980s.

Head north up Wood Lane and left into **Ducane Road**. You can't fail to recognise the familiar gates of **Wormwood Scrubs Prison**, regularly used as cinematic shorthand for 'jail'. This is where Michael Caine emerges at the beginning of *The Italian Job* (though the prison interiors were filmed in Dublin) and Jon Finch is whisked out by ambulance after an attempted suicide in Hitchcock's *Frenzy*. David Warner, though, escapes *into* the prison in Karel Reisz's sixties classic *Morgan – A Suitable Case For Treatment*.

Further west, near Old Oak Common, is **115 Wells House Road**, backing onto the railway line between Willesden Junction and

Quadrophenia: the home of Jimmy: Wells House Road

Acton Central, which was home to Jimmy (Phil Daniels) in *Quadrophenia*.

Further north on Old Oak Lane, near Willesden Junction station, is **Goodhall Street**. A cinema favourite, this quiet street of terraced houses has appeared in *The Last Yellow* and Manchester-set comedy *The Parole Officer*, with Steve Coogan. The **Railway Social Club, 78 Goodhall Street**, becomes one of the 'Hamburg' clubs in *Backbeat*. In *Velvet Goldmine*, its downstairs bar is the 'Midtown New York' bar, where Arthur Stuart (Christian Bale) attempts to track down Brian Slade (Jonathan Rhys-Meyers), while the club's Upper Hall became the 'Last Resort' club, where Bale interviews washed-up Mandy Slade (Toni Collette) in a pastiche of *Citizen Kane*. It's just alongside the club, on **Stephenson Street**, that the young mod Slade picks up a schoolboy in the same film. Further down the street, **29 Goodhall Street** is home to the young Spider (Bradley Hall), where his beloved mother (Miranda Richardson) is replaced by a peroxide floosy (also Miranda Richardson).

If you return to Wood Lane and continue north, the road becomes Scrubs Lane, leading to Harrow Road. Turn right and you'll come to the entrance to **Kensal Green Cemetery, Harrow Road**. Along with Highgate and Brompton, this is one of the city's great 19th-century necropolii. Among the elaborate grave monuments are the last resting places of such Victorian luminaries as engineer Isambard Kingdom Brunel, writer Anthony Trollope and Lady 'Speranza' Wilde, the mother of Oscar. Playwright and screenwriter Terence Rattigan also rests here, unmarked, in the family memorial. On screen, the cemetery can be seen in Cliff Owen's 1972 film of the British TV sitcom *Steptoe and Son*. Dennis Price's body is dragged by horses through the cemetery, and dutiful daughter Edwina Lionheart (Diana Rigg) tends the monument to her late father Edward Lionheart (Vincent Price) in Douglas Hickox's splendidly tasteless Shakespearian black comedy *Theatre of Blood*. It's also the site of Julianne Moore's funeral, where Ralph Fiennes is told of the miraculous disappearance of the investigator's boy's birthmark, in Neil Jordan's 1999 film *The End of the Affair*. Jimmy Porter (Richard Burton) accompanies Edith Evans as she tends the grave of her husband here in the film of John Osborne's *Look Back in Anger*.

The walkable section of the tour ends here. To continue, you'll need to drive or take the tube.

The first stop is Hammersmith.

Theatre of Blood: the resting place of Edward Lionheart: Kensal Green Cemetery, Harrow Road

The Knack: the 'white pad': Melrose Terrace

St Paul's Junior School, in Hammersmith, was the HQ for Lindsay Anerson's *O Lucky Man!* and the cathartic party finale was filmed here. Hammersmith Palais, **Shepherd's Bush Road** (officially it's now **Po Na Na Hammersmith**, but everyone still uses the old name), the famous old dance hall, was the centre of Charles Crichton's 1950 drama of working class life *Dance Hall*. It later appeared in Bernard Rose's WWII-set melodrama *Chicago Joe and the Showgirl*, with Kiefer Sutherland and Emily Lloyd.

Head north up Shepherd's Bush Road to Melrose Gardens and turn left into Melrose Terrace. In 1965, **1 Melrose Terrace** became the 'white pad' where smoothie Tolen (Ray Brooks) effortlessly demonstrates his seduction techniques to gauche schoolteacher Colin (Michael Crawford) in Richard Lester's film of Ann Jellicoe's play *The Knack*. Much of Lester's freewheelingly anarchic movie was shot in the house, which was completely taken over for the production.

Behind Hammersmith tube station, in the shadow of Hammersmith flyover, stands the **London Apollo Hammersmith, Queen Caroline Street** (*© 0870.606.3400*), once the legendary music venue the Hammersmith Odeon. It's down the iron staircase at the rear of the Apollo that the Beatles clamber (supposedly escaping from the Scala Theatre on Charlotte Street, Fitzrovia) for a spot of pixillated fun in the open air –

The Man Who Never Was and **Theatre Of Blood**: Digby Mansions, Hammersmith Bridge Road

Night and the City: Richard Widmark is finally cornered: Hammersmith Bridge

on the helicopter pad at Gatwick Airport, actually. The Apollo is also the venue where fifties rocker Jerry Lee Lewis (Dennis Quaid) gets a cool reception from his English fans in Jim McBride's snappy 1989 biopic *Great Balls of Fire!*

Hidden away inside a modern shopping complex on **King Street** is the **Lyric Hammersmith**, a restored Victorian gem, which became the French Le Théâtre du Grand Guignol in the 1966 shocker *Theatre of Death*, with Christopher Lee. Even more horribly, the same year the Lyric hosted the filming, by Philip Saville, of Anthony Newley's gruesomely self-indulgent stage musical *Stop the World I Want to Get Off*.

Follow Hammersmith Bridge Road down to the Thames. Alongside the bridge stands **Digby Mansions, Hammersmith Bridge Road** at Lower Mall, which in 1955 became '44 River Court', home to Gloria Grahame, where Nazi spy Stephen Boyd checks out the background of The Man Who Never Was. In 1973, the block also became the home of doomed theatre critic George Maxwell (Michael Hordern) in the Julius Caesar section of *Theatre of Blood*.

Cornered weasel Richard Widmark finally gets what was coming to him under **Hammersmith Bridge** at the end of Jules Dassin's excellent 1950 noir *Night and the City*, and Ray (Daniel Craig) suffers a crisis on the bridge after being chucked out of his brother's flat in *Some Voices*. Gwyneth Paltrow and John Hannah row on the Thames beneath the bridge in *Sliding Doors*. While you're here, stop off for a drink at **The Blue Anchor, 13 Lower Mall** (see **Bars & Restaurants**, p20), the pub alongside the rowing club where the pair enjoy a post-rowing "sponsored epileptic fit". It's also on the Embankment here that June 'George' Buckridge (Beryl Reid) mysteriously arrives after having stomped through the back lanes of Hampstead, beneath the credits of *The Killing of Sister George*.

Just north of the busy A4, Great West Road, is the elegant St Peter's Square. **7 St Peter's Square** is home to Peter Finch and Anne Bancroft in Jack Clayton's superb 1964 film *The Pumpkin Eater*. Seemingly almost forgotten, Clayton's adaptation of Penelope Mortimer's novel, scripted by

Sliding Doors: the rowing club pub: The Blue Anchor, Lower Mall

The Pumpkin Eater: the house of Bancroft and Finch: St Peter's Square

The Naked Truth: the scout troop hold-up: Parish Church of St Peter, Black Lion Lane

Harold Pinter, centres on the strained marriage of philandering Peter Finch and fecund Anne Bancroft. Clayton directed only seven features, including the groundbreaking *Room at the Top* and the atmospheric ghost story *The Innocents*. The Regency mansion, home of oboist Leon Goossens at the time of filming, was previously owned by Alec Guinness.

This is clearly Pinterland. Two doors to the right is the home of Ben Kingsley and Patricia Hodge in David Jones' 1982 film of Pinter's stage play *Betrayal* (and this time, there's an Oscar nomination for the writer's own screenplay).

On the south side of the square, look east to the **Parish Church of St Peter**, at the corner of **Black Lion Lane**. This is where the scout troop holds up the police car when a bunch of celebrities cause mayhem for the Met as they abduct their blackmailer Dennis Price, in Mario Zampi's 1957 farce *The Naked Truth*.

Look out for two bits of American history in Chiswick. **Chiswick Town Hall, Heathfield Terrace**, is the site of the IWW (Industrial Workers of the World) meeting in Warren Beatty's *Reds*, and **2 South Parade**, Chiswick, becomes the home of Orson Welles in *RKO 281*, the story of the making of *Citizen Kane*.

Stroll along the Thames footpath, if it hasn't disappeared under one of the river's occasional high tides. The row of houses along **Chiswick Mall** stand in for the 'Chelsea Embankment', where Anthony Hopkins gives a bit of disastrous insider info about the 'Porphyrion' company to Emma Thompson and Helena Bonham Carter as they leave their weekly discussion group at **Strawberry House**, in *Howards End*. The same house is home to James Fox and Anjelica Huston in another Merchant-Ivory production, *The Golden Bowl*, and **Morton House**, immediately to the right, is home to tortured barrister Melville Farr (Dirk Bogarde) in *Victim*.

West of the

Howards End: dodgy advice from Anthony Hopkins: Chiswick Mall

Victim: the home of Melville Farr: Morton House, Chiswick Mall

Hogarth Roundabout stands **Chiswick House, Burlington Lane** (see **Historic Sites**, p32), home to aristocrat James Fox's parents in *The Servant*. The back of the house appears in *Velvet Goldmine*.

Head to South Acton (*tube: Chiswick Park (District line), rail: South Acton*) and on to Acton Lane. In 1986, the cavernous interior of the disused **Acton Lane Power Station, Acton Lane**, was transformed into a temporary film studio for James Cameron's *Aliens*. It had also been used in Ridley Scott's original *Alien*, as the interior of the bizarre craft where John Hurt discovers the developing eggs. Ten years after *Alien*, Tim Burton's *Batman* used the power station as the interior of the 'Axis Chemical Works' (the exterior is another power station in Bedfordshire), where the Joker (Jack Nicholson) plunges into poisonous chemical sludge.

West on Acton Lane is **Central Middlesex Hospital**, where Jim (Cillian Murphy) wakes up to discover that London is strangely deserted in the atmospherically scary *28 Days Later*.

On the **Park Royal Industrial Estate** just behind

The Servant: James Fox's parents' country estate: Chiswick House, Burlington Lane

Velvet Goldmine: Eddie Izzard directs the music promo: Chiswick House, Burlington Lane

The Borrowers: City Hall: Ealing Town Hall, New Broadway

the hospital, a casually tossed carton of milk precipitates the motor smash in Guy Ritchie's *Snatch*. **Acton Town Hall** provided the 'school hall' where Hugh Grant risks his cool to accompany Nicholas Hoult's shaky version of 'Killing Me Softly' at the end of *About a Boy*, and **Trinity Way**, to the south, was used in *Ali G Indahouse*.

Further west is the suburb of **Ealing**, which provided the backdrop to much of *Carry On Constable*, before the massive redevelopment of the town centre. **Ealing Town Hall, New Broadway**, is 'City Hall', where John Goodman tries to register a demolition with Town Planning, in the strangely Anglo-American film *The Borrowers*.

Walpole Park can be seen in *Solitaire for Two*, from Vadim Jean, the director of *Leon the Pig Farmer*. Coincidentally, the Medieval drama *Hour of the Pig* also filmed within the park. In the park is **Pitshanger Manor**, one-time villa of architect John Soane, now a museum (*Tuesday to Saturday, 11.00-17.00*). The house becomes the country retreat of Jack (Colin Firth) in *The Importance of Being Earnest*, and also appears in *The Tichborne Claimant*.

Just north of the park, between Mattock Lane and Uxbridge Road, the blue-tiled frontage of the old Walpole Electric Theatre has been preserved. You can glimpse it and Pitshanger Manor in the background of *Killing Me Softly*, when Heather Graham walks home through the park after an enthusiastic session with studly mountaineer Joseph Fiennes.

On the green to the south, the familiar laurel wreath logo indicates the the old **Ealing Studios**, best known for the series of classic comedies of the forties and fifties. The common theme of these gentle, though sometimes quite dark, films touched a chord in strictly-regulated postwar Britain: resourceful common people subverting pompous bureaucracy. It was at Ealing

The Importance of Being Earnest: Jack's out-of-town retreat: Pitshanger Manor

The old Ealing Studios, Ealing Green

that villagers kept their local steam train on the rails despite the underhand efforts of a modern, efficient (and therefore untrustworthy) bus company in *The Titfield Thunderbolt*, Alec Guinness took on big business as the inventor of an indestrictible new cloth in *The Man In the White Suit*, and the residents of a London borough revelled in gaining their freedom from austerity and rationing on discovering that they had been granted independence in *Passport to Pimlico*.

Films had been made at Ealing since the early years of the 20th century, though the studio itself dates from 1931. In the thirties, northern entertainers Gracie Fields and George Formby scored huge hits with their populist comedies, but it was under the guidance of Michael Balcon that the studio really hit its stride, producing not just the comedies but classic stiff-upper-lippers such as *Scott of the Antarctic* and *The Cruel Sea*. After the studio's fortunes waned in the late fifties, it was taken over by the BBC to be used as television studios. Having come close to being demolished, the studio has been granted a new lease of life – scenes for *Notting Hill* and reshoots for *Star Wars: Episode II – Attack of the Clones* were filmed at Ealing. *The Importance of Being Earnest* was the first production based in the studio since the fifties. You can see the brand new entrance to the complex to the right of the old building.

Almost directly opposite the studio is the **Red Lion, 13 St Mary's Road**, the pub where casts and crews would unwind after filming. The bar is adorned with posters, and photographs of the famous faces of Ealing.

Continue west into West Ealing, until Uxbridge Road becomes Broadway again. **Jesters Amusements, 127 Broadway** at Coldershaw Road, was the games arcade and the office of wide-boy Turkish (Jason Statham) that gets smashed up in *Snatch*.

Westcott Crescent, north of

Snatch: Turkish's games arcade: Jesters Amusements, Broadway

Billy Elliot: Billy rehearses: Hanwell Community Centre, Westcott Crescent

Snatch: the home of Boris the Blade: Tees Avenue

Bend It Like Beckham: Jess' family home: Sutton Square

Hanwell, encircles the looming Gothic bulk of **Hanwell Community Centre, Westcott Crescent** at Cuckoo Avenue (*rail: Drayton Green, Castle Bar Park*), standing incongruously among the modern suburban houses. This was the reception block of the Victorian poor school – and the only part remaining – where the young Charlie Chaplin was a resident after his mother's breakdown. In more recent times, the band Deep Purple came together in the rehearsal space here. Also, although most of the surprise smash *Billy Elliot* was shot in Easington up in the North of England, the Hanwell complex was used as the community centre where young Billy (Jamie Bell) practises his dance steps with teacher Mrs Wilkinson (Julie Walters).

Near the next stop north (*rail: South Greenford*) is **14 Tees Avenue**, Perivale, across the A40, which was home to Boris the Blade (Rade Serbedzija) in *Snatch*.

Continuing on to Southall, and **Southall Broadway**, where Jess (Parminder Nagra) and her friends shop at the beginning of feelgood footie hit *Bend It Like Beckham*. To the west is **Yeading FC, Beaconsfield Road**, the football ground where Jess trains with coach Joe (Jonathan Rhys-Meyers), and even further west, in **Hayes**, is **Barra Park**, where Jess proves she's more than a match for the lads.

South of Southall is **Featherstone School Annexe, Western Road**, the school featured in Todd Haynes' *Velvet Goldmine*. Continuing south, you come to Heston, and **33 Sutton Square**, home to Jess and family in *Bend It Like Beckham*.

Southwest of Hanwell stretches the 140-acre Osterley Park, bisected by the M4 motorway. Within Osterley Park itself stands **Osterley Park House** (see **Historic Sites**, p33), a National Trust property which can be seen in *The Grass Is*

The Grass Is Greener and Kabhi Khushi Kabhie Gham...: stately home and school concert: Osterley Park House

Accident and The Madness of King George: the 'football match' and the Long Gallery: Syon House

Greener, A Study in Terror and Hindi smash *Kabhi Khushi Kabhie Gham....*

Southeast of the Great West Road is another classic mansion, **Syon House** (see **Historic Sites**, p33), set in grounds landscaped by 'Capability' Brown. A frequent film location, the house can be seen in *The Madness of King George*, *The Wings of the Dove*, *King Ralph*, *The Avengers*, *Bullshot*, *Follow Me* and, more recently, Robert Altman's *Gosford Park*. The Great Hall, designed by Robert Adams, is the site of the 'football match' in *Accident*, and the Great Conservatory is 'Heaven' at the ending of the 1967 version of *Bedazzled*.

Far Northwest London: Regent's Park to Wembley

There's a very English cosiness about much of this tour, taking in, as it does, tourist faves London Zoo and Madame Tussaud's, and the well-heeled enclaves of Maida Vale and St John's Wood (home of Lord's Cricket Ground), while name-checking Sherlock Holmes, Alfred Hitchcock, Noël Coward, PC George Dixon and Norman Wisdom. There are, however, two stop-offs in 'New York', a glimpse of 'Washington DC' and, in case you feel too comfy, Boris Karloff inventing virtual reality, a blasphemously sinister immortal and Clive Barker's pleasure seekers from Hell…

Starting Point: Regent's Park

Opposite Great Portland Street Station is Osnaburgh Street. **8 Marlborough House, Osnaburgh Street**, was home to Kenneth Williams until his death in April 1988.

Around the corner is **Park Crescent East (1)**, the pillared semicircle south of Marylebone Road. The eastern curve is where Richard Hannay (Robert Donat) leaves the milkman's horse and cart he borrows after the murder of the mysterious woman at the beginning of Alfred Hitchcock's 1935 film *The 39 Steps*. Hannay supposedly lives at 122 Portland Place, but the exterior was recreated in the studio and the grand six-lane road is reduced to the width of a minor sidestreet.

Take a stroll a couple of blocks south down Portland Place to see a real Hitch location. In Hitchcock's last picture for David O Selznick, the 1947 courtroom drama *The Paradine Case*, lawyer Gregory Peck's luxurious home is **60 Portland Place (2)**, at Weymouth Street. On the way, you'll pass **74 Portland Place**, home to embittered blind playwright Van Johnson in Henry Hathaway's glossy, Hitchcockian thriller *23 Paces to Baker Street*. The title comes from Johnson's directions to a lost soul in the fog. Geography is not the movie's strength. Johnson's apartment not only looks out onto the

The 39 Steps: Hannay leaves the milk cart: Park Crescent East

23 Paces to Baker Street: the house of blind playwright Van Johnson: Portland Place

The Paradine Case: the house of lawyer Gregory Peck: Portland Place

Gregory Peck house but, amazingly, has a rear terrace overlooking the Thames.

Return to Marylebone Road and head west towards Baker Street tube station, and famed waxworks museum **Madame Tussaud's** (**3**; ✆ *0870.400.3000; website: www.madame-tussauds.com*), which astonishingly is London's number one tourist attraction. Not surprisingly, it was used for the backdrop to the 1936 mystery *Midnight at Madame Tussauds*.

The famous address of Sherlock Holmes, '221b Baker Street', is, of course, entirely fictitious, but you can see the Sherlock Holmes Museum at the northern end of Baker Street at Park Road.

Carry on to Melcombe Place, where you'll recognise the elegant glass-roofed frontage of **Marylebone Station** (**4**). A small, rather quiet station serving the northwestern suburbs, its period elegance (lately compromised by the paraphernalia of a modern terminus) and quiet location have made it a film favourite. In 1963 it became 'Bradford Station, Yorkshire', where Billy (Tom Courtenay) bottles out at the last minute, leaving Liz (Julie Christie) to go off alone to, well, London, at the end of *Billy Liar*. The following year, the Beatles evaded screaming fans here for *A Hard Day's Night*. The scientist is abducted from Marylebone at the opening of *The Ipcress File*. The blinded train driver causes panic when he crashes his train into the station in *The Day of the Triffids*. In the 1978 version of *The Thirty-Nine Steps*, Marylebone stands in for St Pancras, where British intelligence officer Colonel Scudder (John Mills) is stabbed by the beastly Prussians, embroiling Richard Hannay (Robert Powell) in the assassination plot.

Outside the station is the **Landmark Hotel, 222 Marylebone Road** (see **Hotels**, p11), the front of which can be glimpsed in

Billy Liar: Julie Christie leaves from Bradford Station: Marylebone Station

Sliding Doors.

267 Edgware Road was the site of the old Metropolitan Theatre, where teenage tearaway Dirk Bogarde establishes an alibi by ostensibly watching the

The Sorcerers: Ian Ogilvy's antique shop: Lisson Grove

act of music hall star Tessie O'Shea in 1949's *The Blue Lamp*. The theatre closed in 1962 and the area has since been extensively redeveloped. No trace of the theatre remains.

Continue on, then turn right onto Lisson Grove. Also extensively redeveloped, this used to be a much more dismal neighbourhood. Michael Reeves began his directing career with the understandably microbudget *Revenge of the Blood Beast*, a campy horror flick made in Italy, and finished with the awesome *Witchfinder General*, before succumbing to a drugs overdose at the age of twenty-four. Between those two films, in 1967, he made *The Sorcerers*. Boris Karloff (in one of his last roles) and Catherine Lacey play an elderly couple anticipating virtual reality with a hypnotic device – operating on the same sixties disco light-show principle as the Ipcress device. Antique shop manager Ian Ogilvy is the youngster through whom they experience the vicarious pleasures of biking, stealing and serial killing. **95 Lisson Grove** (**5**), at Broadley Street, astonishingly unchanged amid the wholesale renovation of the district, is 'The Glory Hole', Ogilvy's antique shop.

Rossmore Road leads to Park Road and the green oasis of Regent's Park, with its boating lake, open air theatre and, of course, London Zoo. A relatively quiet road, the Outer Circle, bounds the park. The small Inner Circle (which really is circular) encloses Queen Mary's Gardens in the centre of the park.

In the southwest segment is the **Boating Lake** (**6**). Richard Hannay encounters the bogus nanny here at the beginning of Ralph Thomas' inferior 1959 version of *The Thirty-Nine Steps*, in one of the few scenes not copied from Hitchcock's original film. The nanny is soon knocked down by a car on the road nearby. Trevor Howard and Celia Johnson go boating

Brief Encounter: the boating lake at Milford Park: Regent's Park Boating Lake

Salome's Last Dance: the Victorian brothel: St Andrew's Place

The Nanny: Bette Davis minds the kiddies: Chester Terrace

on the lake in *Brief Encounter*. The **Long Bridge**, in the centre of the park, is where Howard is left dangling after the accident and has to dry off in the boating shed.

Follow the Outer Circle anticlockwise to the southeast corner of the park. Alongside the modern Royal College of Surgeons building, runs the short cul-de-sac of **St Andrew's Place (7)**. The house at the end of the cobbled road served as the brothel where Oscar Wilde's *Salome* is performed in Ken Russell's fanciful movie *Salome's Last Dance*.

To the north on the Outer Circle are the elegant and exclusive Nash terraces. **Chester Terrace (8)** has proved irresistible to film-makers. Among the screen characters who live here are The Nanny (Bette Davis, acting as a scary Mary Poppins to the kiddies) in Hammer's *The Nanny* and rich girl Fenella (Hayley Mills) in the dated Agatha Christie mystery *Endless Night*. Gertrude Lawrence (Julie Andrews) faces bankruptcy here in *Star!* Robert Wise's ill-fated attempt to recapture the magic of *The Sound of Music*, and blackmailer Dennis Price calls on a victim here at the opening of *The Naked Truth*. The SS march though the terrace's gate in *It Happened Here*. The Ministry's 'mobile HQ' (a double-decker London bus) trundles past the terraces in *The Avengers*. Watch Robert Redford driving to the CIA HQ in Tony Scott's *Spy Game*, and you'll recognise the Nash terraces masquerading as Washington DC.

Continue north to Gloucester Gate and turn left into the park itself. The **Gloucester Gate** entrance leads to the enclosure which once housed the wolves which Withnail (Richard E Grant) recites Shakespeare to at the end of *Withnail & I*. The wolves are now gone, but the enclosure remains.

Take time out to visit **London Zoo (9**; see **Historic Sites**, p33) if you want. A long-estab-

Withnail & I: the wolf enclosure: Gloucester Gate

Harry Potter and the Philosopher's Stone: talking to serpents: the Reptile House, London Zoo

lished film location, it can be seen in *The Fallen Idol*, *The Jokers*, *Arabesque*, *Turtle Diary* and *An American Werewolf in London*. You can see its Reptile House in *Harry Potter and the Philosopher's Stone*, the famous Penguin Pool in *About a Boy*, and the little-known Prince Albert Suite in *Leon the Pig Farmer*

Head southwest on St John's Wood Road to Cunningham Place and south to the corner of Aberdeen Place. **Crocker's Folly, 24 Aberdeen Place (10**; see **Bars & Restaurants**, p21), became the 'New York' writers' club in Warren Beatty's *Reds*, and a gentlemen's bar in *The Importance of Being Earnest*.

Continue down Aberdeen Place to Edgware Road and the Grand Union Canal. **449 Edgware Road** is the flat shared by Charlotte Rampling and ugly duckling Lynn Redgrave in Silvio Narizzano's cynical sixties comedy *Georgy Girl*. The entrance to the flat seen in the film is at the rear of the building, in the tiny alleyway by the red postbox on Maida Avenue. Unchanged in the mid-nineties, an ugly red brick extension to the Chinese restaurant next door has all but obscured the iron staircase Rampling and Redgrave clank up and down.

It's in **Café Laville**, the restaurant over the canal, that Heather Graham meets up with the *Guardian* reporter as she begins to develop suspicions about her mysterious mountaineering boyfriend Joseph Fiennes in *Killing Me Softly*.

Georgy Girl: Georgy's flat: Edgware Road

A blue plaque records that **2 Maida Avenue (11)** was the real-life home of Arthur Lowe. A respected television and film actor, Lowe is

Reds: Gene Hackman drinks in the New York writers' club: Crocker's Folly, Aberdeen Place

Killing Me Softly: Heather Graham meets the reporter: Café Laville

probably most fondly remembered as the pompous Captain Mainwaring in UK TV's classic comedy series *Dad's Army*, brought to the big screen in 1971. His other big-screen appearances include *Kind Hearts and Coronets*, *The Ruling Class* as a scene stealing butler, *Theatre of Blood*, in which he is gruesomely decapitated by Vincent Price, and many of Lindsay Anderson's films from *This Sporting Life*, including his Mick Travis trilogy.

Douglas House, 6 Maida Avenue, is the house where Judy Geeson puts up Chicago cop John Wayne after his digs are blown up in *Brannigan*. It's also here that a potential assassin mistakes Geeson for Wayne. I'll run that by you again – Judy Geeson (27, female) is mistaken for John Wayne (68, male, six foot four). Well she's wearing his hat, you see.

Next door, **Aubrey House, 7 Maida Avenue**, is 'Kipling Mansions', Michael Palin's home, where psycho Kevin Kline is beastly to the little fish (or insects, as he likes to think of them), in *A Fish Called Wanda*.

A little further along, between numbers 15 and 22, is the rear of **St Mary's Church**, where James

Brannigan: Wayne stays with Geeson: Douglas House, Maida Avenue

A Fish Called Wanda: Kipling Mansions: Aubrey House, Maida Avenue

Mason finally proposes to Lynn Redgrave at the end of *Georgy Girl*. The 1974 film of TV sitcom *Man About the House* was also set around St John's Wood and Maida Vale.

The area north of the Grand Union Canal is known as Little Venice, and with its stuccoed villas and brightly painted houseboats, it's not hard to see why. Just over the canal is another world altogether – the bedsit neighbourhoods of Westbourne Park and Notting Hill – but this is staunchly middle-class homeowner territory, and the backdrop for the terribly civilised marital infidelities of *A Severed Head*, Dick Clement's film adaptation of Iris Murdoch's novel. **41 Blomfield Road (12)**, overlooking the canal, is home to

the Lynch-Gibbons (Ian Holm and Lee Remick), as their relationship is put to the test.

Turn right from Blomfield Road into **Clifton**

A Severed Head: home to Remick and Holm: Blomfield Road

Villas, alongside **Warwick Avenue Underground Station** (*tube: Bakerloo line*), where Rita Tushingham feigns pregnancy by shoving shopping into her coat in order to get across the busy road in *The Knack*. Lisa Harrow's possessed son Barnaby Holm follows monk Rossano Brazzi from the tube station to the house of Damien's henchman in *The Final Conflict*, the last of the *Omen* trilogy.

It's amazing to remember that 1964's *The Comedy Man* was considered daring in its day, what with chummy old Kenneth More in the lead, as a down-at-heel actor who finally finds fame in commercials. Tame by today's standards, the sex scenes were considered pretty frisky (gosh, these people weren't even *married!*). The actors' seedily leaky digs, supposedly in Camden Town, were actually northeast of Royal Oak Station in an area since demolished to accommodate the Westway flyover. Off Gloucester Terrace, though, you can see **Ranelagh Bridge, Porchester Terrace North (13)**, where actor-laddie Cecil Parker hails a bus into town.

Westbourne Terrace Road Bridge (14) over the Grand Union Canal in Little Venice is where Police Constable George Dixon (Jack Warner) passes the time with a little improvised verse (such innocent days) in *The Blue Lamp*. This 1949 police thriller cast Dirk Bogarde in an early role as a teenage hoodlum and, although cosy copper Dixon is killed in the film, the PC was resurrected to star in a long running British TV series. The house where Bogarde hides out has been demolished, but on Lord Hills Road at the Regent's Canal you might recognise the site. The old Harrow Road Police Station, too, has gone,

The Blue Lamp: the site of Dirk Bogarde's hideout: Lord Hills Road

The Blue Lamp: PC Dixon's beat: Westbourne Terrace Road Bridge

The End of the Affair and King Ralph: period bar and local boozer: the Prince Alfred, Formosa Street

but the eponymous lamp now hangs outside the new station on the **Harrow Road**.

The dominant feature of the area is the **Westway**, the roaring flyover of the A40, cutting a swathe through West London as it whizzes traffic in from the West to the West End. Beneath the Westway is the playground where the kids hang out in sex-swap comedy *Virtual Sexuality*. Ray Winstone is left under Westway by Ian McShane at the end of *Sexy Beast*, and Brenda Blethyn searches for drug lord Tchéky Karyo beneath its concrete pillars in the 2000 dope-growing comedy *Saving Grace*.

Go northwest up Warwick Avenue itself to Formosa Street. On the corner stands the **Prince Alfred, 5a Formosa Street (15**; see **Bars & Restaurants**, p21). This beautiful mahogany and glass bar appears in *The End of the Affair* and *B Monkey*. It can also be seen, though looking far less impressive, in *King Ralph*.

Maida Vale Underground Station (*tube: Bakerloo line*) has so far escaped the wholesale revamping inflicted on some stations, and retains a thirties feel in the green and white tiling of its stairwell – which can be glimpsed in *The End of the Affair* as Julianne Moore hurries to meet Ralph Fiennes at the restaurant.

Carry on up Formosa Street and across Castellain Road to Warrington Crescent. At the north end of the crescent stands the **Warrington Hotel, 93 Warrington Crescent (16**; see **Bars & Restaurants**, p21), which features in *Bunny Lake Is Missing*.

2 Warrington Crescent was the home of Alan Turing, the gay codebreaker and computer whizz who made such a contribution to unravelling the German codes during WWII. Shamefully ignored by the

Bunny Lake Is Missing: Lynley drinks with inspector Olivier: Warrington Hotel, Warrington Crescent

establishment, he committed suicide in 1954. Turing is clearly a big influence on the determinedly heterosexual Tom Jericho character in 2001's

About a Boy: Marcus tries to set up a date for his mum: Otto Dining Lounge, Sutherland Avenue

Enigma, but for a version closer to the truth, try *Breaking the Code*, a TV filming of Hugh Whitemore's stage play with Derek Jacobi as the troubled mathematical genius.

On the corner of Maida Vale and Sutherland Avenue stands the glass grey slate **Otto Dining Lounge, 215 Sutherland Avenue (17**; see **Bars & Restaurants**, p21), which appears as two different restaurants in the same film, *About a Boy*.

Heading north on Maida Vale brings you to Kilburn Park Road. The huge, rather severe, red-brick **St Augustine's Kilburn, Kilburn Park Road (18**), opposite Rudolph Road, is the 'New York' Church where Connor MacLeod (Christopher Lambert) meets the insinuatingly blasphemous Kurgan (Clancy Brown) in *Highlander*. The church is open to visitors on Saturday mornings between 10 and 12, and Tuesdays between 9 and 12.

Adela Street, a short cul-de-sac off north Ladbroke Grove, running from Kensal Road to the canal, was the site of the scrapyard in both big-screen versions, *Steptoe and Son* and *Steptoe and Son Ride Again*, of the long-running and groundbreaking TV sitcom. It's since been completely redeveloped.

Willesden Old Town Hall became the London mansion of Sir James Burgess (Ralph Richardson) in Lindsay Anderson's *O Lucky Man!*

If you've seen the Norman Wisdom comedy *Press for Time*, you might have wondered why 'Westminster' tube station, outside which Norman sells newspapers, stands in front of an unlikely

Highlander: Kurgan in the New York church: St Augustine's Kilburn, Kilburn Park Road

Press for Time: Norman Wisdom sells papers at Westminster Underground Station: Kilburn Park Station

The Smallest Show on Earth: site of the fleapit cinema: Kilburn Underground Station, Christchurch Avenue

tower block. That's because it's not Westminster at all, but **Kilburn Park Underground Station** (**19**; *tube: Bakerloo line*).

Alongside **Kilburn Underground Station, Christchurch Avenue** (*tube: Jubilee line*), you may recognise the two railway bridges between which stands the old 'Bijou' fleapit cinema run by Virginia McKenna and Bill Travers – with help from Peter Sellers, Bernard Miles and Margaret Rutherford – in the 1957 classic *The Smallest Show on Earth*. The cinema, which is rattled to its foundations every time a train passed in the film, was no more than a frontage built for the movie. A real cinema, though, is the **Tricycle Cinema, 269 Kilburn High Road** (see **Entertainment: Cinemas**, p27).

Chatsworth Road, Brondesbury Park, can be seen in *Leon the Pig Farmer*.

The National Club, 234 Kilburn High Road (see **Bars & Restaurants**, p21), provides another 'Hamburg' location for *Backbeat*.

Shoot up Shoot Up Hill to Cricklewood Broadway for a drink in **The Crown, 152 Cricklewood Broad-**

Backbeat: the 'Star Club, Hamburg': The National Club, Kilburn High Road

way (see **Bars & Restaurants**, p21), which has had a major revamp since appearing as a rather down-at-heel 'Camden' boozer in *This Year's Love*.

If you continue north on Cricklewood Broadway as it turns into Edgware Road, you may notice on your left, on Dollis Hill, overlooking the area, a familiar house. Clive Barker's first foray into directing, *Hellraiser*, introduced Pinhead and those perverse pleasure-seekers from Hell, the Cenobites.

Hellraiser: Pinhead is brought back to life: Dollis Hill Lane

Where else in London would you expect to find the mouth of Hell but Dollis Hill? '66 Lodovico Street', where Clare Higgins bloodily disposes of casual pick-ups to revive Sean Chapman, is **187 Dollis Hill Lane**. It's the rear of the house, much grander than its dilapi-

Tomorrow Never Dies: the Hamburg carpark: Brent Cross Shopping Centre carpark

The Leather Boys: the Ace Café, North Circular Road

dated appearance in the movie suggests, that's used. Interiors were filmed nearby, at the **Production Village Studio, 100 Cricklewood Lane**.

Whitfield Secondary Modern School, Claremont Road, Cricklewood, is the library in Michael Powell's classic shocker *Peeping Tom*.

Brent Cross (*tube: Northern line*) is synonymous with the vast shopping complex. The fourth level of the multi-story carpark of **Brent Cross Shopping Centre** is famously the site of the 'Hamburg' car chase in Pierce Brosnan's second outing as James Bond, *Tomorrow Never Dies*.

Close by Stonebridge Park Station, on the A406, the **North Circular Road**, at Beresford Avenue, stands the legendary **Ace Café**, once again open for business after closing its doors in 1969 to become a tyre depot (*website: www.ace-cafe-london.com*). This was the twenty-four-hour biker hangout where newly-wed biker-boy Colin Campbell meets up with sexually ambivalent rocker Dudley Sutton in Sidney J Furie's *The Leather Boys*. The café also appears in Cy Endfield's 1957 macho trucking movie *Hell Drivers*, with Stanley Baker.

There's little to see yet at Wembley, which was, of course, most famous for its soccer stadium with the famed twin towers. Sadly for those who remember English football's 1966 moment of glory, it is no more, as the controversial new sports venue takes shape. Whether it will find a place in the heart of the nation, as the old stadium did, or whether it's the new Millennium Dome, remains to be seen. You can see the old Wembley Stadium as it was shortly before demolition in *Mike Bassett: England Manager*, which even filmed inside the legendary, if cramped and rather basic, England Dressing Room.

INDEX OF FILM TITLES

ALTERNATIVE TITLES

A

ADVOCATE, THE see **HOUR OF THE PIG, THE**

APRIL ROMANCE see **BLOSSOM TIME**

AROUND THE WORLD IN 80 DAYS see **AROUND THE WORLD IN EIGHTY DAYS**

B

BABY, THE see **I DON'T WANT TO BE BORN**

BIG TIME OPERATORS see **SMALLEST SHOW ON EARTH, THE**

BIGGLES: ADVENTURES IN TIME see **BIGGLES**

C

CABINET OF DOCTOR CALIGARI, THE see **KABINETT DES DOKTOR CALIGARI, DAS**

CASE OF JONATHAN DREW, THE see **LODGER, THE (1926)**

CHANCE MEETING see **BLIND DATE**

COLONEL BLIMP see **LIFE AND DEATH OF COLONEL BLIMP, THE**

CONQUEROR WORM see **MATTHEW HOPKINS: WITCH-FINDER GENERAL**

COUNT DRACULA AND HIS VAMPIRE BRIDE see **SATANIC RITES OF DRACULA, THE**

CREEPING UNKNOWN, THE see **QUATERMASS XPERIMENT, THE**

D

DEFENSE OF THE REALM see **DEFENCE OF THE REALM**

DEVIL WITHIN HER, THE see **I DON'T WANT TO BE BORN**

DEVIL'S BRIDE, THE see **DEVIL RIDES OUT, THE**

E

ENEMY FROM SPACE see **QUATERMASS 2**

F

FINAL OPTION, THE see **WHO DARES WINS**

FIGHTING PIMPERNEL, THE (1950) see **ELUSIVE PIMPERNEL, THE**

FORBIDDEN ALLIANCE see **BARRETTS OF WIMPOLE STREET, THE (1934)**

G

GAY LADY, THE see **TROTTIE TRUE**

GET CHARLIE TULLY see **OOH, YOU ARE AWFUL**

GIDEON OF SCOTLAND YARD see **GIDEON'S DAY**

GOLDMEMBER see **AUSTIN POWERS IN GOLDMEMBER**

GUEST, THE see **CARETAKER, THE**

H

HARRY POTTER AND THE SORCERER'S STONE see **HARRY POTTER AND THE PHILOSOPHER'S STONE**

HAVING A WILD WEEKEND see **CATCH US IF YOU CAN**

HIGH COMMISSIONER, THE see **NOBODY RUNS FOREVER**

HUMAN MONSTER, THE see **DARK EYES OF LONDON**

K

K3G see **KABHI KHUSHI KABHIE GHAM... ('SOMETIMES HAPPY, SOMETIMES SAD')**

KNACK, AND HOW TO GET IT, THE see **KNACK, THE**

L

LONGEST YARD, THE see **MEAN MACHINE, THE**

LOST ILLUSION, THE see **FALLEN IDOL, THE**

LOVES OF ISADORA, THE see **ISADORA**

M

MAN WITH A MILLION see **MILLION POUND NOTE, THE**

MERRY WAR, A see **KEEP THE ASPIDISTRA FLYING**

MONSTER, THE see **I DON'T WANT TO BE BORN**

MORGAN! see **MORGAN – A SUITABLE CASE FOR TREATMENT**

MURDER AT THE BURLESQUE see **MURDER AT THE WINDMILL**

N

NINETEEN EIGHTY-FOUR see **1984**

O

OMEN III: THE FINAL CONFLICT see **FINAL CONFLICT, THE**

OPTIMISTS, THE see **OPTIMISTS OF NINE ELMS, THE**

P

PLAYGIRL AFTER DARK see **TOO HOT TO HANDLE**

PROFESSION: REPORTER see **PASSENGER, THE**

PUBLIC EYE, THE see **FOLLOW ME**

Q

QUATERMASS II: ENEMY FROM SPACE see **QUATERMASS 2**

R

RAW MEAT see **DEATH LINE**

REMARKABLE MR KIPPS, THE see **KIPPS**

ROOMMATES see **RAISING THE WIND**

S

SHARON'S BABY see **I DON'T WANT TO BE BORN**

SIDEWALKS OF LONDON see **ST MARTIN'S LANE**

SOMETIMES HAPPINESS, SOMETIMES SORROW see **KABHI KHUSHI KABHIE GHAM... ('SOMETIMES HAPPY, SOMETIMES SAD')**

SPICE WORLD see **SPICEWORLD THE MOVIE**

S.W.A.L.K. see **MELODY**

SWEENEY 2 see **SWEENEY TWO**

T

THEATER OF BLOOD see **THEATRE OF BLOOD**

TONIGHT'S THE NIGHT see **HAPPY EVER AFTER**

V

VERY THOUGHT OF YOU, THE see **MARTHA MEET FRANK, DANIEL & LAURENCE**

W

WITCHFINDER GENERAL see **MATTHEW HOPKINS: WITCHFINDER GENERAL**

WOMAN ALONE, A see **SABOTAGE (1936)**

WONDERFUL TO BE YOUNG see **YOUNG ONES, THE**

Y

YOUR PAST IS SHOWING see **NAKED TRUTH, THE**

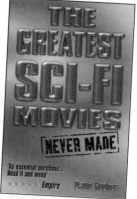